THE

COSMIC FAMILY

VOLUME I

as transmitted through

the Audio Fusion Material Complement

Gabriel of Sedona

THE

COSMIC FAMILY

VOLUME I

The Extension Schools
of Melchizedek Publishing

Although the author of this book claims to be the vessel for bringing through the Continuing Fifth Epochal Revelation (CFER), the interpretations and opinions expressed are not those of the Trustees of the URANTIA Foundation, nor does the publisher claim any affiliation with any organized URANTIA group.

© 1993, 1995
THE EXTENSION SCHOOLS
OF
MELCHIZEDEK PUBLISHING
P.O. BOX 3946
WEST SEDONA, AZ. U.S.A. 86340

ISBN 0-9647357-1-9

REGARDING COPYRIGHT FROM A COSMIC PERSPECTIVE

It was said by Solomon, son of David, "What can be said that hasn't been said before?" Throughout the history of Urantia, those who have made great discoveries in science, the arts, mechanical engineering, in architecture, and writing in relation to philosophy, should have realized within their own consciousness the truth of authorship within the context of the words of Solomon. Living on a defaulted planet one has to protect one's ideas, one's inventions, or one's writings, but this is not the normal process on worlds where beings have nothing to fear from others, nor are they concerned about their survival or self-aggrandizement, for love and divine authority rule these planets at higher degrees. On Urantia where humanity has learned to get rather than to give, and to take rather than to give, and in the process of getting, it does not matter who is injured as long as the goal is achieved.

Christ Michael and his vast administration of Nebadon, from the Bright and Morning Star to the present Planetary Prince of Urantia, Machiventa Melchizedek, would like to make it quite clear that Continuing Fifth Epochal Revelation (CFER) is for the people of Urantia to use in accordance with their own conscience before God. We hope that all spiritual seekers look to Planetary Headquarters and the Starseed and Urantian Schools of Melchizedek in Sedona, Arizona, U.S.A., for unaltered and original books, transcriptions and/or papers. Therefore, Aquarian Concepts Community, the incorporated legal nonprofit corporation that we established in and through the humans we are in contact with, will not at any time now or in the future bring anyone to court for using any of these terms, concepts and truths, for one cannot copyright universal truth or a concept that is from God. It is a gift to the planet to be given unequivocally to all who truly desire it from that same God. It is unfortunate that others who receive divine inspiration at some level feel that they have to copyright their art, their invention, their revelation, or their masterpiece of music. On such a world as Urantia it seems to be the appropriate thing to do. There are two ways to exist. One is within the perfect will of God and the other is outside, to whatever degree, of his permissive will. To the degree that you are in that perfect will is the degree that actualization of life and protection can be granted to you. On this planet, on the mansion worlds and in your ascension process, the extent of your own fulfillment and happiness is the extent you can ascend more in that perfect will, moment to moment, in your own relationship with God. No one can force you to do that.

We send *The Cosmic Family, Volume I*, and all other volumes to Washington D.C. and the Library of Congress in order to establish a date of authorship and copyright so that others in the future who may claim authorship, will not legally be able to stop us at Planetary Headquarters from publishing and distributing Continuing Fifth Epochal Revelation (CFER) to the people of Urantia. We want it to be known that the source of this information first came through Gabriel of Sedona who has the mandate of the Bright and Morning Star, at Planetary Headquarters. We do not want to be stopped from doing the perfect will of God by others who would try to get rich and powerful on the truth of God that is meant to be given unrestricted to all mankind. There is a cost in the printing and distribution of these books, and those humans involved have to financially be able to devote their time processing this massive revelation. If you cannot afford these publications, please write us and state your financial situation.

Those involved in the work of God at Planetary Headquarters do not look to man for their support, but have learned to look to God. In time it is hoped that all on Urantia who are sincerely looking for the highest truth and the highest revelations of God, will come to the conclusion that those in Sedona, Arizona, U.S.A., within the Aquarian Concepts Community, are who they say they are, and that we in Celestial Overcontrol are indeed in contact with them.

March 17, 1993

Paladin, Chief of Finaliters. This transmission is mandated by Christ Michael, Universe Sovereign of Nebadon, for the implementation of the Divine Government of the present Planetary Prince, Machiventa Melchizedek, and for the calling forth of the cosmic and Urantian reservists within the present adjudication by the Bright and Morning Star vs Lucifer which is now taking place on Urantia; as transmitted through the Audio Fusion Material Complement, Gabriel of Sedona.

TABLE OF CONTENTS

PAPER   AUTHOR   PAGE

Regarding Copyright From a
Cosmic Perspective v
Statement of Purpose xvii
Preface to the Second Edition xviii
Introduction .... Niánn Emerson Chase 1
    1. Thoughts on the Father
       Circuits and Authority 1
    2. The Trinity God Concept 1
    3. The Father Circuits 2
    4. Authority 3
Foreword I .... Machiventa Melchizedek,
                         Planetary Prince of Urantia .. 6
Foreword II .... Paladin, Chief of Finaliters .. 14

A.   A Message From the Chief
    Executive of Nebadon Under the
    Order of Our Beloved Universe
    Sovereign, Christ Michael, in
    Relation to the Adjudication by
    the Bright and Morning Star
    Versus Lucifer, to the People of
    the Urantia Movement, Primarily
    Those in the Teaching Mission ..... The Bright and Morning Star . 16
B.   Personal Transmission to Two
    Apostles .... Paladin, Finaliter 20
C.   The State of Our Planet —
    Nearing the Change Point .... Paladin, Finaliter 23
    1. The Fall of Our System
       Sovereign and Planetary
       Prince 23
    2. The Default of Adam and
       Eve 25
    3. The Later Three Epochal
       Revelations 25

PAPER   AUTHOR   PAGE

    4. The Results of the Rebel-
       lion, Spiritual Distortion 26
D. Cosmic Family — Planet of
    Universe Origin .... Paladin, Finaliter 28
      1. First-Time Urantians 28
      2. Second-Time Urantians 28
      3. Starseed from Other
        Universes 30
      4. Cosmic Relatives, Soul
        Mates, Highest Complements 32
      5. Highest Complements,
        Male Female, For Marital
        Purposes and Procreation
        of Children 38
      6. Inappropriate Relationships 41
      7. Man/Woman Roles 43
E. The Reserve Corps of Destiny ..... Paladin, Finaliter 47
      1. Cosmic Reserve Corps 50
      2. Divine Government
        Appointments in the Divine
        New Order 51
197. Explanation of Ashtar Command
    in Relation to Lower-Circle Chan-
    nels of Ashtar, Zoltec, and Others .... Paladin, Finaliter 58
198. Concerning the Entity Semjase ...... Paladin, Finaliter 61
199. Concerning Inner Guidance, A
    Cosmic Perspective .... Ashtar, Finaliter 64
200. Proper Terminology in the Pre-
    Stages of Light and Life and the
    Aquarian Age .... Paladin, Finaliter 67
      1. Masters, a Brief Explanation 68
      2. Recognizing Those Material
        Complements Who Have
        the Mandate of Christ
        Michael, and Mandates of
        Representative Universe
        Personalities 68
      3. Repersonalization and Cos-
        mic Family 70
      4. Closing Statement 71

PAPER   AUTHOR   PAGE

201. Mandates, a Brief Introduction .... Chief of Seraphim on Urantia   73
202. The Cosmic Law of Equivalent
     Reciprocation in Relation to Destiny
     Fulfillment. .... Paladin, Finaliter 76
203. Cosmic Family in Relation to
     Destiny Purpose and the Misuse of
     Talents and Certain other Mindal
     and Innate Abilities. .... Paladin, Finaliter 80
204. Divine Government Appointment
     or the Badge of Social Acceptance ..... Machiventa Melchizedek,
                                            Planetary Prince of Urantia .. 84

     Governmental Appointments of the
     Planetary Prince 86
205. Healing of the Physical, Ethereal,
     Astral Bodies by the Methods of
     Time-Space Warp Procedure of Re-
     trospection, Interdimensional Per-
     sonality Hologram, and the Fusion
     of All Energies Coexistent in the
     Present Body .... Paladin, Finaliter 88
206. The Divine New Order Communi-
     ty, The First Cosmic Family .... Paladin, Finaliter 91
207. The Reorganization of the Cosmic
     Families in Relation to Their Par-
     ticular Ascension Status Before the
     Lucifer Rebellion in Order to Re-
     capture and Claim the Respective
     Genetic Inheritance of that Par-
     ticular Universe Sovereign and
     Michael Son .... Paladin, Finaliter 97
208. The Importance of Genetic Inherit-
     ance in Relation to the Coding of
     the Material Son and Daughter,
     Adam and Eve, and Other Per-
     sonalities of the Caligastia One
     Hundred from Other Systems and
     Universes, in Particular the Third
     and Fourth Generation of Adamson
     and Ratta and Their Present Proge-
     ny on Urantia .... Paladin, Finaliter 102

PAPER	AUTHOR	PAGE

209. Differentiation — A Cosmic Perspective of Interplanetary & Interdimensional Transmissions in Relationship from Highest to Lowest, I.E. Material Complements, Interplanetary Receivers, Channelers, Mediums, and the Differences Existent Therein .... Paladin, Finaliter 106

210. The Bestowal of Michael on Urantia in Relation to the Gift of the Spirit of Truth and the Activation of That Spirit of Truth on Urantia. What is True Spirituality? Does It Differ in the Grand Universe? .... Paladin, Chief of Finaliters .. 115

211. Proper Response in Relation to Mandated Personalities, Spiritual Elders, Cosmic Parents; and Clarification as to Misplaced Loyalties and the Power One gives to Nonspiritual Entities and Other Self-Pursuits of Ego-Centered Passions, Either Tangible, Nontangible or Abstract. .... Machiventa Melchizedek, Planetary Prince of Urantia . 125

212. A Beginning Thesis as to the Coordination of Certain Celestial Personalities in Relation to the Adjudication by the Bright and Morning Star vs Lucifer and the Implementation Thereof Through the Machiventa Melchizedek Government and More Specifically, the Master Seraphim of Planetary Supervision and Designated Mandated Human Personalities .... Paladin, Finaliter 130
    1. The epochal angels 130
    2. The progress angels 131
    3. The religious guardians 131
    4. The angels of nation life 131
    5. The angels of the races 132
    6. The angels of the future 132

7. The angels of enlightenment 133
8. The angels of health 134
9. The home seraphim 134
10. The angels of industry 135
11. The angels of diversion 135
12. The angels of superhuman
    ministry 136
213. The Adjudication by The Bright and
Morning Star vs. Lucifer, the
Establishment of the Government of
the Planetary Prince Using Human
Personalities and The Announcement of Machiventa Melchizedek as
That Planetary Prince of Urantia .... The Bright and Morning Star . 139
214. Hologram Appearance of Machi-
venta Melchizedek to One of His
Potential Material Complements
and Potential Vicegerent First
Ambassadors, with the Announce-
ment of His Elevation to the Office
of Planetary Prince of Urantia;
Clarification of the Title of the
Planetary Prince; and Warning to
Caligastia Regarding Protection and
Safe Passage for All Those Called
to the Starseed and Urantian
Schools of Melchizedek at
Planetary Headquarters in Sedona,
Arizona, U.S.A. .... Machiventa Melchizedek,
                                    Planetary Prince of Urantia . 141
215. Delusion Energy Frequencies,
Distortion Waves and Distortion
Sound Waves in Relation to the
Adjudication of Urantia, Imple-
mented by Machiventa Melch-
izedek, Present Planetary Prince of
Urantia .... Machiventa Melchizedek,
                                    Planetary Prince of Urantia . 144
216. Atavism in Relation to the Various
Cosmic Families on Urantia and to
the Urantian Strain and Linkage to
the Material Son and Daughter,
Adam and Eve, on Urantia .... Paladin, Finaliter 148

| PAPER | AUTHOR | PAGE |

217. Deo-Atomic Triads in Nuclear Structure Within the Ultimaton in Relation to Cellular Physiological Genetics Inherent in Souls Who Are in Harmony with Cosmologic Vibration Pattern .... Paladin, Finaliter 155

218. Apostleship, Discipleship and Faith Believers in Relation to the Pre-Stages of Light and Life and the Establishment of the Machiventa Government Using Human Person-alities Within Respective Mandates as Change Agents, Ambassadors, Assistants, Watchers and Circle Guardians .... Machiventa Melchizedek, Planetary Prince of Urantia . 160

219. Pre-Thought-Adjuster Fusion and Post-Soul and Spirit Fusion in Relation to Soul Identity Function in Respect to Universe of Origin and Coordinating Deo-Atomic Ancestral Inheritance .... Paladin, Finaliter 165

220. The Cosmic Family in Relation to Genetic Inheritance in Respect to the Male and His Various Female Complements in Procreation Which Influences Union of Souls and Group Dynamics Creating Auhter Energies Which Transcend Negative Influences Caused by Rebellion and Lower-Circle Consciousness in the Ascension Process to Paradise .... Paladin, Chief of Finaliters .. 169

221. Mortal Pair-Unit Classification in Relation to Procreation in Ancestral Linkage to Material Sons and Daughters or Other Unrevealed Breeding Personalities, and Their Planetary Administrative Functions in Divine Government Admini-stration .... Paladin, Chief of Finaliters .. 175

PAPER   AUTHOR   PAGE

222. Physical Third-Dimensional Body
     Types, in This Case Those of Human
     Mortal Ascenders, in Relation to
     Mortal Pair Units and the Ovan
     Soul's Etheric Body and Morontia
     Body in Relation to Deo-Atomic
     Inheritance .... Paladin, Chief of Finaliters . . 184
223. The Infusion of Interuniversal
     Diotribe Intraction Cells with
     Intrauniversal Diotribes in Relation
     to the Lucifer Rebellion, and the
     Manifestation of These Unions
     Resulting in Intraction Cosmic
     Language, Which is an Inharmonic
     Pattern That Disorganizes Frequency
     Circuits from Various Headquarters
     Worlds Where These Broadcasts
     Originate, and Are Received on
     Urantia by Mindal Process
     Reflectivity and Other Sensory
     Receptors Innate in Certain
     Orders of Ascending and De-
     scending Beings .... Paladin, Chief of Finaliters . . 190
224. Pair-Unit Classification in Relation
     to Form Units (Body Forms) and
     Their Progeny in Relation to the
     Inheritance of Deo-Atomic Triads
     and Diotribes Resulting in the
     Variation of Those Body Forms, and
     Other Physical Distinctions and
     Characteristics Pertinent to Pre-
     Urantian Body Form Units Where
     Dio-tribe Influence Has Occurred ..... Paladin, Chief of Finaliters . . 198
225. The Dangers Inherent in Sexual
     Intimacy Between Higher and
     Lower Genetic Strains Within the
     Human Race, Including Ovan Souls
     with Urantians and Higher-Circle
     with Lower-Circle Individuals,
     Excluding Procreation and

"The first papers of *The Cosmic Family, Volume I* are given and written in such a manner that it should be easier to understand for the newcomer to Fifth Epochal Revelation. It will begin to interject CFER to complement many of the unrevealed cosmic realities that the beginning one tenth, (the first 196 Papers written in *The URANTIA Book*), left vague or completely unrevealed."

January 29, 1992

"*The URANTIA Book* is the fulcrum for the Continuing Fifth Epochal Revelation (CFER). Even the fulcrum cannot now be understood at a necessary level to bring most of the human beings of Urantia to the fourth circle of attainment."

February 25, 1993

Machiventa Melchizedek, Planetary Prince of Urantia.

STATEMENT OF PURPOSE

The purpose of this book is to introduce new cosmic concepts in words that will be part of one planetary language in the understanding of spiritual reality in which our planet, **Urantia**/Earth, will be operating when the **change point** and shift from **third dimension** to **fourth dimension**, and above, occurs, and a new divine government of **Christ Michael** (Jesus) is appropriated either by his physical return or the physical materialization of the present Planetary Prince, **Machiventa Melchizedek**, and his staff, presently on the planet. We believe that cataclysms will precede either event. Perhaps an **auhter energy** shift will also occur if these two events do not transpire in May of 2000 or 2001 AD. A lower term for this consciousness shift or change point is quantum leap. *It is not a government of arms or military power. We do not teach rule by force of arms, nor do we stock weapons of any kind. We teach only the fatherhood of God and the brotherhood of man/ woman; we teach love.* We will attempt to define each concept as it is introduced; some will be clarified within the text, as well as in the glossary at the end of the book. This volume is the first one in a series to challenge the mind of those who have accepted a nonreality that cannot bring them into true happiness, peace and harmony on this planet.

as one. Paradise is existent and is actually a place, the center of the master universe* around which all superuniverses* and **universes** revolve; all is pulled inward toward it, including each soul. From atoms up through superuniverse patterns, all have a similar motion, circling the center nucleus and held in place by the pull that comes from that center. From the smallest particle to the immense grand universe,* with its billions of worlds, all physical matter is held by Paradise gravity **circuits** and revolves around Paradise. All spiritual matter, including souls, encompassing a multitude of beings, is also drawn towards Paradise and God, the Trinity. The First Source and Center* is the Father; his circuits are Father circuits, and Paladin is a **Father-circuited** being. The Second Source and Center is the Son and the Third Source and Center is the Mother or Infinite Spirit.* At our universe level, our Universe Father, Michael* the Creator Son* (Jesus), came directly from the Paradise Father (First Source and Center) and the Paradise Son (Second Source and Center). Christ Michael's partner in creating and caring for their creatures is the Universe Mother Spirit,* who came directly from the Paradise Mother (Third Source and Center), often called the Infinite Spirit. We beings of universe origin, whether we are mortals or **archangels,** were created by our Universe Father and/or Mother, Christ Michael the Creator Son and the Universe Mother Spirit. But these two universe parents who came from Paradise have no creating powers without the connection to the First Source and Center, for all energy, nonspiritual and spiritual, comes from that First Source and Center, God, the Eternal Father.

3. THE FATHER CIRCUITS

On worlds that have their circuitry still connected, there is a harmonious balance between the Father/Son circuits and the Mother circuits that originate in Paradise and shoot down to our level through our Creator Son and Universe Mother Spirit. Entities with the male essence are properly connected with the Father circuits and those with the female essence are more **Mother-circuited**. All beings have both the yang (Father) and yin (Mother) but each individual has more of one than the other, depending upon his or her dominant essence. For example, the invisible higher beings who have been coming to us are either more strongly connected with the Father/Son or the Mother. Mary, a guardian seraphim* (order of angel), is Mother-circuited, and when she comes through, an aura of extreme gentleness and compassion is prevalent. Her voice, through Gabriel's vocal chords, is soft and high, where Paladin's is stronger, louder and deeper. I sense a soft, white blue connected with Mary and a piercing white and deep red with Paladin. Both come from God, though both are very different from each other. At first I was more comfortable with Mary and her energy, rather than with Paladin's, but that does not mean that Paladin is any less of a ministering spirit. In fact, it is Paladin who has taught me the most and to whom

I feel closest, and it is he who has angered me more than any of the others, for it is he who most challenges my misconceptions and wrong thinking, my anger and bitterness towards men.

It is also through Paladin and the other higher intelligences of Father circuits that I have come to see how beautiful and powerful a truly balanced Father-circuited male is, aligned with God's cosmic laws. As I have studied in detail *The URANTIA Book* papers on the life and teachings of Jesus, and encountered Michael (Jesus) in my own personal spiritual experience, I see the perfection of a balanced Father-circuited man. Yes, I agree with Paladin, this world does need its men to become properly aligned with their God and connected with the Father circuits in a correct cosmic understanding of reality. The men on this fallen planet, with its broken circuitry, do not really know what maleness is and what a real fourth-dimensional man with true spiritual insight is like. For if they did, and became that fourth-dimensional male, there would be no wars, no suppression or oppression of any human, no poverty, no illness, no ecological pollution, no materialism, no starvation, no injustices, no misuse of authority, no betrayals, no unfulfilled and frustrated individuals.

At no time in the history of Urantia (earth) has there been a majority of balanced Father-circuited men; all have suffered because of that fact, and many of the women have become imbalanced and disconnected with the Mother circuits in their anger and hurt and in their fight for justice and sanity. On our world, it is easier for women to be balanced in the Mother circuits, for we have the essence of our Universe Mother within our planet, but in order for true harmony and balance to reign within each soul and upon the planet, all must connect properly with the appropriate circuits. The unbalanced males do not have the proper Father/Son circuits which come directly from the Paradise Father and Son through our Universe Father, Christ Michael. If you knew Jesus, the man he really was when he bestowed here, then you would understand what a balanced Father-circuited male is.

4. AUTHORITY

Paladin also speaks much about proper authority, and I have had to change my attitude about authority. Though in this present life I have personally experienced a more balanced and appropriate authority in my earthly parents and some employers, I was one who still constantly questioned authority on all levels: my parents, my teachers, my employers, the government and even God. Because of what I had observed of authority in general on this planet, I did not think much of it. I saw authority implemented on a lower level as a terrible bullying in individuals who wanted to lord it over another person, controlling, and thus feeling powerful and above the other; I also saw those tendencies at times manifested in myself. I saw this happen between parents and children, between friends, and between lovers. On a larger scale, I saw it in vast bureaucracies and dictatorships that wasted much and got little done. I saw many people put in positions of power and authority who had little vision and little compassion or understanding for the human dilemma, and who just went along with the status quo, though often that status quo was deadly for thousands of people. In many theologies I saw an authoritative God who was hard to please and demanded many sacrifices from his people, and who punished with a vengeance. So when Paladin first spoke of our world needing godly authority, my blood ran cold. But as I got to know him and really listened to his words, I realized that he was speaking of an authority that I had not known completely or observed in this life here on this broken world.

As I began to get past my own pride and to dispel deeply entrenched improper beliefs and attitudes, I opened up to the proper cosmic understanding of *godly* authority, an authority that is manifested throughout the grand universe, on every world and in every relationship. As I studied the subject in *The URANTIA Book* and opened up to the spiritual guides' teachings, I came to see that there is structure, order and administration throughout all the universes. It is not a bureaucratic dictatorship, but a blending of many personalities and complex forces working together to bring forth a more perfected, completed whole. The grand universe is an organic whole with millions of systems* filled with multitudes of worlds and creatures at all levels of material, spiritual and other existence, ever evolving together with various forces in a harmonic pattern towards a higher reality, towards perfection.

Although there is a definite organization to every aspect of the grand universe, given by God the Father, the First Source and Center, this does not mean that there is a dictatorship, a word which connotes stagnation without allowance of diversity or free will. Within this complex organization and structure is the allowance of innumerable divergences. Just because there is a cosmic pattern of order does not mean that there is no movement or change or growth; this order is organic and living and never still, always evolving. In this order is imperfection, because every personality has free will and can choose to flow with the divine pattern and with cosmic law or go against it.

What Paladin meant by "coming under godly authority" is that each one of us is a part of that pattern and our decisions determine whether we contribute to the evolution towards perfection or delay it. Most authority structures and figures on our planet of broken circuitry are not within the divine pattern, are not of *godly* authority, but are of an imbalanced and disharmonious pattern, which creates more imperfection and struggle. We, along with all other material, spirit and other types of personal beings, do have a cosmic responsibility to understand our place in the divine pattern of things, first in our relationships with each other on this world, and then in our relationships with the rest of the universe, superuniverse and grand universe.

Niánn Emerson Chase.

*****

Statement by the Bright and Morning Star

Niánn Emerson Chase, who shares the **mandate** of Christ Michael and the Bright and Morning Star with Gabriel of Sedona, is a direct descendent of Ralph Waldo Emerson on her mother's side, and a direct descendent of Meriwether Lewis of the Lewis and Clark expedition on her father's side. Both of these genetic qualities were necessary for her present mandated position.

She attended Arizona State University and received a Bachelor of Arts degree in English and a Masters degree in education. After receiving her teacher's degree she returned to the San Carlos Apache Reservation and taught for 10 years. She also taught for 5 years at the Globe High School in Arizona as well as at Gila Pueblo Community College and approximately 1 year at the Sedona Montessori School. Presently, besides her administrative and counseling duties, she is also director of the **Starseed and Urantian Schools of Melchizedek** for ovan **starseed** children.

The background given on Niánn Emerson Chase is not to impress the readership, but to state her qualifications for her present mandated position. She received the Spirit of Truth* in this life when she was approximately 9 years old and has walked in the higher counsel of her Father in heaven, which has directed her life from that age to the present time. The degree to which cosmic and Urantian reservists, and even the parents of youth, can hear from God determines the degree to which all find their destiny.

March 1, 1993

The Bright and Morning Star of Salvington.

FOREWORD I

by

MACHIVENTA MELCHIZEDEK
PRESENT PLANETARY PRINCE OF URANTIA

Greetings to the peoples of Urantia. My personal presence on Urantia since December of 1989 was made possible by the circle attainment of two individuals within the **cosmic reserve corps** who reached the third psychic circle and above. They are Gabriel of Sedona and Niánn who co-share the mandate of the Bright and Morning Star. This attainment established an **energy reflective circuit** or **ERC** which allowed my entrance back on Urantia, for many reasons, all of which Celestial Overcontrol hopes you will learn by taking the first steps to become students of the **Continuing Fifth Epochal Revelation or CFER**, which *The Cosmic Family, Volume I* is about. The first papers of *The Cosmic Family, Volume I* are given and written in such a manner that it should be easier to understand for the newcomer to **Fifth Epochal Revelation**, and will begin to interject CFER to complement many of the unrevealed cosmic realities that the beginning one tenth, written in *The URANTIA Book,* left vague or completely unrevealed.

As it is in the evolutionary process, where the mind and heart of human mortals need to grow together, and when this reality is not manifested by mass consciousness, the few, who may have obtained the ability to comprehend higher cosmic reality and absolutes, suffer. The first papers are written in such a way that a beginning reader who has not read *The URANTIA Book* will be able to understand some of its basic truths, which will be complemented by CFER and more fully explained by the later papers which begin to define the cosmic realities, cosmic laws and cosmic absolutes in a more experiential and scientific manner for the more disciplined student of higher spiritual learning. The first papers are written in a more general manner and are also designed to show the series of events which took place among the mandated human personalities which helped to make my personal appearance on this planet again possible. These events also led to their coming together in a union of souls* to represent the **First Cosmic Family** and the first eldership among the first **Divine New Order Community** within the Planetary Prince's government on Urantia.

In the acquisition of truth and logic, it is a common desire among all ascending sons and daughters of all orders of beings to have all the answers at one time once truth becomes their quest. The higher you ascend, each question answered only begins a series of other questions, and it is not the answering of the question that becomes the goal, it is the correct posing of one. In the process of interplanetary communication within a third-dimensional realm, where we will be present, although not visually present, it has been an experiment for Celestial Overcontrol on Urantia as well as on other planets. Limitations as to our mode of communication and what we can and cannot do depends upon what planet we are on, and also the Creator Son's individual mandate pertinent to that planet and/or its home system. Urantia, being a fallen planet whose circuits were cut off approximately 200,000 years ago, has found itself in a unique place when it comes to interplanetary and interdimensional communications when they are allowed from our side to yours. These things are not easy to explain.

I suggest that you go from this point and read PAPER 209 and then, before you continue with me, give it a day or so and talk to the Father within you and outside of you; then come back to this point and continue. You see, we are in a crisis time on Urantia as never before. For many on Urantia, the seeming luxuries of life have blinded them to their own ascension, particularly in Western civilization where capitalism and materialism have added to the Luciferic deception, which has caused a stronger blockage in the reception of what the Thought Adjuster,* God himself, is saying to each and every individual at this hour. The first papers are meant to awaken you as an individual. The later papers can do that also, even more so, but the first ones are meant to speak more to your heart, wherein are found the first circuits, which are the beginning link to the capital of this universe. This is a circuit long closed that we are now so desperately trying to open within each individual on Urantia.

When I first came to this planet, I befriended a godly man who was also a warrior. Some would not judge him as being godly at all. Some, if he stood before them in judgment, would have given him the harshest of sentences, for God has his opinions and you on Urantia have yours. This individual became the father of two present religions and the seed of both of its peoples. Destiny and its application with providence for an ascending son or daughter is eternal in educational reality. If the words written in all the volumes of time and space on this subject were placed on Urantia within one library, the library would be as big as the planet itself. When we look upon your planet for individuals to be given certain mandates of Christ Michael, we have our opinions based upon standards that you cannot see nor measure. We do not look upon the physical; we look within the soul, and if the soul is an **ovan soul**, we perhaps have hundreds of thousands of years to measure; the records of your previous existences as ovan souls, with their individual ups and downs in their own ascension process, is a masterpiece of mercy in relation to those souls. We are humbled by the mercy of God; we are overjoyed and feel secure ourselves the more we learn of that mercy, and know that we are granted the same destiny by the Father in Paradise, the beauty of whose majesty no human adjective can describe.

Gabriel of Sedona and Niánn were chosen in the fourteenth century as candidates for the mandate of the Bright and Morning Star. Several other mortal individuals could have received the mandates of First Ambassador to me. For over half a century all of these individuals were observed; we waited and waited until those who had reached the higher **circles** found themselves and the beginning of their own higher destiny purposes, and then, even harder than that, found each other, which was the beginning of the union of souls. When this union of souls happens on an evolutionary world of time and space by ovan souls, (see PAPER 219) the first stage of light and life is near. How near depends upon the rest of the peoples of the planet who come out of the old order and the many deceptions they have allowed themselves to believe and to follow. For those who now begin to walk into the Divine New Order and the fourth dimension, the reality will be different and greater protection can be given to those individuals from our side to yours. It is a time of cleansing on Urantia and all must face their moment of truth and respond, not to man or the religious institutions of man, but to God and the absolutes of God. These absolutes are recorded and written in the atmospheres and stratospheres of time and space. They are the energies from Paradise that resonate with all individuals long before those individuals try to write about them in books.

The cosmic reservists have been on this planet before, and only a minority of them have met their destinies in accordance with the divine plan and have helped in the spiritual renaissances in the history of Urantia to bring about change and have aided in the planet's evolution. In this era they are asked to do it again, and those who have proven themselves in times past must again prove themselves and meet their destiny purpose. Christ Michael, who was the Creator Son when he was on this planet as Jesus, the Son of Man, had to discover who he was over a period of time. He also walked into his destiny with greater power upon the realization of himself not only as the Son of Man but the Son of God and Creator Son of Nebadon.* Those individuals of the cosmic reserve corps must do the same.

If you who read what I am saying at this point disbelieve what you thus far have read, it matters not to the destiny of your planet, which will be settled in light and life regardless of your choice, for you, if you are an ovan soul, will no longer hinder the coming of the kingdom of God on this planet. As there is a season for all things, the season of rebellion is about to be over. This is a fair warning from me and from your God. You must awaken and you must humble yourselves, for you are either in ignorance or caught in self-deceit and pride. If your true loyalty is to the Creator Son of this universe and to the Eternal Father of all, then you will begin to resonate with these truths — the fatherhood of God and the brotherhood of man — that I taught in the schools of Salem. Those who accepted what I taught then brought peace to themselves, and these words will bring peace to you now and create the New Jerusalem within you. Until it is created within you, you cannot be part of this New Jerusalem which is about to be constructed physically on Urantia. My government is not a government by appointment of man; it is a government by appointment of divine origin. I am a created one and my appointment is an appointment by my Creator, Christ Michael.

The appointments to those humans with the highest mandates on Urantia, the Bright and Morning Star's mandate to Gabriel of Sedona, and the mandate of the **Liaison Ministers**,[2] should be understood with great respect and honor, for these also are not appointments from man to man but from God to man. Within any government, appointments must be given somewhere, and this is where it begins on Urantia. There will be many transmissions to help you and those who are mandated to understand the specifics of these mandates. It is all a part of the process of learning, and God will leave no doubt in the minds of the true seekers that these appointments are indeed from Christ Michael.

As a fusion material complement, an audio receiver and an **interplanetary receiver**, the human Gabriel is also a teacher, counselor and healer, with many other gifts all given for the service of mankind. There is a great difference between the process of communication with him and the mode and process of communication between the first vessel who was used to bring the first part of the Fifth Epochal Revelation, which is now *The URANTIA Book*. That individual did not have the mandate of the Bright and Morning Star. He was not meant to be a teacher of these high truths. As the human Gabriel becomes more perfect in the likeness of his God, as it is with all who ascend to spiritual perfection, it increases his abilities to bring higher and higher cosmic concepts to Urantia. This is his destiny, and for those of you who can be of aid to any of this work, can you not see that this would be your highest calling? You must begin to see the personality of your God in the personalities of your brothers and sisters on this planet. It is these God-seeking personalities and the highest of these personalities

---

[2]It should be noted here that Paper 273 of Volume III designated the seven Liaison Ministers' mandates as the second highest on the planet. Before reaching Deopower, the First Ambassador's mandate will not take full effect until approximately 2040 - 2050 AD.

in their perfection to God who will rule this planet. It is not a matter of monetary wealth, power given to man by man, fame, prestige or education in the universities of man. These appointments are given by Christ Michael in the administration of his universe through various levels to those personalities who resonate closest to the personality bestowal of the Father, Son and Infinite Spirit; Michael is indeed the judge of those things. The power of the Creator Son works first and foremost on the human level through the mandate of the Bright and Morning Star; and then, because of that mandate, the universe administration can begin to be manifested through other human personalities at Planetary Headquarters, in whom the power of Christ Michael is also manifested in various degrees and levels. When any one individual on any planet, fallen or not, begins to resonate with the higher circle of the first creation of the Creator Son and Universe Mother Spirit, which is that of the Bright and Morning Star, and can stay on that circle of attainment a registered period of time, that individual is chosen to be given the mandate for that planet. On different planets it means different things, but it always means a higher dispensation to the whole planet. On fallen worlds it means the beginning of the first stage of light and life, and where ovan souls are gathered, it begins the regathering of the First Cosmic Family and the other cosmic families who originate from other universes.

Urantia has many names, and unfortunately it has come to be known, not only in this universe but in many others, as the planet on which its own Creator was crucified (planet of the cross) and a planet that has suffered default by other supermortal personalities. Because of these facts, Urantia has also become known as a dark planet. It is not a planet that celestial personalities come to for a vacation. We come here to teach and to learn. We are not pleased with what we see. It is a shocking reality for those who have not been here before, even though they have been warned about what they would find on their arrival. To those few individuals who are now beginning to create the auhter energy that can be seen as the light in the darkness of Urantia, we give our honor; we pray for you to persevere and remain steadfast to the reality to which you are awakening, for you have seen through the void of darkness and you have come out of the cave of shadows. To those who haven't come out of their own caves, we pray for you. Perhaps you can see many of the problems of Urantia yourself but are helpless to do anything about them. You too can help create the power to change. It begins within yourself as you walk away from the old order, out of the **Caligastia** system and into the Divine New Order and the Divine Government that I have been appointed to establish on Urantia. As you walk out of the past, you too will create the light and auhter energy that is first observable by sanobim,* cherubim* and **midwayers**, whereupon you personally are brought to my attention. Then all the aid that can be given to you as an individual and to your family is given, and the more you walk into the fourth dimension, the more aid you can receive. The more you leave behind the old order, the closer you become to being a vessel for the divine power which can be manifested to you and to your loved ones. You truly become born again of the Spirit of Truth that resonates with the **Salvington circuit** of Nebadon, the capital of your universe, not with the so-called "spiritual capitals" of this planet where self-appointed men sit upon their thrones of power and arrogance. They have sat upon these thrones for centuries; and still the majority of the peoples of this planet suffer from starvation, mechanized lives of robotic adherence to a system based upon the need for survival, and false allegiance to rulers of governments who would send you and your sons and daughters to die in wars waged so that they, the rulers, can continue to live in their opulence and greed.

The first papers of *The Cosmic Family, Volume I* should be an aid to you in helping you to come out of the old order. The subsequent papers will help you to find your place in the Divine New Order. This part and CFER are not papers that are to be read once or even twice and then put down. They are to be studied, for as you grow you will come back to these papers again and again and again. The truth of these papers is eternal, and you need to grow into it. It is not our position to prove anything to you. It is our position to speak truth, and that is proof in itself. If you are truly a truth seeker you will find your destiny, first as a student of CFER within the Starseed and Urantian Schools of Melchizedek, then in one of the hundreds of positions that will be available to you and to thousands and millions like you, before and after the change point comes to this planet. You are needed to help bring this great change. It is not a change by the force of armies or by the physical takeover of the governments of this world. It is a change of your heart and mind. It is a change of the views of your own reality and in the understanding of yourself as a cosmic citizen with a cosmic destiny, not as the citizen of a country, but as the citizen of a planet within the brotherhood of men and women on that planet, all of whom are destined to learn together the vastness and totality of the masterful creation of the Universal Father.* In the proper recognition of your higher spiritual human teachers who are a definite part of the plan of God, and in your honoring them as such, you yourself may begin to find your own place in the master plan of God. Where false pride in an individual is replaced by true humility and gives its ear to higher instruction in an attitude of submission to others who have acquired a higher degree of godly perfection, knowledge and cosmic insight, that individual and the soul contained within it can become an ovan soul; and on Urantia it can even now transcend the death process and come into morontia* reality just as naturally as going to sleep and waking up the next morning.

You are being called to come into the reality of the first mansion world now, here on this decimal planet, where the first mansion world reality is now made possible by the appointment of myself as Planetary Prince, by the coming of the New Jerusalem, soon with the morontia temple established here, and by the cooperation with those human personalities who have been given the mandates to help implement the Divine Government on Urantia. Do not think it strange that I have physical headquarters on this world. Does not Michael have one on Salvington?* Is it not the divine implementation of creation to first establish headquarters worlds, and then to establish on those planets of the lower evolutionary natures, divine government which begins in geographic locations in cooperation between Celestial Overcontrol and mortal personalities?

The Starseed and Urantian Schools of Melchizedek are first for all those cosmic and Urantian reservists, and their families, where children of all ages are to be taught and trained for the higher learning that will bring the peace and joy to this planet for which all have so long been waiting. I, Machiventa Melchizedek, personally invite you to come and take part, first as a student and then as a co-worker in this new age, in this Divine New Order, in this Aquarian reality.

Urantia is physically beginning to rotate and align itself with those planets which have not fallen in the system of Satania.* The Universe Mother Spirit within and without is beginning to give birth to a new earth, a new seed. Those who do not belong in the new soil will not be able to stay. There is no need for you or your loved ones to face the tribulations ahead alone. If you are reading this book with my words and the contents therein, it is no accident. Take this gift of truth. Take this gift of purpose. Take this gift of higher reality and higher life forward and aid your God, Christ Michael and myself, and create the wave which is necessary at this hour to speed up the process of perhaps the return of our beloved Creator Son, Christ Michael, by helping those whom he has chosen in human form to be his representatives. Give to the Aquarian Concepts Community your dedication and loyalty, your time, your service, and your talents, in any way you can, for they have gone ahead of you. They have sacrificed their own desires; they have been ridiculed by their peers and have suffered at the hands of the very people they were trying to help. Can you do less? Choose wisely, for this is the adjudication of Urantia; it is happening now, and you do have a choice.

January 29, 1992

Signed at this particular hour of time and space, Machiventa Melchizedek, present Planetary Prince of Urantia; in cooperation with the Council of Twenty-four;* the System Sovereign,* Lanaforge;* and the Bright and Morning Star of Salvington; to implement the adjudication procedures pertinent to Urantia in the bringing of these words through the Audio Fusion Material Complement, Gabriel of Sedona of the Aquarian Concepts Community at Planetary Headquarters in Sedona, Arizona, U.S.A.

FOREWORD II

by

PALADIN, CHIEF OF FINALITERS ON URANTIA

My name is Paladin and I am what is called a "finaliter." As you read this book and the books to come, you will become more familiar with just who exactly I am. At this moment in time and space that I am transmitting this through the audio fusion material complement/interplanetary receiver, Gabriel of Sedona, I am second in command to Ashtar of a large fleet of physical vessels, designated by the Creator Son and Sovereign Ruler of the universe of Nebadon, to evacuate all those souls, like yourself, trapped in physical bodies when the cataclysms and/or wars come to this planet. Compared to you, I am a completed personality; I am like a great-grandfather to the one hundredth power. Thus I have much to teach you as a representative of your God to this planet. In the superuniverse of Orvonton* my first experience as a human mortal was in the **Pleiades**, but I am much more now than just a Pleiadian mortal. I existed in the Pleiades 750,000 years ago with a family much like yours.

In order for you to be beamed up, lifted, raptured, evacuated, translated, or rematerialized — whichever term you feel comfortable with — you, the **cosmic family**, must begin to understand what we first and foremost are trying to teach you. With this understanding you will be ready for the fourth dimension, the pre-stages of light and life on this planet, Urantia. If you choose to die a physical death to reach the fourth dimension, that is your choice; but you are nearing a change point in dispensational time that will enable you to transcend dimensions without the experience you call "death."

I am a male mortal being in origin and that maleness is a part of my past and a balanced part of my present. We would say in the cosmic overview that I am more of a Father-Son existence than an Infinite Spirit or Mother existence; I am more of a father and connected to what we hope you come to know in the future as the Father circuits. My mission is to teach the people of your planet what they have forgotten since the fall of Caligastia, your ex-Planetary Prince, and the simultaneous fall of **Lucifer**, your ex-System Sovereign; and that is the authority of the Father circuits. The majority in your generation have experienced unbalanced male energy (too much male energy) in male father figures, or you have experienced unbalanced female energy (too much female energy) within the

14

male father figures. Unbalanced male and female circuitry in both males and females has caused much pain and suffering leading to broken homes, inappropriate relationships and other major problems in modern civilization and in its proper authority structures. A higher understanding is needed regarding what it means to be an ascending son or daughter in relation to circle attainment and destiny fulfillment within the ascension plan.

Some of you human souls who have heard my transmissions may say I am not loving because sometimes I am stern, authoritative, disciplined, logical and action oriented. This is because what is needed on your planet today is the recognition of true godly authority and balanced Father circuits within the males. There is so much confusion and darkness on your planet, and the accepted realities of truth that should be a bright sun are at best just a flicker of light.

To try to explain to you this imbalance would take several years of your learning of cosmic Father-circuit connections. In other words, my friends, there are no easy answers, no quick solutions and certainly no easy way out of your existent problems, no matter who you are. We can only begin to give you ways to take your first baby steps. The first lesson to learn, as in the child's game Simon Says, is to learn to say, "The Father says, 'take two giant steps and begin to put away your childish views of reality and become teachable.'" Until you can begin to see God as your Daddy in heaven, and I didn't say Mommy (there is a difference), you will not be able to enter our ships, no matter how much metaphysical knowledge or how many theological degrees you have.

My prayer to God is that you read this book in true humility and take that first baby step, asking "Father, help me to understand." When you are sincere, the cosmic Thought Adjuster, or fragment of the Father* within you, will help you.

March 21, 1991

Paladin, Finaliter; presently on assignment with the **Ashtar Command,** in cooperation with the **Midwayer Commission** on Urantia; as transmitted through the Audio Fusion Material Complement, Gabriel of Sedona.

PAPER A³

A MESSAGE FROM THE CHIEF EXECUTIVE OF NEBADON UNDER THE ORDER OF OUR BELOVED UNIVERSE SOVEREIGN, CHRIST MICHAEL, IN RELATION TO THE ADJUDICATION BY THE BRIGHT AND MORNING STAR VERSUS LUCIFER, TO THE PEOPLE OF THE URANTIA MOVEMENT, PRIMARILY THOSE IN THE TEACHING MISSION

There are basically three kinds of people in all religious movements. There are those who know God; there are those who know little of God, and there are those who do not know God but are great pretenders, so good that they have deceived even themselves. *These pretenders are basically the controllers.* Some in the Urantia movement, at one time did know God on varying psychic circles.

Caligastia is still existent on the planet today, along with millions of fallen entities, and all are very active in trying to deceive the very elect of God. For every truth there is an opposite deception. In every area of policy-making on every level of divine mandate at system level and downward, there is an opposite rebellious mandate that *seems* like the divine one, but in reality is opposed to the will of God. There is on the world of Urantia that which is called "The New Order"; then there is The Divine New Order. Two thousand years ago, the Fourth Epochal Revelation, Christ Michael, who bestowed himself on Urantia and walked among you as Jesus, the Son of Man and Son of God, taught about the Divine New Order. Those who knew God at some higher level followed him. Those who knew God, the Universal Father, a little, were the very ones, along with the forces of rebellion, who put Jesus on the cross. They sided with the Pharisees of the day, the ones who did not know God at all, but were the religious leaders. Today, in the Teaching Mission, there are these Pharisees.

There are three kinds of mortals on Urantia, as explained in *The Cosmic Family, Volume I*, the continuation of *The URANTIA Book*: those from other universes called starseed, first-time Urantians, and second-time Urantians. The

---

[1]This letter was transmitted when the Bright and Morning Star fused with Gabriel of Sedona on Sunday, September 3, 1995.

majority of the billions on this planet are native first-time Urantians. The Urantia movement has many starseed and second-time Urantians. All have been in rebellion, and even though they have come to Christ and God at some level, the rebellion still lives in many of them, some because they do not want to see the darkness within them. This is why their memory circuits remain closed.

Those who claim to channel other entities are the starseed or second-time Urantians who are either channeling their higher selves, lowest selves, or a fallen entity. *If you, as a starseed, are channeling your higher self, do not make the grave error of thinking it is anyone but yourself.* It is a self that you have long forgotten. If there is truth in what you are saying, that higher self is a part of you that once had higher truth, but you can also channel information that comes from the darkest part of you that ever existed. Some of you are channeling fallen entities: midwayers, angelic orders, even Caligastia and Daligastia themselves. *There was a Paper given by the finaliter, Paladin, on September 3, 1991, and sent then to some of the now-present channelers, leaders, and teachers of the Teaching Mission. It is Paper 209 of The Cosmic Family, Volume I.* There is the Spirit of Truth that is truly available to be activated, by those who are really willing to humble themselves and who follow the Universal Father and Christ Michael. Then there is the spirit of rebellion. This spirit is active and present at very high levels in the Teaching Mission, and those self-proclaimed leaders are the most deceived or iniquitous, or both. Some have lost their first love for the Father. They have begun to think too highly of themselves.

They say, "By their fruits you shall know them." This is true. However, some of the most iniquitous and most controlling evil ones disguise their evil so well and *seem* to manifest the fruits, that even they themselves are fooled. There will soon come a time on Urantia when the truth shall indeed be made known and those false prophets revealed. Their lives will fall apart, and they will become sick. They will lose their fortunes, and they will lose their sanity. The Teaching Mission claims cooperation and unity, yet there are many false teachings and selfish desires for power to control others. These false teachers are not in the will of God as leaders in divine government under true divine mandate authority. They have appointed themselves and claim it is the move of Christ Michael and the Universal Father.

The veil has begun to open, and a great wave of pain will come across these United States. Indeed, it has started. How foolish and vain it is to say that Caligastia is not here when one soul still suffers on this planet. Those in religious power who have the ability to help others with material needs and don't help, are more concerned about their own finances, power, and position. This is not the kingdom of God.

Divine government does indeed have hierarchy. *The Divine Government on this planet is beginning to be implemented, indeed to bring in the first stage of light and life, by those who are together in a geographic location at Planetary Headquarters, as it was in the first, second, third, and fourth epochal revelations, all living within the radius of one mile of each other. At Planetary Headquarters "the third Garden," called Avalon Gardens, is unfolding and supplying organically grown vegetables for those reservists already aligned with the Divine Government.* The people of the Teaching Mission are separated, not only geographically, but by lack of humility. If there is any one person in any one state who cannot meet their rent, would the leaders who proclaim themselves to be such, pay the rent, supply their children with the things they need, put a roof over the heads of those who need it? Those involved in true ministry must be willing to meet the physical needs of others, as well as their spiritual needs. They must first become like Christ. This is divine government, and we see to it that what is necessary to provide those things is manifested. This is the mandate of the Bright and Morning Star. Gabriel of Sedona has proven himself first as one who has fed and clothed the needy, housed the homeless, and visited the sick in prison. He was given public recognition for this ministry long before Christ Michael chose him to bring through Continuing Fifth Epochal Revelation. This true ministry is still happening here at Planetary Headquarters. Do those in the Teaching Mission or Urantia Movement study the Fifth Epochal Revelation three to four nights a week in a formal school setting and have homework assignments? Do they have to live what they speak? Do they have a real eldership that is saying to them, "You are living in evil and sin and you must change"? This is true pastorship.

There is a great difference between the teaching of Continuing Fifth Epochal Revelation and that which is coming as the message of the Teaching Mission. For those who have eyes to see and ears to hear, *The Cosmic Family, Volume I* alone should speak to your heart of hearts. There are too many in the Urantia movement who have become intellectually bent in their minds, and they study the Fifth Epochal Revelation, not to become like God and Christ, but to impress others with their knowledge. The word "love" is not a catchword to be used like you possess it or have a special inroad to its meaning. Those who do this will be held more responsible by the Ancients of Days.

This is a call from the heart of the Universal Father in and through the Creator Sons and Creative Spirits of Nebadon, Wolvering, Fanoving, and Avalon to come back to your Universal Father, to come back to your faith, to truly love. There is a Planetary Headquarters, and it is indeed where the true fruits of the spirit are. Some have come to Planetary Headquarters under false pretenses. They deny the truth here while they continue to use alcohol, marijuana, and other drugs and live in all manner of evil and sin. They can hide parts of themselves in once-a-week study groups, but not at Planetary Headquarters. The truth will manifest.

My cry to all who are deceived, the innocent ones in the Urantia movement, in the Teaching Mission, in the Fellowship, and in the Foundation, is to get down on your hands and knees and ask the Spirit of Truth to live in you. Ask to see the truth, and the truth will set you free. Do not follow the decoys of Caligastia. Many of you are truly called to be leaders and to truly bring in the first stage of light and life, but you must do it under proper authority, just as the apostles and disciples were under Jesus, as the students of Salem were under Melchizedek, those in the Garden of Eden were under Adam and Eve and those at Dalamatia were under the First Epochal Revelation, the Planetary Prince. Each epochal revelation had a leader with a staff and disciples. All of the humble human servants of the fourth dimension and those orders of higher dimensions are located in Sedona, Arizona, the true Planetary Headquarters of Urantia which will soon become the New Jerusalem. Those most humble are invited to apply for admission. "Many are called, but few are chosen."

September 3, 1995

The Bright and Morning Star, Chief Executive to Christ Michael of Nebadon; for the implementation of the Divine Government of the present Planetary Prince, Machiventa Melchizedek; and the calling forth of cosmic and Urantian destiny reservists; as transmitted through the Level Four Audio Fusion Material Complement, Gabriel of Sedona.

PAPER B

PERSONAL TRANSMISSION TO TWO APOSTLES

Machiventa Melchizedek has asked me to try to send this message to you. It should have come to you last week; however, Gabriel would not allow me to finish it, as he is having his difficulty in this work as you have had yours. Machiventa Melchizedek himself will speak to you by **pure impression**[3] about your phasing out your work in Santa Fe. The reason for this is basically the same reason Gabriel and Niánn were asked to leave Prescott: those of cosmic family in these cities who were supposed to get involved in your work have lost the opportunity for the highest forms of interplanetary linkage, divine government and evacuation processes for these areas. We believe that if you search your hearts, the Thought Adjuster will tell you what we are telling you now, or confirm what you already know to be the truth. We would also like to state that presently, February 17, 1991, you are the only appointed team who has the potential of receiving the Vicegerent mandate of Machiventa Melchizedek.[4] It is hoped that upon stabilization on the third psychic circle there will be Vicegerent First Ambassadors that can transfigure by hologram.[5] Only Gabriel of Sedona can be used for direct audio reception, as was the case several weeks ago.

---

[3]**Pure impression**: The opening of the heart and mindal circuits between celestial personalities, in this case, between Machiventa Melchizedek and his staff, and appointed human and nonhuman individuals.

[4]Since the day of this transmission on February 17, 1991, there have been other candidates for Vicegerent First Ambassadorship, and there will continue to be Vicegerent First Ambassadors until 2040 - 2050. It is important that all Vicegerent First Ambassadors stabilize on the third psychic circle. At the time of editing this second edition in April, 1995, none have been able to do so. The leap in consciousness from the fourth psychic circle to the stabilized third circle can take hundreds of years. Native Urantians do this in the mansion worlds of Satania. Starseed through the process of repersonalization. Also the mandate of the Liaison Ministers, which is a higher mandate than Vicegerent First Ambassador, was established since this transmission came through.

[5]*Since February 17, 1995, the apostle that was transfiguring by hologram, no longer does so. At some point in the future we hope that he will be able to do so again.*

In the past, others were also used, such as Lao-Tse in the sixth century B.C. It was required that these others had to give away what was given. However, on the day you leave Santa Fe, Machiventa no longer will speak through any others but Gabriel. If Machiventa had spoken by pure impression to six individuals, which he did not, the other five would have confirmed the transmissions of the one who holds the mandate, for the one who holds the mandate is the clearest and purest impression complement for that particular entity. If further confirmation is needed, Machiventa would speak through the mandated Bright and Morning Star audio fusion material complement, Gabriel of Sedona.

We also would like to tell you that there are no angels of any order presently incarnated on Urantia. There are, however, mortals repersonalized in human flesh who are not human mortals but who were supermortals of other systems and even other universes. It is also quite possible, and this has happened before, that morontia progressors* of the fifth and above **mansion worlds** have been temporarily sent back to Urantia for reasons I cannot explain in this transmission. Other beings of various orders have been incarnated, but I cannot give further information at this time. I hope this information that has been entrusted to you will not be given to just anyone, and we ask you to keep this particular letter, which we will code "TRANSMISSION P-1" for now, between the two of you until we tell you to release it. Much information as to point of origin and the ascension process has been given to Gabriel and Niánn and they have been asked not to give it to anyone until proper alignment occurs.

We are hoping and praying, with cosmic optimism, that all of you will be able to share and learn from each other that which we have entrusted to you.

You two are to become part of the Aquarian Concepts Community. That is and always has been the intent. All the needs of your everyday living can be taken care of upon your union of souls and listening to the Spirit of God within each one of you; and if need be, our very clear words which will always complement the inner direction.

February 17, 1991

Paladin, Finaliter; in cooperation with the present Planetary Prince of Urantia, Machiventa Melchizedek; as transmitted through the Audio Fusion Material Complement, Gabriel of Sedona.

Excerpt of Transmission from Paladin
"TO THE RESERVE CORPS OF DESTINY"

As published in *Six-O-Six*

"We will be asking these two apostles to physically join Gabriel and Niánn in Sedona, Arizona, U.S.A. When you see this transpire, some of you will know that the will of the Father is being manifested in and through us and those four who have been chosen to be the first four leaders and teachers of CFER to your planet, Urantia."

February 17, 1991

* * * * *

Statement by Machiventa Melchizedek
Present Planetary Prince of Urantia

"I, Machiventa, can only continue to appear on this planet through Vicegerent First Ambassadors who have stabilized on the third psychic circle, which will be confirmed by Paladin through Gabriel of Sedona. I have not spoken through any other than Gabriel of Sedona since December 1989."

February 1995

PAPER C

THE STATE OF OUR PLANET — NEARING THE CHANGE POINT

1. THE FALL OF OUR SYSTEM SOVEREIGN AND PLANETARY PRINCE

In order to understand the present state of our planet, with all of its confusion in government, in society as a whole, and in the spiritual realities that exist, we must go back approximately 200,000 years to the fall of Lucifer. In the Christian understanding of these things Lucifer, the devil, Beelzebub, and Satan* are all one and the same. However, they are separate personalities and beings. Lucifer was a primary Lanonandek Son,* created by Christ Michael, who you know to be Jesus Christ, and the Universe Mother Spirit, an extension of the Infinite Spirit of Paradise. There are primary and secondary Lanonandeks. The primary are created to rule approximately a thousand planets, which is called a system, the smallest administrative unit within the grand universe. The secondary Lanonandeks rule planets and are called Planetary Princes. At the time of the fall of Lucifer, our System Sovereign, there were 607 inhabited worlds in our system of Satania, named after a primary Lanonandek Son, Satan, the assistant of Lucifer. Caligastia was the Planetary Prince of our earth. Our planet is called "Urantia" in the universe government, number 606 of Satania, in the constellation of Norlatiadek, in the local universe of Nebadon, in the superuniverse of Orvonton, just a very small part of the grand universe. One hundred supermortals and aides from other planets accompanied Caligastia — the First Epochal Revelation* to this planet — as his staff when he first came approximately 500,000 years ago. Beelzebub was the head of the primary midwayers, beings that were offspring of the supermortals. These offspring were invisible to the evolutionary humans, as was Caligastia himself and other celestial aides.

Throughout various parts of this book, we will make attempts to try to enlighten readers of this text as to the deceptions that exist on your planet and within the individual souls who perpetrate them unknowingly and sometimes with full knowledge of their deceptions. Trying to understand pride would take a text in itself, but there is a good pride and a terrible dark pride. It is this dark pride that so many souls are unable to see within themselves. It is true that "pride goes before a fall," and this is indeed what happened to the System Sovereign, Lucifer, and several hundred million personalities of various orders, from mortals to beings in the celestial realm, who followed him in his fall. At this point it is important for you to know the difference between evil, sin and iniquity.

Evil is error in viewing cosmic reality.

Sin is a purposeful resistance to true spiritual progress.

Iniquity is persistent rebellion against divine will.

When Lucifer rebelled against his Father, the Creator Son, Michael, and the Universal Father of Paradise, it was not a battle of physical weapons; it was a battle of words, concepts and definitions, and a distortion of cosmic truth, absolutes and laws on Lucifer's part. Briefly stated, his manifesto said:

1. There is no God; you are all gods, all creators.
2. There is no need to follow the Father's will; trust in your own self-guidance; do what makes you feel good.
3. There are no absolute truths; all is relative.
4. There is no evil.
5. No one should have any authority over you; be self-assertive; let your liberty be unbridled.
6. You are not a member of the universe as a cosmic citizen and therefore have no cosmic responsibility and obligations to others in the universe.
7. There is no need to spend much time and energy on your spiritual evolution, for you are already perfect.

These distortions of cosmic law and truth not only caused the beginning of confusion on this planet, but on 36 other planets in your system of Satania whose Planetary Princes also fell with Lucifer. Sixty of the supermortals on Caligastia's staff fell with him. Out of the 50,000 primary midwayers, 40,119 joined Caligastia, as well as a large percentage of **seraphim** and cherubim. Naturally most of the evolutionary mortals followed suit. Thousands of beings of various angelic and other orders in the celestial realms went into rebellion with their System Sovereign, Lucifer. Though Lucifer and Caligastia were iniquitous, many others were only in error and repented later when they realized that so brilliant a being as Lucifer could be wrong.

Lucifer was imprisoned on a satellite world near the system capital of Jerusem at the time of the completion of the sojourn of Michael, Jesus the Christ, on Mount Hermon. Satan, his advocate of iniquity in our system, was imprisoned approximately at the time of the bringing of the Fifth Epochal Revelation to this planet, in the early 1930's. Caligastia and tens of thousands of other fallen entities are still active on this planet keeping the people of Urantia in deception and away from cosmic truth.

At the very beginning of the fall, the Creator Son, Michael, commanded that all interplanetary communication be cut off from Urantia, and this planet, as well as the 36 other worlds that fell, became an isolated world. The circuits of universe broadcasts no longer functioned and cosmic news pertaining to spiritual educational processes and growth were cut off. Urantia became a planet of faith, the later generations wondering what exists beyond their small planet in the vast heavens above. The repercussions of the confusion that has entered this planet up to this present day have caused every disease, every injustice, every war, every ecological disaster, and every dream of man to die in despair. Yet still man continues to accept these deceptions of Lucifer under new names and supposed new revelations, cloaked in various disguises. Caligastia continues to perpetrate the lies and distortions of Lucifer in the minds of men and women on this planet.

2. THE DEFAULT OF ADAM AND EVE

In an effort to explain man's dilemma in being estranged from God and God's universe, primitive attempts were made in theological doctrines and traditions which developed into the evolutionary religions. Every so often a great spiritual teacher of the evolutionary races discovered some elementary cosmic truths, but usually their followers distorted the truth that was presented and developed a system of religious thought far from the absolute truth of God and all that God is throughout the worlds of time and space. So the Universe Supervisors* saw fit to send a Second Epochal Revelation in the form of a Material Son and Daughter,* **Adam and Eve**, approximately 38,000 years ago. Although they were informed of the state of your planet before they arrived, they could not believe just how spiritually and intellectually backwards the evolutionary humans actually were. Their function as a Material Son and Daughter was to present a progeny race that would intermingle with the evolutionary mortals and upstep genetically all of mankind. They were supposed to have half a million descendents before this intermingling occurred, but because of much discouragement and impatience Eve decided to step ahead of the plan of God and gave birth to a son of a human partner. Adam himself followed suit and both became mortal as a result. The total benefits of the genetic strain that these superbeings could have given this planet were never realized. Only a very small percentage on the planet today benefit from their genetics.

3. THE LATER THREE EPOCHAL REVELATIONS

Approximately 4,000 years ago a Melchizedek Son, the Third Epochal Revelation, was sent to Urantia. **Melchizedeks** are a high order of beings that exist on various worlds throughout the universe of Nebadon. Machiventa Melchizedek again brought the concept of the one God and First Source and Center Creator, a concept that was almost lost on this planet at the time of his arrival. Though his teachings were spread across the planet by his followers, because of the deeply entrenched falsehoods and confusion left from the Luciferic teachings that were still part of the races' belief systems, these higher truths were not accepted as widely and in the purest sense as was hoped for by the Universe Supervisors.

Approximately two thousand years later a Divine Son, Christ Michael, bestowed himself on this planet as Jesus and brought the Fourth Epochal Revelation, the fatherhood of God and the brotherhood of man. In appreciation for this divine gift, the mass consciousness of mankind crucified this truth upon a cross. The true and pure teachings of Jesus have never really been appropriated on the planet. Much of what are supposedly the teachings of Christ in modern Christianity, in both Catholic and Protestant institutions, are far removed from what Jesus taught and lived. Because of this bestowal and the Spirit of Truth which he left behind upon his ascension back to Salvington, his headquarters world, much good and divine purpose has been accomplished in universe administration, planetary government, and in reestablishing the broken circuits between our world and the others of our universe. In the two thousand years since his bestowal, Urantia has become worse in the area of evil, sin and iniquity. Not only do humans suffer (and there are more humans on the planet now than there have ever been since the beginning of mankind), but the very earth itself, the reflective spirit of the Universe Mother which has come to be called Mother Nature, has been dying. She is soon to give birth to new life within and upon her.

To prepare her new children and the seed of the offspring of those who follow the Father's will, and that of her Co-creator, Christ Michael, the Fifth Epochal Revelation is being given to help ease the pain of her birth which is a change point, that could very well happen anytime within this decade. We believe that the extension of grace and mercy of the Universe Father, Michael, in allowing the rebellion to take its course, is about over, due not only to the many injustices and sufferings on your planet, but also to the very deterioration of the essence of the Mother God within the earth herself. Because of certain earth changes that we believe will take place around May of 2000 or 2001, it is of immediate urgency that all those who can hear what the Spirit of God is saying to the seeds of light respond to the Fifth Epochal Revelation, that which is in print and that which is continuing to come through the mandated audio fusion material complement, Gabriel of Sedona. This revelation is brought to the planet by a composite of beings, of which I, a finaliter, am one.

4. THE RESULTS OF THE REBELLION — SPIRITUAL DISTORTION

As I have repersonalized on your planet several times, I understand very well what it is to be human and what it is to experience total and complete hopelessness, suffering of all kinds, and the experience of human death, mostly caused by my own adherence to the very deceptions that I believed to be truth, which I perpetrated upon others, also leading to their sufferings and deaths. Although I experienced error, I never willfully chose sin. When I realized my error, I corrected it. I never consciously fell to any of the deceptions of the **Lucifer rebellion**. I understand what it is to have misplaced compassion, to misunderstand God and be unknowingly disloyal to my fellow brothers and sisters. I have seen the insensitivity of man to man. I have watched the good die hungry, be tortured and abused by the evil and powerful. I have watched the dreams of the idealistic and artistic die within the reality of circumstances that they could not change, due to the fact that others less creative than they feared the poets' dreams of flight and beauty, and I have watched the fires of change quenched with the chains of suppression and control. I have seen the abuse of man to man and the suppression of woman by man. I have experienced prejudice of every kind and have died through violence by the hands of those who disliked me merely because of the color of my skin. I have watched my own children and grandchildren being tortured by others because they could not control me, and so they attacked the innocent. For when one becomes strong and wise enough to fight back and come against evil, sin and iniquity, those who notice your light and your courage will stop at nothing to destroy you, as they did to the most beautiful being who set his foot upon this planet, Jesus Christ, the carpenter of Nazareth.

This book is an attempt to awaken you to the bondages that you have been in, perhaps not just for this lifetime but for many others. Throughout the rest of this book, attempts will be made to express in more detail some of the statements that I have made in the previous paragraph.

Paladin, Finaliter; as transmitted through the Audio Fusion Material Complement, Gabriel of Sedona.

PAPER D

COSMIC FAMILY — PLANET OF UNIVERSE ORIGIN

Each Creator Son, who is of the order of Michael, decides the ascension process to Paradise for all the various beings created within his universe. *The URANTIA Book* gives information about the ascension process in the universe of Nebadon. CFER gives further information concerning some neighboring universes and their ascension plans. This book will only cover some introductory information that complements what is already written in *The URANTIA Book* for the reader who is open to the threefold Spirit* within. This book in no way intends to give the complete ascension process to Paradise for the universe of Nebadon or any other. But for a more detailed description of the Nebadon ascension process, you may want to study *The URANTIA Book*.

1. FIRST-TIME URANTIANS

Since the Fifth Epochal Revelation has come to this planet, more detailed cosmic truth has been given as to that wondrous reality of mortal life, and on this planet, of human mortal life. As the evolutionary process took its course, the first male and female human, who called themselves Sonta-an and Sonta-en, left their primate family members because they felt so different, and began to make moral decisions, and as such were the father and mother of the human race on this planet. The Planetary Supervisors, who monitored this awakening from a more animalistic nature to a human nature, announced to all the worlds of Nebadon that Urantia had now become number 606 of the inhabited worlds of humans seeking moral perfection. Up into modern history, the majority of souls upon this planet are in existence for the first time, their point of origin being Urantia. Whether one is primitive or with the mindal capacity of the twentieth century, when one leaves this world one proceeds to the first of the seven mansion worlds which are some of the satellites of the system capital, Jerusem; then on to the constellation worlds and on through the universe and superuniverse worlds to the central universe, Havona,* and finally inward to Paradise.

2. SECOND-TIME URANTIANS

Sometime since the beginning of this century, there has been an adjudication of some sleeping survivors, for what purpose is known only to certain of the Universe Supervisors. What we do know is that certain **Urantians** have been

28

allowed to come back to this planet for the second time. In the history of Urantia, this has been the first time that this has been allowed to happen, and we speculate that it is because your planet is about to transcend into the fourth dimension, which is close to what the first mansion world would have been for them.

There are two groups of **second-time Urantians** on Urantia today:

1. The first group are souls who will hopefully be able to help in this transition, for they had higher genetic coding implanted within them in their first life on this planet. Despite this coding they were not able to synthesize much of their higher insight into practicality and virtue, continuing to fall into error on Urantia in their first life. They would have been detained as sleeping survivors but it was decided by Overcontrol for them to return to Urantia to become students of the Fifth Epochal Revelation, which would stabilize them so they could teach others. They themselves are destined, as they spiritually mature, to meet their higher teachers and cosmic family who were their first parents, children, grandparents, etc.

2. The second group of second-time Urantians also had higher genetic coding, but became iniquitous because of their higher mindal abilities. Because of the special implantation in these souls, instead of a continued sleep state until adjudication, it was decided that they'd be given another opportunity on Urantia where the adjudication was now taking place. In a sense they are being adjudicated, but given a second opportunity. They will have to overcome whatever pride that is within them that caused their failure to ascend to the first mansion world. This point of truth will happen for them when they humble themselves in this era upon meeting the mandated teachers they are to be in submission to. Many of these second-time Urantians may be better off financially and educationally than the teachers that God has appointed for them. If they have not learned to look for the right things, they will base credibility on wrong values and will miss their appointed teachers and their destinies. It is quite possible that they will not be able to be translated or evacuated at the time of the change point. Many of them may have to die a physical death and go into a sleep state to await yet again another judgement by the Ancients of Days,* who in turn may order them to one of the other 36 fallen planets in Satania; but they will not be allowed to return to Urantia, where their first human parents and relatives are, for they rejected them when they met, being entrapped in the Luciferic deceptions from which they could not break away.

There are under 2000 second-time Urantians, which is a very small number in comparison to the billions of **first-time Urantians**, and 170 million ovan souls/ starseed of other universes and planets. A vast number of these starseed have defaulted in their ascension and are now on the cosmic fence. They also would have had to go to one of the 36 other fallen planets, but chose Urantia because some of their cosmic family were here.

3. STARSEED FROM OTHER UNIVERSES

Usually the only extraterrestrial genetic mixture of evolutionary races on a normal world would be that of a Material Son and Daughter, an Adam and an Eve; but on Urantia Adam and Eve themselves had incorrect relations with humans, as did the fallen staff of Caligastia (the one time Planetary Prince). Many of these supermortals were not only citizens of Jerusem (the capital of our system of Satania), but they were descendents of finaliters on assignment to the Jerusem capital at the time and fully embodied in a morontia reality. Also present were many Jerusem citizens of other universes who had gone through the prescribed ascension plans of their particular Michael Son including a sojourn on a system capital of a neighboring universe. What adventures would await them at that point would be entirely up to the Universe Sovereign, the Michael Son of that particular universe of their sojourn. Thousands of years ago, many evolutionary humans inherited the genetic codes of their ancestors' point of origin and ascension process; these humans are not starseed, but they have starseed genetics. Many of the processes are very different from the ascension plan of Nebadon; although to some degree they have to obey much of the ascension rules of Nebadon. It has been a universe fact in Nebadon that starseed have repersonalized over and over again on one particular planet. On Urantia, in the teachings of ancient times, humans began calling the process of these souls traveling back to this planet "reincarnation," which in reality is based more on superstition than on fact. However, approximately 170 million starseed/ovan souls have returned to this planet as part of their ascension process to be with their cosmic family (at least that was the Universe Supervisors' design time and time again). So, those souls who have extraterrestrial genetic coding within them, have been allowed to return to Urantia by the Sovereign Ruler of Nebadon, some of them up to a dozen times. Gabriel of Sedona and Niánn have had more than a dozen **repersonalizations**. They are the two oldest souls on Urantia. The exact number of their repersonalizations is unrevealed at this time. Gabriel has had more than Niánn. All 170 million starseed are from another universe. Most of these ovan souls have repersonalized, on average approximately ten times, with the higher spiritual types averaging 12 repersonalizations. Any soul who says that she or he is a very old soul and has had hundreds, thousands, or millions of incarnations on this planet and others is either an ignorant and arrogant soul and/or most likely a fallen starseed who has only been here, at the most, a half dozen times.

Much information about these ascending sons and daughters must be withheld from the contents of this book. Until the reader can assimilate this text, in its proper context, these cosmic truths and laws will not be understood. What can be said at this time is that there are presently in human form, born of human parents (and many of them born of first-time Urantians), souls from another universe or another superuniverse. Until you understand the ramifications of these things, you will not quite realize the immensity of instructions that would have to be given to properly teach such a subject. However, the Michael Sons of these universes all have their own unique plans of ascension to Paradise, and part of those plans are intermediate sojourns on planets of neighboring universes and superuniverses. Urantia is a very well-known planet because your Creator Son himself chose to be born of the very beings that he created, a human mother and father. When a Creator Son, a Divine Paradise Being, chooses to become the very lowest of personalities, that particular world on which it happens becomes known as a special "planet of visitation." So, your planet, Urantia, is a Mecca of spiritual assignment throughout all of the superuniverses of time and space. I, Paladin, a finaliter, am not originally from your universe, nor am I from your superuniverse. However, the very first time that I became a mortal human in your superuniverse was in the star system you call the Pleiades, on the third planet from Alcyone which you call Electra and we call **Tora**. There, I had many children in several repersonalizations, not only on that planet but on several other planets within that system. To those children who came into existence for the first time as a human mortal Pleiadian, I am their cosmic father. To those who have ascended into a higher mindal (intellectual) and spiritual attainment, I rejoined them in many lifetimes, sometimes as their father again and sometimes as their grandfather, uncle, or friend, always as an elder teacher and always someone they loved and respected. It is the plan of the gods, not only in this universe, but in all the universes of time and space, for the union of souls of the very highest spiritual commonality and cosmic understanding of the universal absolute truths, to be reunited time and time again. This is uniquely happening now, not only on the lower evolutionary world, Urantia, but also on the higher worlds of light and life. It has been and is, up unto this very hour, an unfortunate reality that because of your pride, you seldom recognize your ancient ancestors when you meet them. You have developed loyalties to false friends and career associates who can perhaps give you material things, while those of your cosmic family can only give you truth and love. These other friends are those who expect you to remain in their social norms and religious institutions because they are your employers, and the politicians that you have voted for and who control your daily lives, as opposed to your other acquaintances who may be your garage mechanic, your supermarket manager, an idealistic artist who has not become financially successful, or who perhaps, like Jesus, as your local carpenter, would also be rejected today and never become your friend or cosmic family member and spiritual teacher. Your attitude today seems to be "Can any good thing come out of a laborer, an artist, a noncelebrity?" Yes, I have heard those words before; they were said 2000 years ago in Galilee, "Can any good thing come out of Nazareth?" (John 6:47)

4. COSMIC RELATIVES, SOUL MATES, HIGHEST COMPLEMENTS

All humans are mortal, but not all mortals are human. On the evolutionary worlds of time and space within various universes, life as you know it is quite different . However, there is a consistency of what you on your world call "friendship," "family," "procreation," and "marriage." No matter in which universe you first come into being, you will have a mortal mother and father who are bipeds, meaning they walk upright on two legs. All other features may be quite different from other human mortals. Human mortals exist on planets other than Urantia and in systems other than Satania. The first time a soul comes into existence as a mortal, that particular planet is his or her planet of origin. As a human mortal, or perhaps a nonhuman mortal, the associations that you have in that life with your nuclear family and friends, and more importantly, with those who come to understand the higher spiritual principles of cosmic order and law, and particularly the fatherhood of God, come to be your first cosmic relatives. Many of these relatives and friends repersonalize over and over again with you on other worlds in various universes. These relatives become your soul mates,* twin flames,* and an eventual union of souls. Females can consistently become wives with the same male(s) in various lifetimes and give birth to the same children with those male(s).

In the universe of Nebadon under the sovereign rule of Michael, no ascending mortal son ever becomes an ascending female or a descending female. In other words, if you are now presently a man or woman, you have always been either a male-circuited personality or a female-circuited personality, more Father/ Son-circuited or more Infinite-Spirit-circuited. The false belief by some that they have been a male in the past when they are presently a female or vice versa, stems from superstition and continual propagation of this falsehood by those fallen personalities of the Lucifer rebellion. Also, in no circumstances do the Universe Supervisors allow past mothers and fathers to become present husbands and wives of their past children. However a past female complement can become a present mother but under no circumstances would this justify incest as the child matures. In some circumstances[6] on Urantia it is quite possible that past sisters and brothers who have reached a seventh stage third-dimensional relationship

---

[6]Further explanation in future volumes.

can become marriage partners and procreate children, with the hopes that these cosmic brothers and sisters can become twin flames of fourth-dimensional reality and, more properly, **complementary polarities.**

It is within the plan of most Creator Sons that the members of these cosmic families reunite on various planes/planets in the many ascension processes, in order that they together can be a force for cosmic truth and the Father's will throughout the universes of time and space. On Urantia it has been the aim of Caligastia and the forces of rebellion to keep these cosmic family members from uniting. On Urantia, with the fall of the Planetary Prince and the Material Son and Daughter and the misinterpretation of the message of Michael/Jesus Christ, it has been next to impossible for humans here to receive continued revelation about the cosmic family. Even at the time of the first papers of *The URANTIA Book* in the early 1930's, it still was not time for Urantians to receive these higher truths. It could only be partially given to some starseed of the fourth to the first order, and there are seven orders in the universe of Nebadon. Presently, now in the early 1990's, there are 170 million of these starseed from the first to the fourth orders who can now receive and understand these higher truths and cosmic connections. Still, the majority of them will not be able to break free from the many chains that bind them and from old thoughtforms, traditions, religious dogma, etc. The actualization of finding one's cosmic family and higher soul mates and complementary polarities will be almost an impossibility presently in the third dimension on Urantia. But it is not totally impossible, and it is the hope of your Creator Son, Michael, and all of the Universe Supervisors down to the present administration on Urantia that, Divine New Order communities with cosmic families can be appropriated so that Urantia can have a prototype of a civilization that will exist after the purification of your planet is over and the Divine New Order and the first stages of light and life begin.

Basically, on the evolutionary worlds where mortals have children and raise them, there is some method of social organization in which these children can be raised and educated, but it may not be in a monogamous family unit. On the higher spiritual worlds children have relationships with grandparents, great-grandparents, uncles, aunts, cousins — just like you do on Urantia — with the exception that on these worlds that have not fallen the societal structure is quite different. But the teaching of cosmic law and truth is a prerequisite for all to learn in all the universes of time and space; so there is a cosmic norm. In your universe of Nebadon, a monogamous marriage is the ideal, but on other worlds in other universes, marriage of one husband to one wife is nonexistent, and higher spiritual mates can all join together in unions of families for procreation and spiritual education. As far as the Urantian human is concerned, it seems that the monogamous relationship between male and female works best and is consistent with the rest of the worlds in Nebadon. However, there have always been a high representation of starseed of other universes on this planet, particularly the males, who have never been able to adjust to monogamous relationships and/or marriages. Because of the social standards of modern Western civilization, they have had to adapt to the norm of the first-time human Urantian reality. For those first-time Urantians, the group guardian angel who observes that one of the souls he or she is overseeing has advanced to a seventh stage third-dimensional relationship with a present mate and a higher psychic circle, will see to it that this soul is properly matched with his or her complement of highest potential, as long as both of these souls continue to seek the Father's will, with the hopes that they will be able to obtain fourth-dimensional reality, which became quite possible with the Fifth Epochal Revelation being brought to this planet.

The following is a list of the seven stages of third and fourth-dimensional relationships.

Third-Dimensional Soul Mate Relationship:

Stage   1. Physical sex drive
Stage   2. Need for children/procreation
Stage   3. Intellectual attraction
Stage   4. Emotional attraction
Stage   5. Commonality in interests, hobbies, etc.
Stage   6. Shared inner vision
Stage   7. A shared sense of spirituality

Fourth-Dimensional Complementary Polarities (Twin Flame Relationship):

Stage   1. God can be realized and both are actively seeking the Father's will.
Stage   2. Shared realization of God as a trinity and both have received the Spirit of Truth as well as having the fragment of the Father.
Stage   3. All three aspects of the Trinity are activated within both (the Thought Adjuster, the Spirit of Truth, and the Holy Spirit*).
Stage   4. Both knowing when all three aspects are in themselves and in their mate.
Stage   5. A common understanding of the cosmology of the master universe, which includes the physical worlds and the various personalities who exist in them (Fifth Epochal Revelation knowledge).

Stage   6. Both have a sense of shared destiny and have not fallen back into institutional entrapments or man's doctrinal interpretations of Fifth Epochal Revelation, which can only be interpreted by the threefold Spirit within, and those celestial personalities who are in attendance with **third-circler** mortals.

Stage   7. Both are learning CFER in order to bring about the Divine Government on the planet, and to bring about fourth-dimensional and above consciousness and the pre-stages and first stage of light and life on the planet.

Although there are many first-time Urantians who reach the first stage of fourth-dimensional God-realization together, very few follow through with seeking the perfect will of that God because of many reasons:

1. Improper religious affiliation which teaches too many of the doctrines of men.
2. An unwillingness in one or the other to give up ways of selfishness and false desires.
3. An unwillingness to leave family and old friends behind who are themselves unwilling to change.
4. An inability to hear from one's God because of lack of proper listening and prayer life.

Fourth-dimensional complementary-polarity relationships were actually possible when Christ Michael came as Jesus and taught some of the basic truths about the threefold aspect of God. Unfortunately, the true message of Jesus became greatly compromised with pagan, Hellenistic and Roman thinking. Those who reach the second stage of the fourth dimension on Urantia usually lead lives of higher reality and have a sense of security with their God amidst the problems that life may deal them.

Many who reach the third stage of the fourth dimension have an even higher life together, and God is able to use them more because of the balance that they have as individual male and female. The children will be better adjusted, and family life as a whole will run more effectively.

When both individuals know that they have received the threefold Spirit of God within them, this knowingness enables them to control their individual tendencies toward imbalances and therefore adds to the individuals' abilities to perform at work as well as in the home, and to accomplish more as light workers within the kingdom of God on the lower evolutionary worlds of time and space where rebellion has occurred.

Each stage should flow and create the energy force to shift into the next stage quite naturally; however, because of the fallen state of Urantia with its myriad confusions and problems in the spiritual realm, many highest complements of fourth-dimensional reality, even starseed who have lived through many repersonalizations on the fallen worlds including Urantia, do not reach the fifth stage easily. This stage is of the Fifth Epochal Revelation; it is the stage of shared common terminology of cosmic law and truth; it is the stage of the mutual understanding of the master universe, to the degree that it can be comprehended between both mates. Usually at this level each individual is ready to enter the third psychic circle; but they are always, without exception, on the fourth circle before moving up to the third. This is the stage where complementary polarities can become highly used by God as of teachers of higher cosmic universal truths. This is the stage where the couple together can realize a higher existence, freer from the timetable of Caligastia, secular work and bondages, and more able to receive higher communication from the Universe Supervisors, and protection in the material as well as the spiritual realm. It is the breakthrough stage in the reopening of the circuits which were cut off at the time of the Caligastia rebellion. It is the beginning of this couple's entering into a union of souls with higher cosmic realities and personalities. On the fourth psychic circle and first-through-fourth stages, one can have a realization of and even have contact with celestial personalities, but it is quite impossible for those personalities to truly reveal who they really are. This has to do with a cosmic law concerning the free will of the individuals on the fourth psychic circle and the pride that they may have within them which would be inconsistent with true humility, therefore keeping them from a higher circle and higher stage. No celestial personality can give information through and over the pride of obstinate souls who are unwilling to humble themselves to human teachers and/or become students of higher cosmic truths, which are written and have been given to this planet by the Universe Supervisors in the writings of *The URANTIA Book* and CFER through the mandated audio fusion material complement, who presently also has the mandate of the Bright and Morning Star.

When the couple together realize some of the elementary aspects of the master universe in both physical and nonphysical hierarchical structure and have some idea of their own ascension process to Paradise, they together, in reaching this sixth stage, can be even more highly used by God in a moment to moment situation in life, as opposed to perhaps God being able to use them for half of the moments of the day. Their every word, every action, every movement is a reflection of their God to others, and they become living and breathing representations of their Creator Father and Mother and represent the totality of God wherever they are present, on whatever plane they are on. When both individuals are flowing together, they become a single unit, fully aligned with the triune purposes of the Father, Eternal Son,* and Infinite Spirit, as represented and actualized in evolutionary men and women.

On Urantia there are only approximately 977 couples who are in the fifth stage of complementary polarity relationship. (There are many more who may have an understanding of the cosmology of the master universe, but who have not yet acquired the previous stages of a fourth-dimensional relationship.) It is hoped that by the turn of the century, this number will be increased to 10,000 couples. There is presently only one couple who has reached the seventh stage of fourth-dimensional status. This is Gabriel of Sedona and Niánn who co-share the Mandate of the Bright and Morning Star. It is not always necessary for complementary polarities to be male and female in physical body; the fourth-dimensional complementary relationship between two people is focused on the spiritual union rather than on the sexual. However, when male and female complements of this stage can be put together, the children of such a union will always be first order starseed. Those children, would have reached a stage of sixth and seventh mansion world progression in the universe of Nebadon, and would erroneously be called "**Ascended Masters**."

So you see, it is quite possible for complements to be cosmic father and son, father and daughter, mother and son, mother and daughter, sister and brother, sister and sister, brother and brother, grandmother and grandchild, etc. Again, it has nothing to do with the sexual; and when these souls can be brought together, (and they are brought together on worlds settled in the first stages of light and life), great and marvelous things can be accomplished for those individuals and for the betterment of the planet on which they are presently located.

Since the time of the Caligastia fall, the forces of confusion have done all that they can to:

1. Separate those humans with superhuman genetics which keeps them from actualizing their higher mindal capacity and their ability to attain higher **cosmic circles**.
2. Keep first-time Urantians on the sixth stage of the third-dimensional reality.
3. Misrepresent what true spirituality is on the seventh stage of the third dimension.
4. Confound the true concept of God as a personal Father and to present the Eternal Father as nonpersonal and only a Force and Energy.
5. Teach against the experiential aspect of God* and speak only of the existential aspect of God,* preventing the individual from ever fully realizing in totality the vastness of the beings/personalities that God has

created for our brother/sisterhood.

6. Confound the cosmic understanding of the Father and Mother circuits and the incorporation of those circuits and energies within the evolving male and female, therefore causing unbalanced men and women.

7. Keep cosmic family members from finding one another and then joining one another for the work in the kingdom on the rebellious worlds.

8. Teach the distortions regarding the ascension/descension processes in Satania, bringing in false and superstitious concepts such as reincarnation and karma as opposed to repersonalization and cause and effect in order to create further misunderstanding and prevent the coming together of cosmic family.

5. HIGHEST COMPLEMENTS, MALE / FEMALE, FOR MARITAL PURPOSES AND PROCREATION OF CHILDREN

In the universe of Nebadon, in the various systems that exist, the highest orders of sexual beings are Material Sons and Daughters. They are not human and are not mere mortals. They are created by the Michael Son to act as teachers and administrators, and to introduce their genetics by the intermarrying of their offspring with the human mortals of the evolutionary worlds. Adam and Eve defaulted by having sexual relationships with human beings. There were to be about half a million of their offspring on Urantia before any intermarrying between these offspring and evolutionary humans took place; therefore:

1. The genetics of the human races were not uplifted by the offspring of Adam and Eve as planned.

2. By having sex directly with mortals, Adam and Eve created offspring who would genetically inherit the desire to give of their life plasm through sexual encounter, which to the offspring was an act of love, but to Adam and Eve an act of misplaced compassion in the original default.

In societies where monogamy is the norm, this inherited psychological and spiritual personality trait is more difficult to deal with and little understood by the offspring themselves or society as a whole. The Christian concept of original sin was actually developed by some of the apostles because of a misunderstanding of one of the teachings of Jesus which is not mentioned either in the New Testament or in *The URANTIA Book*. Jesus himself, over a period of time, had to learn what he could and could not teach his apostles. It is said that he spoke to them and said, "I give you milk now because you are not yet ready for the meat." This was true of so many higher concepts and cosmic realities which he tried to share, but later concluded that he could go no further trying to instruct them. Jesus knew that there were seven of his apostles who were not first-time Urantians. He also knew that they genetically were linked to the Material Son and Daughter, Adam and Eve. He tried to explain this one day to Andrew, John, Thomas, Nathaniel and Peter but realized that in giving them this information he only confused them more, and so had to hold back in giving them higher cosmic truths, as they had not reached the circle of attainment capable of understanding these higher cosmic realities. They understood that the descendents of Adam and Eve inherited some kind of difference, and when Jesus used the word "default" to explain the Material Son's and Daughter's default, they naturally thought that whatever was inherited from their offspring was also a default. Since they were also trained in the Genesis understanding the fall of Adam and Eve, they passed on the false teachings that all mankind originated from Adam and Eve and inherited their default or sin. In reality, all mankind did not come from Adam and Eve. The highest genetic strain present today on Urantia that actually has the Adamic genetics of highest physiological and astral inheritance is approximately half a million souls, mostly among the present day Caucasian races of mankind. Those with the purest genetic link are less than one dozen on the planet. These one dozen, if united together, could create a higher race of human beings on Urantia. The breakdown of the half million can be put into various groupings, very specifically and exactly, by the recording angelic overseers and Life Carriers* who know exactly who these people are and who try their best, with the help of certain midwayers and group seraphim, cherubim and sanobim overseers, to match them in marital relationships without interfering with their free will. In a future book more exact and detailed information will be given regarding these half million descendents of the highest genetic strains of Adam and Eve. It is intended that all of the 170 million starseed at one time in some repersonalization on Urantia marry and procreate with the Adamic offspring. When the starseed chose to come to this planet, it was part of their purposes to marry within that genetic Adamic strain, therefore producing in their human children an even higher genetic coding that would aid in the spiritual and mindal development of the human race as a whole. Again, it is Caligastia's plan to keep the Adamic strain separated from other cosmic starseed and to keep the offspring from marrying their highest complements. Because of the various defaults that have occurred on Urantia by the Planetary Prince and the Material Son and Daughter, and because of Urantia being an **experimental planet**, human pair marriage has not usually functioned on the very highest level. When the highest spiritual realities are not understood by the individuals on the planet, it is next to impossible for two human beings to come together as husband and wife or mates/partners, to have a working relationship between themselves in the highest capacity and to give birth to and raise children in the highest of spiritual realities.

Presently, there are seven orders of starseed who can be repersonalized through human parents. These orders have nothing to do with point of origin, but with the last planet of ascension. They have nothing to do with the seven cosmic circles, though sometimes there is a correlation. The seven orders have more to do with the spiritual ascension of that particular soul. When higher soul mates produce children together, that enables a higher soul to come through that union.

1. First-order **star children** can only come through highest complements of cosmic origin who are on the fifth stage of the fourth dimension. First-order star children are souls who come from planets that have settled in the first stages of light and life and above in any universe in the superuniverse of Orvonton. First-order star children on Urantia have usually been here previously.

2. Second-order star children come from planets that have not fallen in the rebellion in the system of Satania and are usually **sixth and seventh mansion world progressors**. There are none on the planet at this time.

3. Third-order star children come from other universes whose planets are in the first stages of light and life. They are new to the experience of Urantia and relatively new to Nebadon, are less adaptable to the normal maturation process of the human child and certain motor and psychological functions take a little longer to develop than those of the first-order star child.

4. Fourth-order star children come from other universes in Orvonton, where they have erred or fallen but have supermortal ancestors who have been to Urantia.

5. Fifth-order star children are always finaliters who are purposefully on assignment on this planet, for whatever reason, and are of another superuniverse. At this time, however, there are none of this order on Urantia.

6. Sixth-order star children are the same as above but have been to Urantia through repersonalization at least once before. Again, there are none of this order here.

7. Seventh-order star children are unrevealed personalities, either from this universe or another, who repersonalize either by assignment or ascension. It is never a descension for these personalities.

In the reality of the cosmos, these ascending mortals and other ascending orders of beings reach a certain spiritual status based upon their fusion with Father, Son and Spirit (Mother) circuits. The highest of oneness (fusion of the threefold spirit), denotes a status of spiritual ranking gained in the celestial realms. When these mortals and other personalities, for whatever reason, repersonalize or incarnate on Urantia or any other world of lower evolution, they still retain their spiritual status/ranking. Even on worlds as confused as present-day Urantia, they are meant in destiny arrangement to become leaders and teachers, with the full understanding by others that their spiritual ascension has nothing to do with that present world's social or educational degrees or titles.

In a future book, more detailed explanation of these children and the seven orders will be given. However, for now the first-order starseed are the highest order because of their assignments to become spiritual teachers and spiritual governmental administrators. They usually come to a planet when it is about to shift from the third to the fourth dimension. The other orders can come any time during the evolution of the human races on that planet. Because these souls are so badly needed on the planet today, it is of the utmost importance that the very highest complements of cosmic family come together to bring forth these children. Just as important, those others who are cosmic relatives need to come together to help in the raising of these children, as it never is the total responsibility of just the mother and father to raise such children in the education of higher cosmic truths, laws and universal concepts.

6. INAPPROPRIATE RELATIONSHIPS

On planets settled in the first stages of light and life, the divine governments see to it that soul mates and complementary polarities are united together in community environments of cosmic family and higher genetic strain. Even on some planets that are in the pre-stages of light and life and have not defaulted in their epochal visitations by celestial overseers, the human administrators know full well the value of cosmic family organization and community life for the benefit of the nation and planet as a whole. Even on such fallen worlds as Urantia, with third-dimensional humans on the seventh circle, some nationalities pride themselves in their family ties, and many organizations, some even unethical in practice, pride themselves on family unity and loyalty. They are able to accomplish great things in a third-dimensional secular sense, and they become powerful forces in the accomplishment of their own goals. The forces of evil know full well the power of such unions. That is why they try so very hard to come against the higher spiritual reality of the truths of the union of souls and cosmic family, for then the light would overcome the darkness and the forces of evil would not be able to perpetrate their designs upon humankind.

Because we are very near the purification time of Urantia and the change point into the Divine New Order and the pre-stages of light and life, the forces of light can give more aid now to certain souls to help them break free of old thoughtforms and confusions within their personality makeup. Even first-time Urantians can be complemented with their very highest seventh-stage mates in order to move into the fourth dimension and complementary relationships in the higher stages. But many confusions hold these first-time Urantians, who are the majority on the planet, from finding their highest soul mates and marital partners.

Most relationships between male and female are based upon the first six stages of the third dimension, and an unfortunately high percentage (70% to 80%) are based upon the physical attraction alone, which is the first stage in the third-dimensional relationship. Many of these couples remain physically united, even though the individual souls themselves have no commonality of interests, no spiritual harmony and lead lives of utter desperation outside of their sexual unions, which in reality does not really satisfy them. In fulfilling the other necessary commonalities needed for higher complementary relationships and not realizing or knowing what is truly needed for themselves, they seek fulfillment by trying to acquire other sexual unions, never really satisfying the inner evolving soul. Many others marry just to have children, without even having attained the first stage, and the first stage is important, for there must be some physical attraction between human mortals. This is consistent with a one million year study by Universe Overseers on this planet and of much longer periods on other planets, where human mortals like yourselves function. In these inappropriate unions of first-time Urantians or mismatched starseed with first-time Urantians where children are born, they are always, without exception, giving birth to first-time Urantians; and higher orders of star children cannot be born from the mothers of such unions. Some children born through these unions may have physical and psychological defects. This is no fault of the children themselves and is not related to any karma, but it is an error and perhaps even a sin of the parents themselves not seeking the will of the Creator to the fullest extent in the choosing of their mates and having these children.

Concerning the third stage of a third-dimensional relationship, intellectual attraction can breed pride within both of the individuals and an inward deterioration of both, which can lead to various cancers and other diseases. In the fourth stage many souls come together in marriage because the other has a strength that they lack, and they become emotionally dependent upon each other. One also could be inappropriately attracted to someone who offers financial security. There is only one commonality in the fifth stage that should be sought for in a mate, and that is the spiritual commonality. All others are meaningless unless this one is met first. A couple cannot truly grow together unless both individuals can bring the other closer to God and closer to the actualization of the other's purpose in the plan of God.

A couple can have a shared vision of a certain dream or desire that may not be God's purpose for them and together they may achieve their goal, but when they reach it they will find themselves still empty and will have to set another goal, until one or both together come into alignment with the Father's purposes for their lives. When a couple truly reaches the seventh stage in a third-dimensional relationship, both should come to realize that there is some power outside of themselves that has an influence in the destinies of men and women. As they seek that power together, their relationship strengthens. As long as they are on the same path of seeking, they can have somewhat of a fulfilled life together; but they can never serve the highest purposes in the Kingdom of God until both come to total God-realization and know him as a personal Father.

7. MAN / WOMAN ROLES

In the universe of Nebadon, the very highest models of male and female embodiments in flesh are the Material Sons and Daughters, the Adams and Eves; they are the highest examples of male/female to the lower evolutionary worlds of time and space. In the universe of Nebadon, the pair relationship of one Material Son to one Material Daughter is the basis for human marriage and the highest ideal set by supermortal intelligences. However, in other universes there may exist systems where the Material Son is mated with more than one Material Daughter. In none of the universes of time and space, nor in all the grand universe, does the Material Daughter have more than one Material Son for a mate. However, on many of the rebellious worlds, and other interuniversal evolutionary worlds, where there are unbalanced females strongly connected to the Father circuits, they have many husbands, in much the same manner as where in your earlier civilizations the men had many wives and/or concubines.

Because of the fall on your planet of 60 of the **Caligastia one hundred** and the default of Adam and Eve, your Material Son and Daughter, there has been great division and strife between individuals to find fulfillment in relationships with the opposite sex in both physical and spiritual unions. Throughout all of the universes in time and space, those ascending beings who are closer to the Father-Son circuits have certain attributes that distinguish them from those of the Infinite Spirit circuits. On the lower evolutionary worlds this takes form in ways that have to do with family, marriage and procreation of children. In all of the universes of time and space, where the male personality is spiritually balanced and in a relationship with one or more females, that male will have certain connections to the Father circuits that will give him authority over the female and responsibility before the Creator in the authority that he has. Because of the fallen state of Urantia, the abuse of authority by very imbalanced males has greatly confused the reality and cosmic fact of male authority within a relationship between male and female personalities. Even in those religions where the partial truth is appropriated, such as in fundamental Christianity, Islam and Judaism, the abuse of male over female continues because of the incomplete spiritual truths of the particular religious affiliation incorporated by the males.

Also because Urantia has such a variety of starseed and first-time Urantians on it, when they intermarry without cosmic perspective as to who they are, it is next to impossible to have a harmonious working relationship, due to the fact that:

1. Their understanding of male/female roles is based upon man's religion or no religion at all.
2. Their understanding of roles are based upon social ethics.
3. They may be from two different universes.
4. One soul may be much older than the other and neither may have an understanding of who they are.
5. The starseed, if married to a first-time Urantian, has not discovered who she or he is in cosmic perspective and therefore married far below the level of relationship needed for her or his fulfillment.

For first-time Urantians, it is always the job of the acting group seraphim and cherubim to bring the highest psychic circle obtainers together, as well as those who have reached the seventh stage of the third dimension, therefore putting them into the category of third-dimensional **highest complementary polarities**/twin flames. However, this seldom guarantees happiness together, nor does it guarantee the couple remaining together. In most situations, third-dimensional complementary polarities can only be brought together after several broken relationships and in their later years of life. There are instances where first-time Urantians are brought together early in life at the seventh stage of the third dimension and they remain together at this stage throughout the rest of their lives without obtaining the first stage of the fourth dimension. The second-order starseed can come through seventh stage third-dimensional marriages.

In the twentieth century on Urantia, because of thousands of years of male imbalance, females are connecting more with the male energy, the yang, more appropriately termed the Father-Son circuits. These women think they have to do this in order to obtain equality in the home and work place. In monogamous relationships where the female has actually more yang than the male, or is more Father-circuited, the marriage can work and actually prosper, as long as the male remains imbalanced himself, therefore never taking his appropriate role as leader and spiritual advisor within the household. If he does begin to assume his rightful position, the female needs to then submit herself to his awakening. If she does not, there will be friction between two male energies or, more correctly speaking, two Father-circuited opinions in relation to numerous circumstances that have no authority in actualization, leaving all concerned, particularly children, void of a decision-making and goal-fulfillment ability within the family setting. Many females who are intuitively connected by program to the Infinite Spirit/Mother circuits have had to use leadership capacities in educating themselves and family, particularly children, as to spiritual realities.

Where the male is balanced and has proper connection also to the Infinite Spirit circuits, he himself should assume, and usually does, the spiritual leadership of his household. It is, however, always the responsibility of the male, no matter how imbalanced, to take the spiritual lead, even though the female may be unwilling to follow. Examples of this would be in the seeking of higher spiritual truths, in the study of these truths, in family worship, and so on. If the female chooses not to follow, then the male who may have this higher spiritual truth should follow the higher revelation, in spite of the unwillingness of a female mate, who may or may not practice a spirituality of her own. In other words, continuing revelation should first be received by Father-circuited males and acted upon. However, in most cases, particularly in Western civilization, it is usually the females who respond to the spiritual first, but are quite hindered by imbalanced males who do proclaim their authority but have no sense of spirituality or true leadership. In many cases, they hinder not only their wife's growth, but also their children's.

Because of the imbalance in females who obtain an incorrect understanding of male energy and who rule their husbands and children, it has been observed in the twentieth century by the angelic orders that these women usually die before the men or are very frustrated and become diseased with various life threatening illnesses.

Women can also prevent their men from growing spiritually by not submitting to the male's desire for expansion and refusing to follow their husbands into a possible higher way. We have found this to be the case when many men have discovered the truth of the Fifth Epochal Revelation with excitement in their spirits and souls, but were held back or stopped in their pursuit by their wives who were not interested in the Fifth Epochal Revelation now present on the planet. We further discovered that one of the core reasons is because the Fifth Epochal Revelation, when properly understood in the home, speaks very strongly of male leadership; and these women did not want to give up their positions of self-imposed authority, which they indeed had in their lives with their mates and children. In a third-dimensional relationship, in many instances, this causes the husband/mate not to find his proper livelihood, therefore decreasing the financial flow that would come to that family and even causing the female authority herself to seek employment outside of the home to meet the needs of her family. She will not be able to find her true livelihood, for an ascending son and daughter of God cannot truly hear from the Thought Adjuster at a high level where control manifests itself over godly meekness and submission.

It is true, however, that a balanced male properly connected to Father and Mother circuits is hard to find on Urantia. But the women now make it even more difficult for the males to take their proper positions in the home because of lack of trust and fears over the many abuses that women have suffered at the hands of imbalanced males. However, until those ready for mating and procreation of children can be brought together with their highest spiritual complements, these imbalances will continue on Urantia, up until the time of the dimensional shift, for the majority of mankind.

Paladin, Finaliter; as transmitted through the Audio Fusion Material Complement, Gabriel of Sedona.

PAPER E

THE RESERVE CORPS OF DESTINY

There always has been existent on Urantia a group of humans chosen by the celestial overseers for a specific purpose in regard to the spiritual upliftment of humanity. Presently on Urantia, this corps consists not only of first-time Urantians, but a cosmic reserve corps numbering now, as of this writing, between one and three thousand. It is broad because the majority of these cosmic starseed of the reserve corps are fourth-order starseed. Many of them are on what we call the cosmic fence in their spiritual ascension. Many of them have remained on the same psychic circle in other repersonalizations on this planet and on others. It is always hoped that when these souls begin to find themselves as cosmic citizens once again and come to the Fifth Epochal Revelation, and all of them no doubt will, they will also then understand the essence of this knowledge in the heart and not just give intellectual assent in the mind. Those who cannot fuse with the **heart circuit** will not gain the I AM presence and will not open up the circuit of circuits and will remain on the lower circles and on the lower worlds. Because Urantia is shifting to a higher dimension, if they do not attain the third circle of attainment, they will not return to Urantia and will be separated from their cosmic family for at least one other lifetime and perhaps more.

The majority of starseed on Urantia are of the fourth order. This has come about because of an adjudication by the Ancients of Days and the Bright and Morning Star versus Lucifer which began around 1911. Approximately 170 million of them have been sent to Urantia, both to learn and grow. Previously, along with the fourth order, second, fifth, sixth and seventh orders of starseed have been on Urantia with the first-time Urantians. It is hoped that the fourth-order starseed who have continued to come to Urantia will now ascend to higher circles. It is possible for a fourth-order starseed, for example, to ascend to a higher circle and a higher order when Urantia moves into the first stages of light and life, therefore becoming a first-order starseed upon leaving the planet and going to another. All finaliters who come here, the fifth and sixth-order starseed, will always be on the first circle. They can never fall backwards, for they have proven themselves in eons of time, and in their highest overself they are Havona and Paradise citizens. First-order star children have entered this plane only as of November of 1988 and come to the third psychic circle or above and all will attain the first circle while on Urantia. It is highly improbable for them to default, as they are sent to be teachers and leaders and administrators in the divine governments of the pre-stages and first stages of planets in light and life, which Urantia is about to come into. However, if their fifth-stage fourth-dimensional parents default and they for some reason are raised with other parents of lower circles and ascension status, they themselves may not meet their destiny for many years. But in cases where this has happened on other planets, amazingly these children find themselves and their calling in their later years of 40's and 50's. Many of the first-time Urantians who are of the **reserve corps of destiny** in this era may also default in their calling because of narrow-mindedness, which leads to fundamentalism and false loyalties. The present-day *URANTIA Book* movement, that consists of thousands of possible reservists, fits into this category. Those starseed of the cosmic reserve corps who have been true to their destiny without default and, while on Urantia in this life, have ascended at least to the fourth psychic circle, have the most difficult task moving to the third. Those who do attain the third circle are presently the highest spiritual teachers on Urantia, mostly unrecognized by their peers and even rejected by those reservists of narrow minds who themselves have not escaped their own blindness. These starseed of the third and above circles, along with first-order star children who have come to Urantia, will be the first administrators and leaders in the planetary government after the change point, followed by those of lower-circle attainment who have not defaulted in the years following.

After the change point, higher circle attainment will continue with Urantians as well as starseed and will be made easier because of the Divine New Order of the planet. It will be more common for Urantians to obtain all seven circles within one lifetime; therefore, when they leave Urantia and arrive on another planet, they will be known as first-order starseed. It should be noted here that many first and second-time Urantians, who are of the highest Adamic strain, have the adaptability within them to attain higher circle development even now before the change point and can even excel their defaulted cosmic starseed in spiritual attainment. Based upon this fact, being a starseed does not necessarily mean that they are higher in ascension or circle attainment. Being a fallen starseed on Urantia can make it much more difficult to ascend to a higher circle because of their inability to overcome their pride in what they think they know, therefore creating a stumbling block that can keep these starseed and second-time Urantians repersonalizing on fallen worlds over and over again, until the basic fruit of humility is learned and submission to proper authority is understood. The fact is that the majority of the 170 million starseed on Urantia are on the fifth, sixth and seventh circles and are fallen and of the rebellious mode. So being a starseed does not necessarily mean spiritual superiority.

If you are a fourth-order starseed, which the majority of ovan souls are, and you come to realize who you are because of some inner search that has led you to these revelations, we highly suggest that you take these steps in self-discovery:

1. What souls have you met in your past that you have envied the most? Ask yourself why. Perhaps they were right and you were wrong. Why did you not submit to their higher insight?
2. Could it be that in times past you have thought too highly of yourself at certain points?
3. Have you ever had a human spiritual advisor, teacher? If not, why not? Do you have one now? Cannot the voice of your God speak to you through the voice of an older soul or a soul who has greater humility, therefore being higher in spiritual ascension than you?
4. Can you really see your envy of others? Why do you envy them?
5. If you have lost some of the most precious gifts that God has given you, why has this happened? If you justify the loss, you will never overcome the problem of the loss.

You, who are fourth-order starseed, are sitting on the cosmic fence of transcendence and yet think that you will be evacuated from Urantia in the times of tribulation through light-body transcendence or even spaceship transference. Or you may think that if you die you will go to a higher plane. Perhaps your own arrogance keeps you in what we call "static spirituality." Many of you have been in this static stage in numerous repersonalizations and all the while so blind to your own arrogance that you die a physical death thinking that you are ascending to a higher plane, when in reality you do not go to a mansion world, but to another fallen planet of the third dimension. Static spirituality causes both physical and psychological illness in the third dimension. It creates a tremendous imbalance, and even though you can accomplish certain achievements, such as college degrees and career attainment, you will never find your true calling and may possibly find yourselves emotional cripples.

Many of you will go through many relationships, seeking a higher soul mate or complementary polarity. You may be able to draw certain soul mates to you, but you will never draw your highest complements until a degree of humility is resonant within your consciousness and you become more of a listener to the voice of God within you and to those higher human teachers designated to be your spiritual advisors, placing yourselves in the Divine New Order of the Aquarian Age under proper leadership and spiritual direction. Many of the visions and dreams that you have tried to accomplish will begin to be more reachable as others come to the same place of consciousness realization as you, therefore recognizing you for who you are. In the kingdom of God on planets that have not fallen or are in the dawn of the first stages of light and life, a higher recognition of one another's gifts, abilities, qualities, talents and mandates at various times is the norm rather than the exception. As you begin to humble yourselves to your leaders and teachers, others will do the same with you.

There is no competition in the kingdom of God, only recognition as to each other's unique place and being in all that one is and has accomplished, both spiritually and experientially. In the greatest symphonies a violin cannot be a bass. When the individual instruments of God recognize who they are, what they can do and what they can't do, what things their brothers and sisters do better than they, and admit their shortcomings as well as recognizing their own abilities, then harmony can come within the human race and there will be no need for even a monetary system. Such evils as envy, pride and jealousy will be sins of the past, and the spirit of cooperation and humility will reign, for truly the meek shall inherit both the earth and the journey to Paradise with the countless billions of worlds of humble spirits of God.

1. COSMIC RESERVE CORPS

Those starseed of the cosmic reserve corps who have been chosen to become **change agents** of the Divine New Order, consisting of all the present orders with the exception of the fifth and sixth, have a relatively difficult time existing on Urantia for many reasons. Basically this is because Urantia is and always has been an alien world for them. These starseed may have been thousands of years older than their first-time Urantian peers, their parents discovered that the maturation process in the earlier years was much slower in developing. Perhaps the child did not walk as soon, or talk as soon as others, and when he or she did, talking may not have been a priority with the child, for perhaps he or she came from a planet where communication was complete telepathic transference. Also abiding by the many cultural and social norms can be difficult for the starseed child, causing him or her to be tagged a rebel, a beatnik, a hippie, etc. while growing into young adulthood. As some of these starseed grew older and compromised with the norm, they became more accepted but less happy, even to the point of despair for some, for they had come to dislike themselves. Perhaps some felt like a caged animal. The truth is that these starseed are like eagles in a cage, chained by the opinions of others and the ruling class who provides their sustenance. Some have found themselves, at various points in their lives, trying to obtain the very things that in their highest selves disgust them. They feel that if someone in power would only recognize who they are, by using the influence and financial ability of the powerful one, they would be put into a position to obtain their dreams. As long as these starseed have these mixed motives, they will find that the more they pray "Father, thy will be done," the less they are likely to succeed in many of the areas that they think they belong and should excel in. Let us hope that they have at least come to the place of recognizing

God as their Father, for if they have not at least come to this place, they are still fumbling in the third dimension. The fact is that if they forget about God the Father and his will, they might just succeed in some of their dreams. For instance, they might become president of a large corporation, a rock star, a famous actor or actress, a high officer in the military, or a doctor in a certain field; but any of these "accomplishments" obtained without being in the perfect will of God are, in cosmic perspective, defaults and regressing rather than progressing in spiritual ascension and psychic circle attainment. Many souls who have reached these places of so-called accomplishment have found only emptiness when they got there. If they had obeyed the will of God, they would have found their total fulfillment, perhaps as a carpenter in a small town with one's highest complement and children, as opposed to the architect in Los Angeles or New York, whose fame has brought nothing but added responsibilities and emptiness. The first-time Urantian who does not find his or her destiny for whatever reason, is one thing; but an older soul, a starseed, who does not find his or her destiny is quite another thing, for the pain in the soul is greatly magnified. There is always a voice within these souls that recognizes that they should always be somewhere else, never completely enjoying the moment, drifting through time and space, in rebellion to cosmic law and order.

Being on a planet that is in such confusion as Urantia also adds to the isolation of starseed and blocks them from coming into the cosmic families in which they would find their own realization, both of self and of cosmic identity. One cannot do without the other, for when one becomes truly realized, he or she recognizes the need for others higher than themselves to learn from and for others lower than themselves to teach. All suffer on a planet when one soul cannot recognize another in totality. Magnify this a billion times, and you have a planet of chaos, a planet where might rules and power dictates, where authority can only be recognized by force; and the multitudes struggle for mere survival instead of developing the gifts and talents within them for the benefit of all humankind. It is the cosmic starseed, particularly the first, second, third and seventh orders, who will help bring about the transition from the third dimension to the fourth and the true Aquarian Age, the pre-stages of light and life on Urantia, and perhaps even the first stage if Michael decides to return at any time.

2. DIVINE GOVERNMENT APPOINTMENTS
IN THE DIVINE NEW ORDER

We believe that within this decade, perhaps even before the change point, Machiventa Melchizedek, along with others of the Council of Twenty-four Elders, will rematerialize in physical form on Urantia. They will use as staff, extraterrestrial and interdimensional personalities who will become visible to other human staff members who will be of the Urantian and cosmic reserve corps. This preliminary organization of higher intelligence and human intelligence working together can greatly ease the suffering of thousands, perhaps millions, in the great tribulations to come, and quicken the orderly setup of the Divine Government after the change point, because human personalities will have been trained in what the magnitude and functioning of this new world system will encompass. Many of the cosmic seed presently working minimum wage, for example, may be put into positions of great leadership when the divine takeover occurs. Most of the jobs in Western civilization and the present social and economic structures of the world will be eliminated. Many of the latent abilities and memories of the cosmic starseed will be restored, enabling them to perform in a supermortal function and accomplish tasks that in their previous life existences on Urantia were impossible for them. Many of the motor skills will also be actuated, and many starseed will find total enjoyment and fulfillment in their daily realities. Many of the Urantian reserve corps with various potentials of service will be functioning in schools of development to realize their fullest potentials, where in their pre-change-point existence these potentials could not be realized because of survival concerns due to the monopoly and greed of the controlling elite. Many of the career fields, such as medicine, the building trades, and of course all commercial and merchandising positions, will drastically change. Agriculture and many of the health related sciences will also undergo tremendous advances in a short period of time. All disease on the planet can be completely eliminated within a few months, provided that there are enough human **assistants** of the reserve corps, both cosmic and Urantian, to fulfill certain tasks that would be highly inappropriate for certain angelic orders and supermortal beings to be assigned. It is not a matter of humility for these beings to accept these positions, for they would be willing vessels; it is a matter of efficiency in using the higher intelligences for the more difficult tasks.

Much of what has been thought to have been supernatural in reality has always been superscientific. Both physical and nonphysical sciences, such as parapsychology, will take great leaps in the early stages of the Divine New Order. As the links between the system, constellation and universe headquarters increase, particularly among individuals functioning with clearer circuitry within their own central circuits, a higher degree of self-fulfillment for the totality of humankind can be realized. The closer that each individual, on any plane of existence, is functioning with the perfect will of the Divine Father, the more light is shed upon that particular plane of existence. This creates more harmony and ease of existence, particularly for those material (flesh) and morontia (spirit and flesh) beings. Those not ready for morontia bodies who, by the adjudication of the Ancients of Days may be allowed to remain on Urantia (these are the ones who have survived the cataclysms and still remain sane or have returned after being physically evacuated), will continue to procreate children in pre-morontia bodies. However, because of the setup of the new government and its overcontrol, the children of these marriages will be categorized specifically as to their appropriate cosmic designation and order of starseed, and they will be placed into the proper Melchizedek schools of higher learning.

Those who already have translated into light bodies (some stage of morontia form) will be more useful in that they will no longer have certain tendencies of inward struggle in self-realization and much more easily be able to be taught the higher abstract cosmic truths of interplanetary linkage and communication, therefore creating a much more expanded understanding of universe family than just the newly developed concept of planetary family. As far as the planet is concerned, nationalism is extinct, and one planetary government is functioning and overcontrolled by the system headquarters on Jerusem and the universe headquarters on Salvington.

Most student visitors on Urantia in the early years of the Divine New Order will be students from planets within the local universe of Nebadon. These student visitors will be from planets that have never fallen, and all will be visible. Many of them will be human mortals, but many will not. Also, interplanetary travel by Urantians to other planets will be accelerated, with higher technology given to allow physical transport to neighboring planets in other solar systems; but a "distance barrier" will be in place up into a certain period in the Divine New Order, and technology will not be given until a certain higher consciousness is developed on Urantia. Always within the lower evolutionary worlds and up into the morontia worlds there is a limitation to information of divine origin that can be given; it is never revealed to ascending sons and daughters of God until they themselves ascend to that particular plane. One of the greatest lessons for the ascending son and daughter to learn is what *not* to tell a fellow ascender. As one becomes more in attunement with cosmic law and has a higher grasp of universe citizenship and above, one understands that certain information given to undeserving rebellious personalities can be most harmful to the loyal beings of light on that realm. Information given even to loyal personalities can be detrimental to them and the planet. The individuals may take this information in an inappropriate manner because they were not ready to receive in totality the fullness of conceptual understanding. This is why even in the lower worlds of third-dimensional planes, educators have to learn to give information at the level of their students; if they cannot organize their own thoughts to meet the various levels of their students, then in reality they are failures as teachers, for their students cannot grasp at their level what they as individuals need to structure within themselves as the first foundations so that higher learning can take place.

Teachers too often try to place the building blocks one upon another without first laying the various foundations, therefore making the learning process most confusing and even unattainable for their students. If one teaches from a point of arrogance, one is not a teacher, but a sounding board. When one teaches from humility, one may not appear to be a teacher to the prideful and arrogant, but to those who can recognize this, she or he becomes Christlike. The bread and water of life is truth in simplicity, given step by step in creating the masterpiece of cosmic truth.

Geographically the Divine New Order government will be divided into **sectors**, which will incorporate large land masses and many previous countries. In a future work a complete detailed description will be given of these various sectors. For now it should be known that the reserve corps of destiny and starseed who transcend to the fourth dimension will be part of this divine sector government.

Although there are many opinions as to the geographic center of this divine government and where the New Jerusalem will be placed, the reality is that it depends upon the gathering of the cosmic family into a particular location near one of the existing energy reflective circuit (ERC) areas on the planet. As of this present writing, the highest possibility is where the archangels' headquarters is located, and few humans have been given this information. The archangels' headquarters, which now represents the gathering of the nonmaterial and semimaterial cosmic family, has been moved several times because the human members and relatives that were hoped to be awakened and linked with the unseen family have not aligned with Divine New Order concepts and the perfect will of the Universal Father. Therefore, other geographic locations were found where other cosmic family members of higher spiritual potential were located in conjunction with existing ERCs (vortexes*) and **ley lines** (grid links and star routes*).

The cosmic reservists have the difficult task of first discovering who they are, then awakening their cosmic relatives, and after this awakening, finding the geographic areas where their elder cosmic relatives and teachers, who usually are their **cosmic parents** and grandparents, are located. On many of the mortal fallen worlds in time and space where many of the defaults of mandated personalities have taken place, it has been found by Overcontrol's observations that the quickest way to change the consciousness of the planet is when those of the highest spiritual ascension, both cosmic and native, can be brought together in geographic proximity of one another under proper leadership and administration. These prototype communities usually expand into cities, states, and countries, and on some planets are the most advanced civilizations, with other countries on their planet being thousands of years behind in relation to the government of cosmic family. Even on third-dimensional Urantia, tribes and clans have prospered where extended and nuclear families have stayed together. At first, in early civilization, the family and tribe stayed together for mere survival. This beginning recognition of the union of souls should have remained intact on all levels of cultural and individual development, particularly at the dawn of the industrial age. Gradually, as new technology and transportation advanced, the family unit and extended family became separated. It has always been the plan of the Universe Supervisors to repersonalize starseed in close geographic proximity to one another, and it has always been the work of Caligastia to separate them or keep them from meeting one another or keep them, as individuals, blind to their cosmic origin. On a fallen planet such as Urantia, this has been accomplished to a high percent by the rebellious forces. Even with methods of transportation as basic as the camel and horse, a further separating of cosmic family occurred on Urantia. With the invention of the steamboat and the automobile, the breakdown of cosmic family accelerated to the point where it became a near impossibility to bring together the highest Adamic strains in geographic proximity. Many individual family members have become chained to various third-dimensional, materialistic, but factual bondages. These include:

1. Ownership of property where the human family resides, but not where the highest cosmic family members are located
2. Inappropriate marriage or relationship
3. Wrong careers
4. False obligations
5. Misplaced loyalties
6. Static spirituality

In America, in the second half of the twentieth century, the highest orders of starseed have had to move from place to place for both self-discovery and the awakening of others, due to the fact of the present conditions of the scattered cosmic family. Many of the Adamic Pleiadian strain have been placed in various geographic locations around the U.S., Canada, England, Australia, New Zealand, France, and Israel for the purposes of the regathering of cosmic family and primary Divine New Order centers. The majority of the cosmic seed can be found among the present-day Caucasian races, but it is not an exact rule and there are many exceptions: starseed can be found in every existing race on Urantia. However, most starseed of countries with the mass populace of first-time Urantians will find themselves being called by divine providence to other locations where their genetic cosmic family is located, to meet their own individual destinies, particularly in the mid and late 90's. The Universe Supervisors will see to it that no entrapment by man or man's government can keep these starseed in the countries of their human origin and lower spiritual realities. If they indeed seek the perfect will of the Universal Father, doors will be opened so that they can find and come to the primary cosmic family centers. Presently, a prototype for these communities exists only in the U.S. The mandates of the Bright and Morning Star and Machiventa Melchizedek represent the authority of the Father/Mother community that is located in the U.S. where sector 1 will be and where the New Jerusalem is planned to be located. This prototype cosmic family community and first primary **sacred/protected area**, the Aquarian Concepts Community, is organized with a functioning administration, proper leadership, the beginning Starseed and Urantian Schools of Melchizedek; the call to all starseed worldwide is to come to this community. At this time, when all of the highest mandated personalities are geographically together, as well as spiritually united, that area becomes more functional as a planetary headquarters. The messages that are going out to the world from Planetary Headquarters are contained in the concepts of CFER.

Paladin, Finaliter; as transmitted through the Audio Fusion Material Complement, Gabriel of Sedona.

I, Paladin, Chief of Finaliters on Urantia, interject this statement at this time, to explain that the audio reception from us to Gabriel is a process which is very difficult to understand. We ask you at this time to read Paper 209, if you have not already done so. There is only one mandated audio fusion material complement on Urantia at this time to bring Continuing Fifth Epochal Revelation to the people of this planet. The transmissions through Gabriel of Sedona, Arizona, U.S.A., will continue to come in a series of papers in higher Ascension Sci terminology and definition, which is the fusion of cosmic science with the spiritual, as more members of the cosmic family find their own individual destiny purpose at Planetary Headquarters with Gabriel and the other elders of that Divine New Order community.

As you read through CFER, you should be able to notice the increase in cosmic insight, definition and higher universal absolutes being presented in the highest of procedures in which we, on our side, can presently give revelation to you on your side.

January 29, 1992

PAPER 197

EXPLANATION OF ASHTAR COMMAND IN RELATION TO LOWER-CIRCLE CHANNELS OF ASHTAR, ZOLTEC AND OTHERS

My name is Paladin; I am second in command to Ashtar. My associate, Zoltec, is also second in command, and communicating with those of the fourth psychic circle and below, such as Tuella. Gabriel, whom I communicate through in like manner, is of the third psychic circle and rapidly moving to the first. Those who come through Gabriel will bring a higher revelation of CFER language. Since we are in contact with Machiventa Melchizedek and Lao-tse, we speak to you (human at this time) vessels. As you are agondonters right now, and although you are potential mandated vessels, your imperfections of spirit and need of spiritual growth purification (as also with the vessels Gabriel and Niánn) prevents us from giving you information that you are not ready for. As you have found out, I am sure, we will give you information that will hopefully enable you to begin a process of alignment with, at this time, the human vessels Gabriel and Niánn of Sedona and their work there.

Since approximately 1947, when we as finaliters came to this plane in physical spaceships, we have been using channels based upon their mindal capacity and spiritual evolution. There has only been one vessel who could be used to bring the higher truth of CFER to Urantia, and that is Gabriel of Sedona, who has the mandate of the Bright and Morning Star of Nebadon. Those others who were spiritually advanced we did use, but they did not have the mindal capacity to teach the Fifth Epochal Revelation and Continuing to Urantia. They could talk about the evacuation to some degree, such as Tuella did; but 95% of what we would have liked to have said to her concerning some very basic information, we could not use Tuella for. Those channels we have used to the highest potential have never themselves seen a physical spaceship, let us say, in a close encounter. Those who have, like Billy Meier in Switzerland, are of the sixth psychic circle and cannot be used to bring higher spiritual truths. They are used to open up people to the reality of cosmic citizenship with other beings, in hope of expanding their consciousness. We never intended, and are unhappy with, the various UFO cults that have surfaced as a result of the misrepresentation of the information we gave certain contacts. As soon as we saw that we could no longer use them, we left them and they began to "channel" on their own, claiming our sponsorship. This has happened to at least 99% of those contacted. Thus we can account for the confusion perpetrated by the New Age prophets concerning certain cosmic data and truths about the master universe. There is only one foundation and that is the Fifth Epochal Revelation, that which is already written and that which continues to come through the mandated vessel. *In December, 1989, with the arrival of Machiventa Melchizedek, present Planetary Prince, audio transmission through lower-circled channels was ended.*

One important element that is needed between those leaders whom we are calling out and using is the virtue of true humility and the understanding of the spiritual hierarchy that exists not only in the morontia bodies and above, but also in human form. Though Caligastia has done an admirable job in the breakdown of authority on this planet, unbridled liberty can never be the accepted norm in the spiritual arena when it comes to recognition of those souls who are on a higher plane than others. This recognition has nothing to do with financial status or formal education. This recognition begins first among the human leaders chosen to be of the council and staff of Machiventa Melchizedek, just as Machiventa, must recognize those who are his superiors in the government of Nebadon, as John the Baptist recognized the Christ. As Urantians, it can become quite confusing when various entities speak through the human vessel; all of you are just beginning to understand the process of repersonalization and **rematerialization** (referred to in New Age terminology as a "walk-in"*). The present-day understanding of the term "walk-in" is limited and mostly in error. It is not the intent of this transmission to educate in these areas. At present *The URANTIA Book* only touches on these processes in relation to the mansion worlds, but there is a much higher understanding that you will come to learn, as we have been teaching Gabriel and Niánn for the last three years.

It is of the utmost importance that an alignment occur between the future mandated persons, those who receive by pure impression and other leaders, and that proper recognition of each other's work and office be understood, that all resources be shared and that you aid one another wherever possible, for a new garden must be built. This third garden will be host to many celestial overseers who will come to help us establish the Divine New Order on Urantia. This will take continued great sacrifices of those appointed vessels. Whatever must be done to get out of all debts and to help those leaders to do the same must be done by all of you. If you, as appointed human leaders, are not willing to come together to form a council of elders, blessing one another and recognizing each other's mandate, then the mandate will be taken from you, and you will not be recognized. You may have followers, but you will not be working within the third psychic circle and potentially moving to the first; you will not truly aid in the coming implementation of the Machiventa Government, light-body transference into the morontia body,* and if necessary, physical evacuation of this planet, and you will not be given the true information of how this will be done. We have hundreds of decoys, and thousands of books have been allowed to be written so that those truly of the light will not be hampered by the government and other unethical organizations.

It is of great importance that you can all come together for a first meeting. Although specific names of the individuals who were contacted will be left out, we will state that one who went by the name of a prophet was in Canada, one was a reader of *The URANTIA Book*, also in Canada, who received by pure impression beginning messages from Machiventa, and the third was also a *URANTIA Book* reader well known within the Urantia movement* presently living in California. These individuals were contacted previous to 1989, but the first two did not respond at all and the third is undecided. In the future, many other individuals will be contacted by Machiventa's Vicegerent First Ambassadors to align themselves with the Machiventa Government and CFER and possibly to be given mandates themselves.

There is much going on of which all of you are unaware, and it is not time for you to know. One thing is certain, all of you who feel called to spiritual service and can align with the Machiventa Government must be free to do just that, be free of financial debts and worries and have adequate financial resources to effectively reach the masses with CFER.

We of the Ashtar Command in cooperation with the Midwayer Commission on Urantia and so many millions of others, that's right, millions, are blessed over the simple fact that now the first potential Vicegerent First Ambassadors and Gabriel and Niánn have met at least by letter. We have been trying for two years now to have Aquarian Concepts' materials fall into your hands. You see, we work with the wills of men (and that is a subject in itself that the satellite schools of Jerusem will teach you much about), when it comes to actualizing the Fourth Epochal Revelation (which has never really been actualized), and bringing the Fifth Epochal Revelation and Continuing to the human consciousness of your Urantia.

December 7, 1990

Paladin, Finaliter; with the Ashtar Command in cooperation with the Midwayer Commission of Urantia; as transmitted through the Audio Fusion Material Complement, Gabriel of Sedona.

PAPER 198

CONCERNING THE ENTITY SEMJASE

The following is given with the hope of clarifying the issue of Semjase and her messages to the planet Urantia through various appointed vessels of communication. First of all, we would like to state that *The Keys of Enoch* with all of its truth, also has much human error. Much of it is written in archaic Hebrew conceptual language and thought because this was the level of ascension that the channel had come to in soul evolution. When cosmic truth and continuing revelation could be introduced in this vessel's mind, it was done; but many times it was done with the human vessel combating what we were saying with his understanding of words, concepts and spiritual realities. It is the purpose of this transmission to point out only one particular aspect of all the errors in *The Keys of Enoch*.

The original Semjase was indeed of fallen hierarchy, but *she* was never a *he*. This supermortal did unfortunately choose the side of Lucifer; but before her fall, like Lucifer, she was a brilliant and loyal being, serving Michael and the universe of Nebadon for thousands of years with faultless character. Because of this, thousands of mortals on various planets were named Semjase in her honor, as I likewise named one of my daughters, the Pleiadian **Semjase of Tora**. It was she who came to Billy Meier of Switzerland and to one other, whose name I cannot mention, in your country of America, and gave purely scientific information to him.

It is quite common today for many fallen entities to come and speak to human vessels and call themselves by names of those of the light with whom they try to identify themselves, such as the archangel Michael. Anyone who has an understanding of our universe knows that Michael is our Creator Son, not an archangel. Yet because so many believe that Michael is an archangel, those fallen beings identify themselves as such and give truth interspersed with lies, just enough to poison the spiritual mind of those who receive this information and try to live by its spiritual concepts. How many St. Germains do you know about? How many Djwal Khuls? How many Mother Marys? Once again, if one understood the ascension process and what various beings can and cannot do in the third-dimensional plane, that person would be able to determine more clearly the true from the false. This ascension process is found in part in the Fifth Epochal Revelation, *The URANTIA Book,* which should be the guide book for all truth seekers on your planet. Information from other mandated channels can also be used as a guidebook, but at this time their writings are not published in a book, though some of the concepts have been written in letters and articles, given on tapes and circulated around the world by word of mouth.

Semjase of Tora did not contact Billy Meier after the spring of 1976. Whatever Semjase followed, was not the Semjase of the beginning. It is quite common for contactees who do not understand higher spiritual concepts and cosmic truths to allow themselves to be deceived once they have originally been contacted by the beings of light. Any information that does not coincide with the Fifth Epochal Revelation could not possibly come from any being who has been loyal to Christ Michael and the Universal Father. Once a soul is contacted, she or he has a wonderful opportunity to advance his or her growth; and all of these contactees were in one way or another introduced to the Fifth Epochal Revelation, which they either believed or rejected or just did not understand at the time. Many of them became prideful, and when this happens we leave, and others, perhaps of the dark forces, come and take our place.

As for Billy Meier, he is a first-time Urantian and the work with him was solely to bring physical evidence to your world of Pleiadian reality and contact. It is not impossible for first-time Urantians to understand Fifth Epochal Revelation; however, in the decades following the giving of the revelation to your planet, it has been observed by planetary supervisors that mostly starseed and those of the reserve corps of destiny become students. And of those, only a small percentage are open to CFER.

My daughter, Semjase, is much more than just a Pleiadian mortal, but it is not time yet to reveal her stage of ascension and cosmic identity. However, as she said to Mr. Meier, she is not a god and is only a fellow ascending daughter and servant of our Universe Father, Christ Michael. Because of the confusion that exists, from now on, when she does contact human personalities, she will identify herself as "Semjase of Tora." All beings of light who transmit to this planet either identify themselves by order or by planet of origin, and no fees of any kind are charged to hear us speak. As of August, 1990, we of the light ask human contactees to charge no price for our transmissions or teachings. We of the light ask our contact personalities to be ministers of faith, accepting donations only for their work and service in the bringing about of these revelations to the planet today.

January 26, 1991

Paladin, Finaliter of the Ashtar Command; in cooperation with the Midwayer Commission of Urantia; as transmitted through the Audio Fusion Material Complement, Gabriel of Sedona.

PAPER 199

CONCERNING INNER GUIDANCE — A COSMIC PERSPECTIVE

Many souls on your planet of Urantia claim to have a divine connection with their God. They claim to hear from God personally and uniquely. Yet throughout history, in the name of the voice of this inner God, they have murdered one another, ruled over one another, and have taken what little their brothers and sisters had in order to build temples where some have said they heard from God even better. There has always been a mixture of those who have truly heard from their inner God, which has led them to great and wonderful ministries in the service of their fellow brothers and sisters on your planet, and those who also claim to hear from their God who wished to control others and hinder the true moving of the Spirit upon the earth.

The voice of God within an individual can be quite distorted, confused and vaguely heard, even by the most decent of people. This is due to pride, selfishness, vanity and the many perplexities of living in social orders that are inconsistent with the divine government which has not been able to take root upon this planet. Many people have claimed innate contact or objective communion with the Creator Son of Nebadon, Christ Jesus, whom we know to be Michael of Salvington and they know as their Father. They claim to be able to hear from him individually, independent of even those their Master gave to help them in their daily sojourns in life, as lived on a third-dimensional fallen planet. Did not Jesus say that he gave some as apostles, some as evangelists, and some as teachers for the edification of the church, (the church being those who claim to understand the threefold Spirit within them)? Yet those who make the claim to hear from the Spirit of Truth (the gift of the Creator Son, Michael, which is only one-third of the Trinity's voice), seem to have found themselves, even up to this day, in wars against their brothers and sisters they call infidels and pagans, in improper marriages and relationships, and in careers of unfulfillment and wrong livelihood, many dying from diseases brought about by inappropriate thinking and living. From the pope upon his throne to the lone monk in the solitude of the forest, this self-same Spirit seems to say different things to different people concerning cosmic truth.

But does this Spirit of Truth differ in cosmic revelation? Or could it be that the listener has a limited capacity to hear what the Spirit of Truth is actually saying because of the many obstacles that have been built into the listener's programming? Over 200 different denominations in the Christian world claim to be the authoritative interpreters of that Spirit of Truth, and several thousand independent sects also make that claim. Why is it that all of them seem to differ in interpreting what that same Spirit of Truth is saying?

In the Piscean Age there always were those who said they would choose no sides, join no institutions, and that they would be the interpreter of that inner voice and have no teachers to guide them except the Spirit of Truth within them. The number of these are legion. Some, more proficiently educated in their religious training than others, have come to their mindset by intellectual assent. Others have made this decision by pure heart acquiescence, divorced from mindal influence and intellectual pursuit. Regardless of the reasons for the decisions of those who choose to alienate themselves from the appointed teachers of the universe administration that does exist, they hinder their own growth as ascending sons and daughters and impede the very kingdom of God with which they claim to be so in touch.

The Creator Son, Christ Michael, came to this planet as the Fourth Epochal Revelation with its premise of the fatherhood of God and the brotherhood of man and the teaching of the threefold Spirit within. Two thousand years later, that same Creator Son has endorsed the Fifth Epochal Revelation, so that those who are ready to enter the Divine New Order and true New Age can learn of the many hundreds of orders of beings that he has created to help in the administration and ministry of not only this planet, but the millions of planets and thousands of systems that exist in his universe of Nebadon. It is not the will of God, the Eternal Father, for us to know only of him, for if we did, we would not know of his Creator Son nor would we know of the angels. It is time for all mortals of Urantia (earth), who are willing and capable, to learn of the vast family of beings which exist, many of which will be totally present and visible when the change does come to Urantia.

It is our prayer that you will truly come to know who we are and to seek out those human instructors on your planet who have been divinely appointed to be your teachers. This is what the Spirit of Truth is saying to the people of Urantia this hour; and if you are truly listening, you will receive that same message. No one book can contain all of the cosmic truth of God; and as the Book of John states in the New Testament, if all the words of Jesus were written down, there would not be enough books in all the world to contain his words.

The Fifth Epochal Revelation, that which is written in *The URANTIA Book* and that which is coming through appointed vessels, is the latest and highest revelation of divine love and a divine gift given to the people of your planet.

If these words have reached you, it is because the Spirit of Truth is reaching out to you in that which is known as the printed word, as God has many ways of speaking to you. Our prayer, and the prayer of the angels of the heavens, is that you put aside your personal viewpoints and opinions and truly follow that Spirit of Truth that is trying to reach you, inwardly and outwardly.

January 31, 1991

Ashtar, Finaliter; in cooperation with the seraphic hosts of Nebadon and the Midwayer Commission of Urantia, under the direct orders of Michael of Nebadon to give this transmission through the Audio Fusion Material Complement, Gabriel of Sedona.

PAPER 200

PROPER TERMINOLOGY IN THE PRE-STAGES OF LIGHT AND LIFE AND THE AQUARIAN AGE

No evolving planet can experience a oneness of spiritual unity until there is on that planet a common conceptual understanding of God and the master universe and a common language to define those concepts. Urantia, with its many languages, has greatly helped Caligastia in dividing the human race. In the spiritual realm, many of the same truths, even at the same level of understanding, are spoken in language using different names, tags, etc. It is important that you of the reserve corps of destiny and you teachers who are aware of the sovereignty of Christ Michael in his universe of Nebadon, begin to speak and teach in common conceptual language to prepare the way on Urantia for the common tongue to be appropriated, as it is on the mansion worlds. Some of the Fifth Epochal Revelation that you are presently receiving in this era on Urantia has been received by other spiritual seekers thousands of years ago, but they used other words to describe some of the cosmic information they were receiving with their limited circuitry connection to Salvington and Jerusem. We are asking that the ancient terminology be replaced with cosmic terminology, and I will attempt to define some of the specific areas:

1. *Circuit* rather than:
   a. Mayan Zuvuya.
   b. Tibetan Antakarana* or Rainbow Bridge.
   c. New Age chakra* or channel.
2. *Fifth Epochal Revelation* rather than:
   a. Tibetan understanding of the Fifth Initiation.
   b. The Hopi Fifth World.
   c. Buddhic Plane, Nirvana or a higher mental plane.
3. *Morontia Mota** rather than the Monadic Plane.
4. *Havona* level rather than the Logoic Plane.
5. *Office of the Planetary Prince* rather than Tibetan Sanat Kumara. (The Tibetan masters, including the human Djwal Khul, were also mistaken about who the Ancients of Days were.)
6. *The Caligastia one hundred and aides* rather than the 104 Kumaras.
7. *Sixth and seventh mansion world progressors,* who choose to descend to a more primitive world in their ascension to teach, rather than ascended masters.

8. *Bestowal Son* (a Divine Son incarnating) rather than **Avatar**. (There has been only one "Avatar" who has ever come to Urantia, and that is Christ Michael, Jesus.)

9. *Repersonalization, reconstruction, or rematerialization* rather than reincarnation and reiteration. (Until the time that proper understanding of these terms can be used, in place of reincarnation and reiteration we would prefer that you use the word "repersonalization." There is no reincarnation in the universe of Nebadon as taught by the evolutionary religions of Urantia.)

1. MASTERS, A BRIEF EXPLANATION

To those who understand the cosmology of the master universe to some degree, those who have been called "masters" by humans and have repersonalized on Urantia from the sixth and seventh mansion worlds are, in the ascension process, like kindergarten students in comparison to the Master Architects, Master Sons, Master Physical Controllers,* etc. Those in the present New Age circles, whose understanding of ascended masters as great and high beings of all knowing and divine orientation (some even being called gods), are quite incorrect in their understanding and are antiquated in their language. When you speak of the Divine Government that is now being set up on Urantia and of those beings who are speaking through certain human complements, *it is of utmost importance* that words such as "ascended masters" not be used and that their ascension progress and status be recognized. For example, I, as a finaliter, would prefer to be called such rather than an ascended master, which is several hundred thousand years below my ascension status. You of Urantia must come to understand these things and who is speaking to you.

2. RECOGNIZING THOSE MATERIAL COMPLEMENTS WHO HAVE THE MANDATE OF CHRIST MICHAEL, AND MANDATES OF REPRESENTATIVE UNIVERSE PERSONALITIES

Many starseed who have been used as channels by both the forces of light and darkness really have no understanding of who is speaking to them, nor can they until they submit themselves in godlike humility as students of the Fifth Epochal Revelation and come under proper authority to human teachers who have the mandates of Christ Michael to teach these higher cosmic realities. It will become increasingly evident that even those of the light if they do not do this, will find themselves cut off from all transmissions and will only be receiving the voices of fallen entities of the rebellion or their own higher or lower selves.

The Bright and Morning Star is mandated to speak through only one audio fusion material complement on Urantia, and that human complement is Gabriel of Sedona. At the present time, the Bright and Morning Star is not transmitting because it takes a certain number of cosmic family aligned with one another in physical proximity to create an ERC. which allows the mandate to be actualized. However, this has happened with Aquarian Concepts Community in the past, and certain transmissions from the Bright and Morning Star that were recorded, will be given at the appropriate time. All other transmissions that have come from "archangels" called Gabriel were either from angelic beings of the light named after the Bright and Morning Star, or they were from fallen entities of various orders misrepresenting truth and title of identification.

Many who think they are in contact with angels have actually been in contact with midwayers who could not tell their contacts who they really were, for this would have gone against divine ordinance.

Only by the channels' free-will choice to become students of the Fifth Epochal Revelation can concepts be given to them; and if they do not have the language in their mind already, the concepts are difficult to transmit in the very highest manner. The Fifth Epochal Revelation language is not to be given to the channel before he or she has agreed to become a student of that material (as many *URANTIA Book* readers have given information of the contents of the papers to undeserving and unready spiritual neophytes). When this takes place, these souls, who have not chosen to receive the free gift of the Fifth Epochal Revelation to some degree, use some of the terminology in their attempts to portray knowledge that they really do not have and to gain position over others, because the words of the Fifth Epochal Revelation are powerful cosmic realities. The beginning seventy were given this information by the Midwayer Commission, and that is why, from its origin, the URANTIA Foundation chose not to proselytize the book to just anyone. They were told to publish the first edition of the papers in 1955 because it was believed that the book would find itself in the hands of those who were willing to be its students.

You must still seek these earnest students. However, you must be careful what information you give out to others. How can you tell who to give information to? First of all, those who are called to be teachers will be led to their students and vice versa. Then you must discern the humility of their hearts; be slow to speak and wise in your choice of what part of the Fifth Epochal Revelation and Continuing (if you know any) to give. You will find in the days ahead, those of you who can discern just how terrible pride is, that you will give less and less information to those undeserving. In this manner, by the mid 90's there will be a dividing line between those loyal to Christ Michael and the

Universal Father and those on the path of the Lucifer rebellion, be it first-time Urantians (which most are) or those repersonalized starseed who have chosen to continue making the wrong choices on this planet and on the other 36 fallen planets in the system of Satania. Many first-time Urantians are unwittingly in the grasp of the rebellion and will most likely be unable to get out of their deceptions before the change point.

3. REPERSONALIZATION AND COSMIC FAMILY

The following are some excerpts from a transmission by the Bright and Morning Star when he "walked in" for three days in July of 1989.

"Ascending sons or daughters can be repersonalized on a planet by various technical methods, of which rematerialization, reconstruction and repersonalization are just three. In actuality, this process is always an ascension and never a descension stage. Participants may have had to go to one of the 37 fallen worlds of Satania, but some could choose their planet. Usually their planet of choice would be where others of their cosmic family were sojourning, and they were destined to meet and have some commonality of friendship and spiritual union. Some of the reasons that starseed have returned to Urantia have to do with:

1. Their planet of origin *outside* the universe of Nebadon and the vast ascension varieties of the other Michael Sons.
2. The location of their highest complementary polarities' or twin flames' material body (because at one point in the evolution of these ascending mortals, they were separated due to the default of one or both).
3. Interuniversally accepted error as a result of post-rebellion teaching to the relatives of the staff of the fallen Planetary Prince.
4. Repersonalization by choice of sixth and seventh mansion world progressors from another universe.
5. Default of various nonhuman and nonmortal celestial personalities.
6. Assignment of a descending son in mortal form to a lower world.

"The point of origin of a mortal ascending son or daughter of a particular universe is some of the most important information that an evolving soul can come to know. Because of this fact, there are many of the Luciferic persuasion who claim to give this information to others and also to regress others to past lives through hypnotherapy and so on. Any of these who claim to give specifics as to what and who a person was in a past life with detail of city born in, career, cause of death, etc. are giving false information that is most dangerous and confusing, particularly when they claim to give a starseed's planet of origin.

Starseed in this context is any mortal soul who came into origin outside of Urantia. Many channels and clairvoyants can tap into celestial circuits and can know the era a starseed lived, up to the very year of their birth and approximately when they transcended, and whether it was a violent or a natural death. But they cannot give any other specific information; and if they do, it is either imagined, fabricated or misinformation given by a fallen entity. The only universe intelligences who can broadcast points of origin are myself, the Bright and Morning Star; a finaliter on specific assignment; and my attendant seraphim who are of the order of the **angels of enlightenment** under my jurisdiction and mandate.

"*Presently, the only human vessel on Urantia mandated to give the planet of origin is Gabriel of Sedona.* Information as to who a person was in a past life and specifics about that life can also be received by those humans in contact with the recording seraphim under my jurisdiction, Melchizedeks, certain Mighty Messengers* and certain finaliters who work *in cooperation with the Midwayer Commission* to serve in this capacity. Many of the genetic strains of the Urantian races have extra-terrestrial ancestral linkage. Because of this, they have a different code concerning their spiritual ascension to Paradise, and this has to do with their extraterrestrial ancestors' point of origin.

"Many of you who have had past lives on this planet need to come into the union of souls with your cosmic family under proper leadership and authority so that the pre-stages of light and life can begin to manifest."

(Transmitted by the Bright and Morning Star of Salvington through Gabriel of Sedona and paraphrased by Paladin, a finaliter, presently on assignment with the Ashtar Command.)

4. CLOSING STATEMENT

This paper is for those in the Urantia movement, and particularly of the reserve corps of destiny, who have ears to hear what the Thought Adjuster is saying to those who have received the gift of the Spirit of Truth and who have become one of Michael's independent voices, independent in that you are capable of hearing that Spirit of Truth as opposed to the teaching of man and man's organizations. This is for those who can become eagles rather than followers of the flock of social prestige and organizational status. You may mistakenly choose to deny all or some of this paper, but that will not change the validity of its truth, and because of its truth, you will one day have to accept the reality of these truths and place yourselves under the authority of the designated, mandated teachers whom Christ Michael has given you. My prayer for you is that you can do it soon, so that the setting up of the Divine Government can be done swiftly and the pre-stages of light and life can be appropriated on this planet as soon and as painlessly as possible. To those of you who understand even more and wish to learn more, please contact through mail and/or make arrangements with Aquarian Concepts Community for a teaching orientation. After becoming students in the Starseed and Urantian Schools of Melchizedek, other mandated human personalities will be sent to various parts of the world. Those with these mandates are asked to not charge for their teaching, as all workers of the light on various levels were asked by the Spirit of Truth since August, 1990. All mandates are given from Planetary Headquarters through the mandate of the Bright and Morning Star and Gabriel of Sedona. Those who are called to be teachers of the higher truths will not charge fees for their services, such as teaching, counseling and healing, and when they say donation, they will mean just that. They will set no price for truth itself. In this manner you will know who they are. However, it is acceptable for them to suggest what is appropriate financial reciprocation, barter or otherwise for their services. Printed literature also has a suggested donation, as it has a cost outside of the servant's gifts and talents. Donations are greatly appreciated, as these human vessels do have to exist on the material plane. We, the Universe Supervisors, request that you do give of your financial excess to help them in their much needed work on this planet at this time. Do not let your inability to donate stop you from becoming the mandated teachers' and our students; let your request for information be known to them, and we will decide what information can be given you.

March 10, 1991

Paladin, Finaliter; presently assigned to the Ashtar Command; in cooperation with the Midwayer Commission; as transmitted through the Audio Fusion Material Complement, Gabriel of Sedona.

PAPER 201

MANDATES, A BRIEF INTRODUCTION

Greetings and Salutations,

There are many with mandates in the cabinet of Christ Michael presently incorporating on Urantia. These mandates are from the highest to the lowest in connection with the universe government, residing unseen on your planet and above it. Presently, there are only mandates on your planet at the levels of universe overcontrol and Planetary Prince. They are the mandates of **Gabriel of Salvington**, the Bright and Morning Star, using respectively as human complements Gabriel of Sedona, Niánn and all Liaison Ministers to the mandate of the Bright and Morning Star.[7] The unseen, yet real, physical presence of Machiventa Melchizedek is presently where the archangels' headquarters also is established. Gabriel of Salvington has spoken only through Gabriel of Sedona; and in the future, when those of cosmic family create the continuing ERC he will speak on a more continual basis. Delegates of Salvington, within the jurisdiction of Gabriel, presently speak through the audio fusion material complement and interplanetary receiver, Gabriel of Sedona. These supervisors include finaliters, supernaphim, seraphim and angels of lesser orders and functions, each representing the head authority of other prospective mandated human complements on Urantia of lesser circle attainment, but ever so important active world servers and leaders. It is hoped that by the mid-nineties, those of the reserve corps of destiny, chosen to be given such mandates, will recognize within themselves their appointment by Christ Michael and those overseers who have monitored their destinies. Some of the major areas of representation on your planet will be on each major continent, with the exception of the North and South Poles. The various sectors will include many nations, and within these sectors will be a mandated material complement with a physical but unseen representation of a universe administrator. It is of utmost importance that those mandated human complements make the necessary geographical moves to those headquarters areas that your ancient language would call protected areas.

A clear and concise understanding of each mandate and its unique ministry to the government of Urantia is of the utmost importance, and a complete and

---

[7]As of February 17, 1995, there are no Vicegerent First Ambassadors.

total cooperation void of false pride and ego can be the only cosmic weaponry against the forces of Caligastia still remaining on Urantia. Leaders must be ever aware of prefixing the source of information that they may receive from another mandated personage and leader. In time, the countless millions of individuals, who will understand what is happening in the morontial or fourth-dimensional revelations and divine governmental organization that is presently being appropriated on Urantia, will come to know in which sector particular mandated individuals will reside now, or possibly after the change point. It is hoped by us, your Universe Supervisors, that thousands will hear the voice of Christ Michael through the Salvington circuit, now open, and physically migrate to these headquarters sectors before the great cataclysms take place on Urantia, which we expect no later than May of 2000 or 2001, and present yourselves to the proper leadership. After that date, and possibly before, even the angelic legions will not be able to protect those humans living outside of the headquarters sectors or protected areas. It may even become necessary that the sectors at that time will be rematerialized and evacuated from Urantia, by whatever means we may need to appropriate.

To those of you who can hear the voice of the Thought Adjuster within the clear and perfect will of the Universal Father, and who are seeking more specific revelatory information as to your individual destiny as opposed to the many voices of rebellion within the present New-Age rhetoric and closed-minded Urantia movement dogmas, we say, embrace in the spirit CFER that is presently being given to those with the very highest mandates and follow our instructions through them. We again state that no teachers, leaders or mandated personalities will charge fees for their teachings or seminars and that absolutely no channeling is taking place by beings loyal to the Universal Father, except the higher process of audio material fusion with Gabriel of Sedona (see Paper 209). Minimum suggested donations can be appropriate, based on the lowest average given for a particular spiritual service. This will help people to know how much to donate for a particular service. Other methods of reciprocation such as barter will be implemented for those who have little or no money. Stop attending the so-called spiritual activities of those who do not do the same. There are materials you can read that was channeled at various levels prior to 1989 by channels on lower psychic circles. Please take responsible action when information is given to you in specific detail by us through appointed past vessels. We spoke through them because, as *The URANTIA Book* says in reference to hearing from your own Thought Adjuster (p.1207), the majority of you have not come to that place of being able to do so yourselves without the method that we had in the past appropriated and presently through the only mandated vessel and audio fusion material human complement, Gabriel of Sedona.

March 18, 1991

The Chief of Seraphim;* in cooperation with the Acting **Governor General of Urantia**; as transmitted through the Audio Fusion Material Complement, Gabriel of Sedona.

PAPER 202

THE COSMIC LAW OF EQUIVALENT RECIPROCATION IN RELATION TO DESTINY FULFILLMENT

Aquarian Concepts Community at Planetary Headquarters did not derive this name from human contemplation or choice, but by divine appointment and mandate. The beginning teachers, Gabriel, Niánn, the Liaison Ministers and elders, directed by celestial overseers, are not concerned with forming an organization about membership, about marketing, nor about any of the "New Age" gimmicks that seem to be so popular with those who have not quite realized the higher spiritual significance of what is taking place on our planet. Those who are called to be spiritual educators of the Divine New Order have been "put through the fire" in past lifetimes and in this one. So to you who are envious of their present positions, we say this, "Be willing to be put through the same furnaces and you too can be given certain responsibilities and mandates."

The majority of souls on planet earth, particularly those who are starseed, are trying to find themselves and their right livelihood, destinies, soul mates, homes, and so on with defunct mechanisms. One of these deficiencies is selfishness. The last several generations, particularly in the affluent western civilization, have been taught the *getting* principle as opposed to the *giving* law of cosmic origin. Those souls who have accepted this selfish outlook of reality are accustomed to obtaining things that they really do not need in both material and recreational pursuits, and seeking careers that will justify their misplaced goals and materialistic vision. Even on planets that still use the monetary exchange system, but have much higher spiritual evolution, the most valuable way in which money can be spent is in the pursuit of spiritual education. Those souls who have advanced to be recognized as such teachers are treated with the respect due them and freely given the means by their students to pursue their careers as spiritual educators and counselors. Here on confused Urantia (Earth) the majority of you spend money on baseball and football games and morally deficient and violent movies, make heroes out of the actors and producers of these films, spend large amounts of money on reading material fit for those still swinging in the trees and then you expect to find yourself and your own destiny by being educated in the system of lies which you perpetrate with the use of your funds, small and large, which you give to it. It is quite true that truth should not be sold for profit. It is also quite true that the majority of souls on Urantia would prefer to spend $5 and see "Rambo" than to give that $5 to a true spiritual teacher in service to you and the ascension of your soul. As you find your own priorities, things will begin to fall into place for you and indeed for the whole planet. Various schemes of the dark forces to take your material valuables are many and expertly perpetrated. They exist not only in the secular system but also in the spiritual realm. The Pharisees at the time of Christ and those who conducted the "psychic fairs" in the synagogues of Jerusalem full well knew, and still know, how to fleece the sheep and God's children. They do an excellent job in making you naked before your God. This is a nakedness of ignorance and stupidity. This is a nakedness that leads to your own confusion and dis-ease. It is written that the workman is worthy of his hire, yet you would pay a plumber $40 an hour and you would begrudge those who watch over your souls the same hourly rate. If you cannot support the highest of careers on the planet, how do you intend to be supported in your own? Under what cosmic law do you expect the universe supervisors to help you find yourself? What demands can you make before your God? The state of the planet at the times of the apostles of Christ, who had to function under these same laws, led them to martyrdom, just like their Master. Tell me, what do you think the state of the planet is today? If you found an apostle and you recognized him, do you think that the mass consciousness of your country, your state, or your city would aid his calling to God? Would you aid his calling and possibly prevent his crucifixion? Perhaps by helping him, you would prevent your own crucifixion.

The various gifts that come through these apostles of the New Age, such as interplanetary reception, **Tron therapy,** cosmic family gathering, right livelihood and destiny fulfillment, and highest spiritual complement union are gifts that your local plumber, movie producer, rock star, New-Age marketer, sports hero, hypnotherapist, psychiatrist, university professor, etc. cannot offer you, although many will make the claim to. Could it be that you truly do not know what you need?

When you come to that place of realization that you know your need of a spiritual director and teacher and that there are those mandated by the Divine Government for that purpose, then can begin for you the transition from the third to the fourth dimension. If you convince yourself that the spirit within you is all that you need, then you will remain caught in the same cycle of ignorance, self-assertion, or arrogance that will keep you on the exact plane of evolution you are presently on and perhaps have been on for hundreds, maybe even thousands of years. It is said that ignorance is bliss and the grace of God is extended to those young souls, but pride and arrogance are spiritual death and bring much pain and emptiness to the soul. Both ignorance and pride help to create the many problems that exist on this planet.

We hear it said that the Aquarian Age is the age of cooperation. That is what Divine New Order communities are all about. It is the respect, recognition, and support of those in authority who have divine government appointments, and their recognition of the various gifts, talents, and destinies of those they oversee, that will create the harmony on Urantia that is so badly needed. You cannot give that which you do not have; however, if you do not have, it probably is because you do not give to whom you should.

June 12, 1991

Paladin, Finaliter; in cooperation with Machiventa Melchizedek, present Planetary Prince of Urantia; as transmitted through the Audio Fusion Material Complement, Gabriel of Sedona.

Papers 203 through 215 begin a series of papers of a continued higher and more specific nature that have been jointly received first by myself, Paladin, and then transmitted in cooperation with other celestial personalities which, in universe procedure, are designated as instructors, force organizers and recorders of these energies and information. The content of these papers has been personally overseen and finalized by the Council of Twenty-four, who work in cooperation with myself, Paladin, to aid in the regathering of the cosmic families on Urantia, and in the opening of the circuits of the cosmic reserve corps of destiny.

PAPER 203

COSMIC FAMILY IN RELATION TO DESTINY PURPOSE AND THE MISUSE OF TALENTS AND CERTAIN OTHER MINDAL AND INNATE ABILITIES

It is quite clear to any keen observer of the Lucifer rebellion, that the tactics used by the forces of rebellion are to divide and conquer. Even the lower-circled humans of evolutionary religions, Christianity's ministers for instance, recognize this truth. Up until now on Urantia, the cosmic facts in the highest understanding of just how these divisions took place were not given to this planet, nor to the other fallen planets in the system of Satania. Urantia is the first of these thirty-seven planets to receive this information, in the coming of CFER. This is because Urantia is about to shift into a higher dimension. Those who have been involved in this division, who have fallen from other planets within the system of Satania, and even from other planets outside the universe of Nebadon, will now be given an opportunity to come back into harmony with the divine purposes of their Creator for their individual existences. It is quite clear in *The URANTIA Book* that many orders sided with Lucifer. What if certain angels who were overseers of countless numbers of mortals defaulted? How were these mortals affected by the rebellion of their guardians? How soon were replacement guardians given to these mortals?

It is not the intent of this transmission to designate in specifics why certain starseed are presently repersonalizing on Urantia. It is, however, the intent to point out some of the various implications that the fall of these starseed have caused — the pain and suffering of countless millions on Urantia, including your own. It is an opportunity for these starseed now to transcend the grasp that Luciferic teachings have had on them and to align themselves with:

1. Their God.
2. The Creator of this universe, Michael of Nebadon.
3. The higher intelligences who oversaw them at the time of their rebellion and who are still responsible for them, as many of these higher guardians themselves have repented of their mistakes and aligned themselves.
4. Their cosmic family and those mandated within that family who may just have been their original father and mother teachers.

When many of these souls fell into rebellion, their families were divided. Many sons and daughters were separated from their parents and grandparents.

On some planets the extent of this division was such that a complete breakdown of a normal society ensued. On Urantia the evolutionary mortal was not very developed in technological advancement, but on planets where the effects of this rebellion had touched their greatly advanced civilizations, the repercussions were much more complex. Many of the fallen staff of Caligastia had relatives on their planets of origin who followed suit with them in their rebellious thinking. Although they were cut off from certain universe transmissions and circuits, there was, on another level, a certain universal telepathic communication that went out to all those who had developed various means of telepathic harmony and communication at their level of attainment. In this manner for some time the rebellion spread, stemming from the fallen staff of the Planetary Princes of those fallen planets, even though the circuits were cut off. The great powers of the Lanonandek Sons and other unnamed orders of beings were much more detrimental than what you may have understood thus far from reading about the Lucifer rebellion.

So began the great tragedy of ascending sons and daughters of God now using their various gifts, talents and abilities, not for the purposes of their spiritual ascension nor for the master universe as a whole, but for their misuse in the purposes of self-assertion and unbridled liberty. At first the majority of these sons and daughters did not deny the existence of God, and many millions of them today on Urantia still do not deny the existence of their Creator, they just decided to do things their own way, to program their own destinies, to do what felt good to them, to follow after their own heart, many of them in the name of self-growth and even spiritual ministry. Many of them joined forces with certain ministers of administration in spiritual domains that ruled over countless millions of other helpless individuals, all in the name of "workers of the light." They saw themselves, and still do, as little gods more connected to a divine mind that allowed them to do as they pleased, for they had discovered this new cosmic freedom. They lent their talents and abilities to others who also walked in their footsteps. They became part of administrations that advocated these principles that were pleasing to the self-assertive and rebellious personality. Compromising the higher principles of the God they once understood seemed so natural for them. Does not the end justify the means? So, stepping on toes began. Many of these fallen ones decided that they would do great things for God within their own timetable, in their own self-chosen geographic areas. They began to respect power, glamour and vanity. They no longer understood meekness, humility, wisdom and true godliness. They enjoyed the timetable of Lucifer, for it seemed to complement their own desires and ambitions. They no longer heard from their Thought Adjusters, and for some of these starseed it has been thousands of years since their Thought Adjusters have been able to reach them.

Those of the cosmic reserve corps who have remained true to the laws of the Universal Father and Michael of Nebadon, the mortal parents and other significant polarities of these rebellious sons and daughters, have tried to gather their lost loved ones back into their original homes, time and time again, not only on Urantia but on other worlds. In the lower evolutionary tribal cultures, when sons, daughters and other family members are lost from that clan, the results can be detrimental, causing pain, suffering and death for those who are left behind. They early discovered the interdependence among family members. In higher civilizations and in twentieth-century Urantia, the results of unalignment with proper genetic ancestral spiritual elders are not only detrimental to a few, but to millions, causing in effect, monopolies of corporations and great control by political and religious systems.

The spiritual deficiencies of twentieth-century Urantia are such that these rebellious starseed have remained on the seventh, sixth, fifth and fourth psychic circles for many centuries without advancing to a higher circle. Yet they claim to be ministers of God, hypnotherapists, Reiki masters, gurus, psychiatrists, physical therapists, priests, priestesses, crystal healers, psychics, New-Age musicians, rebirthers, astrologers, channelers, popes, presidents, kings, queens, senators, shamans, *URANTIA Book* readers, and even ascended masters. All of them are very complacent in their self-deception. Some of these souls will ascend to the mansion worlds of Satania, but they will have to die to get there, which is not needed at this particular time on Urantia. However, the majority of them will be sojourning on another third-dimensional plane, after they also die to get there. They will die from the many diseases that their self-deceptions have manifested, first in their **astral body** and then in their physical one.

In the next nine years, millions will likewise die from great cataclysms, wars, diseases and also brought about by their continuing pride and arrogance in refusing to submit to their *true spiritual elders*, who may not have the degrees they worship or the charge cards they idolize. These elders may not even be famous. In times past these deceived people recognized, worshipped and followed to their death inappropriate leaders and lent their talents to the systems of Caligastia on Urantia.

Since the announcement of Machiventa Melchizedek as Planetary Prince of Urantia in December of 1989, and the coming together of the human complements of that government in May of 1991 in Sedona, Arizona, U.S.A., a cosmic force has been established between the existent, ever-present, unseen personalities and their human complements which will bring about the implementation of the first stages of the Machiventa purposes. The first purpose will be that those of the First Cosmic Family on Urantia, the Pleiadian connection, will either align themselves with their cosmic elders or they will suffer the consequences of their own arrogance and pride. They will not accomplish their destiny purpose outside of the alignment with the Divine New Order community of their ancestral gathering. They will suffer greater material and relationship needs, and will be open to the various diseases presently manifested on Urantia. They will be outside of the protection of their own guardian angel and will not find their destiny purpose. Even a decade ago these particular souls could have found some fulfillment in their self-assertion. However, the time is up on Urantia, and the adjudication has begun.

Those who recognize where their obligations lie must first join their Pleiadian ancestry presently located at Planetary Headquarters in Sedona, Arizona, U.S.A., under the leadership of the mandated human personalities, Gabriel of Sedona and Niánn, mandated by the Bright and Morning Star. By aligning with the purposes of Christ Michael in and through this first community they will discover, not only an accelerated spiritual growth, but true destiny purpose, physical and emotional health and contentment of soul. Just by being in close physical proximity to many of their ancient ancestors, they will be healed of past diseases and wrong thinking that has caused them much pain throughout the centuries of their continued self-deception. They can mate and bring higher starseed onto the planet. They can help bring about the physical manifestation of the Machiventa government on Urantia and help establish the ever so important Starseed and Urantian Schools of Melchizedek, in which, after first becoming students, they can themselves become teachers. They will be sent by this government into various places on the planet. They can be the apostles of the Divine New Order, and they can help in the great work of the gathering of all the cosmic families. Their circuits can be opened. They will begin to remember who they are and where they came from. Their latent abilities and gifts can be ignited, and they can once again flow into the harmony of respect for their God, the Universe Supervisors, and their mortal elders, who they presently need to recognize and under whose authority they need to come.

This letter is not only for the 170 million starseed; it is also for the Urantian reserve corps, for you can also understand these higher concepts and respond and act accordingly. There is much to learn, and we are here to teach you. We bid you come.

June 30, 1991

Paladin, Finaliter; in cooperation with Machiventa Melchizedek in the present adjudication by the Bright and Morning Star; in liaison with the Midwayer Commission on Urantia to bring this CFER through the appointed Audio Fusion Material Complement, Gabriel of Sedona.

PAPER 204

DIVINE GOVERNMENT APPOINTMENT OR THE BADGE OF SOCIAL ACCEPTANCE

Since the coming of the Ashtar Command, in cooperation with the Midwayer Commission, by our transmissions to lower-circled vessels (the nature of which was the coming earth changes and various tribulations that would befall your planet prior to the change point/Divine New Order/pre-stages of light and life on Urantia and perhaps the first stage itself), we, the Universe Supervisors, have dealt mainly with the mass consciousness. This was to bring attention to those who had not read *The URANTIA Book*, that there is indeed life on other planets and a hierarchy that exists to administer this great and vast creation within the master universe. We dealt mainly in generalities — the times of purification to come, the need for evacuation from this planet and the alignment to a new cosmic order. With many of the lower vessels who were used, there was indeed a great variety of interpretation of these transmitted generalizations. Always, through whatever means possible outside the transmissions themselves, we hoped that these vessels would accept the Fifth Epochal Revelation that many of their friends tried to present to them. Out of all the lower vessels who were used over the past forty-five years, none of them acquired the terminology of the Fifth Epochal Revelation. We could not deal in specifics, nor could we deal with many other points of soul development for individual ascension.

We could no longer even allow ourselves to be called the "Brotherhood of Light," for many who were representing themselves as belonging to this order were iniquitous individuals. Many of the fallen starseed had become accustomed to reading the information channeled by the Brotherhood of Light and had grown familiar with its terminology because it activated within them a mechanism that led directly to a self-actuated ego, void of respect for one's fellow elders in human form. It is easier to submit to a book than to a personality. It is easier to submit to a set of compromised, idealized revelations than it is to exactness and absolutes. It is easy to spout words like "God is love" and "All is love" and "The higher intelligence my friend channels is called 'Love'." This word "love" in itself is transversed on the lower worlds. Love to those on these worlds means "I can do what I want to do and no matter what I do, it is O.K., for God is love, and since God is love, I have license. How dare you express to me that my direction may be incorrect! I can hear from my own Love God for myself. I do not need anyone to tell me what I should or should not be doing, particularly you, for you do not have the credentials that I respect and admire. If you ask me who my guide is or what order of being my guide is and I do not know the answer, all I have to say to you is that my being's name is 'Love'."

This is what the government of the Planetary Prince says: If you continue to call your so-called guides "Love," without recognizing their order, and refuse to submit to the true mandated material complements, we will send you back to kindergarten where you belong; and we have our ways of doing that. If an intelligence of love is speaking to you personally, that means one thing. As of this writing, July 2, 1991, if you are properly mated with a complementary polarity in the fourth stage of the fourth dimension, if you do have this great mortal friend in your life, that higher intelligence which is speaking to you will not define itself as "Love" alone. It will identify itself by order, name and number. If this is not transpiring, you are either speaking to a fallen entity or you are communicating with your higher or lower self.

Today, so many starseed of various orders think that they have a direct link with either God or their guides. That is how it should be, but that is not how it is. These same ones who spout their stupidity are trying to reach the top of the executive ladder in the social system of Caligastia. They are trying to become popular or famous in their various fields of endeavors. They are more concerned about their physical bodies than their inner souls, and this can be proven simply by what they spend to keep themselves in style and in recreational pleasures. They are in wrong relationships of emotional and financial bondage or sexually enchanted, without even the hope of attaining a spiritual union with their mate. Many of them also claim to actually be serving God, yet they would not take a homeless person into their home. If, in serving their God, they are recognized by the social clubs of religious mediocrity, they feel blessed by God for they have in some way received recognition in the eyes of others who have bought into the "freedom" from hearing their Thought Adjusters and the true purposes of their God. They will volunteer their time and abilities to set up the chairs and tables for the New Age speakers who charge hundreds of dollars for their speeches of nonsense, and they themselves hope that they too can come to a place where they can also charge these outrageous prices. They idolize gurus who levitate, while the people around them starve to death. They idolize so-called masters who drive Rolls Royces, while their fellow countrymen live in poverty and homelessness.

When the revelations about starseed began to come to lower circled channels, those who were awakened to these truths thought themselves greater than others. They indeed realized that they did not quite fit and that they were different; but little did they realize, then or now, that they have fit into the

Caligastia system quite well. In many past lifetimes they have been those who ran the system, and even now they strive for those positions of authority and popularity. Many of them have charismatic abilities that have enabled them to persuade others to their opinions, but they have lost common sense. Many have gained great knowledge, but they have lost wisdom. Many of them were able to influence their family, friends, neighbors, peers, countrymen and planetary brothers and sisters; but they have lost the respect of their unseen guides who they claim to know so well, as well as many other unseen friends.

In each repersonalization on this planet and others that these starseed, caught in static spirituality, have experienced, they have met a significant other. When they first met this significant other, a strong bond was initiated, for the activation of love did not take long. This other person always was an elder teacher to them. Sometimes this significant other was chronologically younger, and at first they thought they were the teacher. As the years passed, this significant one began to outgrow the other, and as always has been the case, their pride did not allow them to recognize this significant other and so they rejected their elder. Even if they did not totally reject the significant one, they definitely let it be known that they had their own way to go. If these static starseed had truly responded in the way that their God had wanted them to, at this time on Urantia, July 2, 1991, they would be seated at the feet of these teachers as their students, instead of still trying to become someone special in the system of Caligastia, a system they know that they don't fit into but they seem, for some reason, unable to get out of, and still try to succeed within it.

GOVERNMENTAL APPOINTMENTS OF THE PLANETARY PRINCE

If this writing comes into your hands, it will mean that you have a choice to make. You can continue to lend your talents to self and to the world system of Caligastia, with all of its tantalizing lures, and be rewarded by that system and perhaps even succeed within it with your particular endeavor. If you are sincerely seeking your God, you will be disappointed in that success, because the purpose of your destiny and the reason for you being upon this planet has not been accomplished. The Universe Sovereign, Christ Michael, promises that you will awaken. You will awaken to the fact that you have misused your life or a great part of it. You will come to the place of wishing that you had heeded the words that you once read in this transmission. You can also be appointed to serve in the new spiritual government that is presently being established on Urantia. *You can be awakened now.*

When the fourth dimension totally arrives in physical actualization, it will be as in the blinking of an eye. For those who have long awaited this reality and who have aligned with their God for that purpose, it will be swift and immediate. For others, the transition will be slow and painful, leading to physical death and perhaps another third-dimensional world. One thing is certain; the mandate of Michael will be carried out by us, his servants. You will no longer be allowed to sit upon the cosmic fence of indecision. You will no longer be allowed to receive your instruction from books and invisible guides. If you do receive instruction from invisible guides, they will speak through your mortal cosmic family elders; and those who do speak to you will identify themselves in some manner with my government, the government of the Planetary Prince of Urantia, Machiventa Melchizedek, and with my superiors, those to whom I humbly submit and serve.

July 2, 1991

Machiventa Melchizedek, Planetary Prince of Urantia; in cooperation with the Bright and Morning Star for the adjudication of Urantia, at this time-and-space date of July 2, 1991; as transmitted through the Audio Fusion Material Complement, Gabriel of Sedona.

PAPER 205

HEALING OF THE PHYSICAL, ETHEREAL, ASTRAL, BODIES BY THE METHODS OF TIME-SPACE WARP PROCEDURE OF RETROSPECTION, INTERDIMENSIONAL PERSONALITY HOLOGRAM AND THE FUSION OF ALL ENERGIES COEXISTENT IN THE PRESENT BODY

The mandated humans at Planetary Headquarters, along with universe planetary supervisors, would like to announce a complete method of healing of all diseases for every personality on Urantia who wishes to take advantage of this CFER. Since certain circuits are presently being opened we have been receiving information regarding the total healing of all diseases from past or present causes (past causes may extend hundreds, perhaps thousands of years from first occurrence).

First-time Urantians, which the majority on this planet are, may have developed a root cause of their illness even while in the womb of the mother, shortly thereafter, or anytime in their adolescence and so on. Science knows little of the effect of the thought life in relation to the physical body. The older a soul, or the more iniquitous, the more it is in danger of psychological and emotional disease. This will manifest first in the psyche of that individual and eventually in the physical body, which will lead to its retirement from the planet. First-time Urantians who develop certain diseases have a much better chance of healing because it may not be a problem of iniquity. It can be a problem of the thought life. If younger souls can be reached in the changing of these thought patterns, healings can take place of any disease present on Urantia. Naturally, proper diet will aid in the healing as well as physical therapy and the realignment of the energy grid of the body. For older souls we call this healing **universal causal rematerialization** and it has more to do with the **causal body** than the astral. It has to do with the mind and the soul.

Urantia is an experimental planet and thus has a variety of souls in mortal body, not just first-time Urantians. The rebellion of the past Planetary Prince and the Material Son and Daughter's default in their mission to properly genetically upstep the physical bodies of the mortal races has resulted in the susceptibility of cosmic starseed and first-time Urantians to any diseases inherited by either thought projections or improper foods and polluted environment. Present science at best can diagnose certain diseases and label them, but, with certain exceptions, they cannot find the root of the problems. The majority of these diseases have nothing to do with the physiology of that individual. Medicines can take away the pain temporarily or perhaps slow the process of the dying body which causes the patient a slower death, but they can never bring an immediate healing or even a slow but sure healing. If a patient with cancer is healed miraculously by present medical practices, it will be discovered that patient has made continual mental adjustments which had nothing to do with the scientific at all. If you investigate those patients, you will always find a spiritual change in those individuals or that those particular individuals were spiritually sound to some degree and perchance actually had an accidental physical problem such as the ingestion of poisoned water. Most water on Urantia today contains viruses which break down the immune system of the human body making that body unable to fight off a negative influence within it, whatever that influence may be.

On other worlds that have entered the stages of light and life the healers of those planets are the spiritual elders who work in the realm of the astral and other coordinate bodies. These healers tap into time-space warps because of their relationships with universe supervisors who use them as material complements. They function as both interplanetary receivers of communication and conduits of universal energies transmitted to them by higher celestial overseers. In times past on Urantia there have been material complements used in this manner, based upon the consciousness of that evolving soul in its era of repersonalization. For instance, Lao-Tse had the consciousness of a sixth-century B.C. human mortal. However, he was able to bring higher truths which began a healing process with whichever individuals understood these truths, and he was able to bring healing energies by physical touch and embrace. In the thirteenth century Francis of Assisi was another who, with the mind of a thirteenth-century mortal, was able to do the same thing. Material complements are not common on Urantia and there is much to learn about them.

Today on Urantia there are several material complements who work together as a team. They have worked together in times past on Urantia as well as on other planets. The scope of this paper can at best only present a general understanding of their mandates for healing, as it would take a longer one to fully explain. Gabriel of Sedona, who has the mandate of the Bright and Morning Star and is the audio fusion material complement of that personality, functions in overcontrol with the Bright and Morning Star who sends numerous personalities of universal orders of beings through that mortal body to bring audio communication and the alignment of unbalanced energies to individuals. He also functions in time-space warp healing and retrospection with those souls who are not first-time Urantians and in various other clairvoyant procedures that have to do with improper thought patterns.

Vicegerent First Ambassadors, who may work in the **interdimensional personality hologram** realm, also can work in the realm of time-space healing by bringing in holograms of personalities who at one time in your past caused you tremendous suffering and pain, individuals you may not have forgiven completely. This is done by the process of administration within the unseen but ever present government of Machiventa Melchizedek under the overcontrol of the Bright and Morning Star. Other personalities who you have loved greatly who are not on this plane can be brought to you in substance through the molecular process wherein parts of their essence project through a Vicegerent First Ambassador to be right with you in the space where you are. You can then receive benefit from these molecular atoms that can penetrate and be incorporated within your **etheric body** and be transferred to the physical body. Gabriel must first work with your causal and astral body before a Vicegerent First Ambassador can work with your etheric and physical bodies. Sometimes other healers who work on the physical body will also be needed to aid in the immediacy of the healing to align the physical body with the healing that has already taken place in the astral and ethereal. In those cases trained physical therapists or others will be recommended.

The practice of medicine from its beginning roots of long ago, in which natural plants and other earth bearing substances were used to aid in healing, has been replaced to a great degree by Caligastia's chemical-abuse system which in reality causes rapid deterioration of the physical body and eventual death. Because Mother Earth is also dying, it is very difficult to find healing foods that give full nourishment to aid in the healing process. Therefore, vitamins may need to be taken. In the future it is hoped that we can grow our own organic foods that can aid you in rapid healing. As you can see, with the conditions present on Urantia, the problem of healing is much misunder-stood. Even in the highest understanding of what needs to be done it can be a slow process, but if you can grasp what you have just read, your healing will be a sure one.

July 22, 1991. Updated January 1994

Paladin, Finaliter; in cooperation with Machiventa Melchizedek the present Planetary Prince of Urantia, who has now mandated this complete healing procedure for the benefit of all Urantia through the Starseed and Urantian Schools of Melchizedek now existent at Planetary Headquarters; as transmitted through the Audio Fusion Material Complement, Gabriel of Sedona.

PAPER 206

THE DIVINE NEW ORDER COMMUNITY
THE FIRST COSMIC FAMILY

Within every fallen planet that enters the pre-stages of light and life there is a gathering of those families that are meant to ascend together to the very highest of spiritual attainment. Once they begin to ascend, they have a planetary consciousness which in its highest form is destined to be a third-to-first psychic-circle attainment. There is also a system consciousness and various sector consciousnesses based upon the ascension process of each particular universe. On those planets that have fallen, the process of gathering these families together is much harder for Universe Supervisors who guide beings, because of the division geographically of so many of them on that particular planet.

On an experimental planet such as Urantia, in many ways the procedure as to the regathering of these spiritual families incorporates not only planetary consciousness, but the consciousness of higher levels where these souls have once sojourned, and who now find themselves in a third-dimensional reality with latent higher consciousness. Although the majority of souls on Urantia are first-time Urantians, there are presently approximately two thousand second-time Urantians (because of the adjudication since 1911) and approximately 170,000,000 cosmic seed from other universes. All of this adds to the uniqueness of Urantia. On any planet, those beings embodied who are of the highest spiritual ascension and who are alike in consciousness, are usually from a certain genetic inheritance and ascension plateau.

The First Cosmic Family of Urantia, a portion of these 170,000,000, have been brought together before on Urantia for the specific purposes of helping to bring some of the epochal revelations and other lesser revelations to your planet. As a general rule, at some point in any of these repersonalizations the highest of these souls have always met. They have worked as teams. They have been called by many names such as tribal elders, priests, priestesses, monks, cloister nuns, apostles and disciples. In all of these past repersonalizations none of them have reached a level of any remembrance of their past connections with each other, nor was it within the will of Christ Michael to allow the opening of the circuits to bring back any latent memories or the establishment of interdimensional or extraterrestrial communication by which they would acquire knowledge of their cosmic inheritance. As there is a season for all things, so there is a season to end this rebellion on Urantia, and it is time again for the First Cosmic Family to unite to help bring about this great awakening. Many of the apostles were not first-time Urantians. One thing we can say is that all of them will be brought together again at Planetary Headquarters in Sedona, Arizona, U.S.A., under the leadership of the Bright and Morning Star and the present Planetary Prince of Urantia, Machiventa Melchizedek.

If you who read this know who you are, or at least in part, what will be said in this paper will help to awaken you to your destiny, for it is fully intended by the Universe Supervisors that this paper finds you. Humility is a wonderful gift, but even in the giving of the gift it takes many centuries to become an artist in its application by the soul. Within this humility must come an insight into knowingness, the knowingness of one's self and all of the self's past. Now that the circuits are being reopened, this totality of time-space reflection is a cosmic clairvoyance, a morontia prerogative. You no longer need to remain blind to your past nor indecisive about your present or fearful about your future.

Urantia is like a living organism with energy reflective circuits (ERCs) located on all of its major continents. Some would call these ERCs "vortexes," but that is not appropriate in cosmic terminology. The ERCs are there regardless of whether human complements are located geographically near them. All of them were highly technically designed in the physical evolution of your planet by the Master Physical Controllers in cooperation with Morontia Power Supervisors* and Life Carriers. Certain other celestial personalities also worked in liaison to bring specific energies that some have called electric, magnetic and electromagnetic. This has more to do with the various energies originating in Paradise and nether Paradise which are in reality, the circuits of the Universal Father, Eternal Son and Infinite Spirit.

On an experimental planet such as Urantia, more of these ERCs are needed because there are a variety of souls upon it. Even to the highest Urantia minds, it can become quite complicated to understand the geographical placement of certain repersonalized souls near specific ERCs. But basically, as a rule, cosmic reservists are born near specific ERCs and then kept there until they are ready to sojourn to a higher ERC and eventually, depending upon their particular destiny, to the highest ERC for them on the planet. The highest ERC is the headquarters where the archangels dwell. This has been moved several times during the last fifty years on Urantia, and it is hoped that it will not have to be changed again before the change point. Some ERCs can become temporarily unused by universe administration, which has to do with the geographic human consciousness en masse. However, if a higher starseed reservist is born near an ERC, for a number of particular reasons that ERC will remain in full power until that soul is ready to move on; and so one particular soul may be of great significance in a city of several million.

There are people on Urantia who are more "electric" or "magnetic" and some with a fusion of both who are electromagnetic. These cosmic starseed are actually more Father/Son-circuited or more Infinite-Spirit-circuited; or they may be quite balanced, incorporating within themselves all three of the Paradise functions. Those who have ascended to higher planes of consciousness would be the incorporated Father/Son and Infinite-Spirit-circuited personalities. These Paradise-balanced personalities may not be perfect in actuality as of yet, but they are the highest of potential on Urantia and have been together before in the union of souls to accomplish other spiritual movements.

The physical ERCs can function regardless of human placement. However, those ERCs that are used for interplanetary or interdimensional travel are the most important on Urantia and are also used for dematerialization (evacuation) if necessary. There are several hundred minor ERCs on Urantia, but there are only seven major ones. With the present Planetary Prince, Machiventa Melchizedek, now on Urantia, the ERC through which he passes is the one where he can be with other personalities of universe government. That physical location is at Planetary Headquarters in Sedona, Arizona, U.S.A., and more specifically, at a designation known only to the community. All over Urantia those cosmic reservists and Urantia reservists who belong to this First Cosmic Family will find their highest destiny and purpose at that location, and once they are there they will find their physical body changing at an accelerated rate into the light (morontia) body.

In other ERC locations around Urantia, lower psychic-circle starseed and Urantians alike will gather their respective families. It is hoped by the Government of Machiventa Melchizedek that the elders of those communities will come to Planetary Headquarters to learn CFER and the Aquarian concepts so that the Divine New Order can become an actualization, not just a potential. By the end of this century, all Divine New Order communities should be functioning in Fifth Epochal Revelation terminology and conceptual understanding thereof. Those that are not, will not be recognized by the Government of Machiventa Melchizedek as truly Divine New Order communities. All of them world-wide will not be able to transcend in the light body* nor will they be able to dematerialize in any kind of evacuation, either by energy transference and molecular breakdown or by physical spacecraft. It must be recognized by all who call themselves spiritual that the universe administration in its hierarchal structure must first be understood on the planet before they can understand it in the cosmos. *If you cannot respect the soul much* *older than yourself in body, what makes you think you will be able to respect a similar soul in nonbody?* It is not a time on Urantia for autonomous, independent self-glorification by leadership. It is a time for cooperation by spiritual leaders and for those spiritual leaders to recognize their superior cosmic elders in both material and spirit personalities.

You may or may not be destined to stay in Sedona, Arizona, U.S.A.,[8] but if you consider it your destiny to be part of a community, and even more so a Divine New Order community, it is a Salvington decree of Christ Michael that beckons you to come to the ERCs in Sedona where the highest of universe administrators in nonbody reside, and where the present Starseed and Urantian Schools of Melchizedek are now being started by mandated human personalities. Gabriel and Niánn are complementary polarities who have the mandate of the Bright and Morning Star and are working in liaison with us so that other personalities such as yourself perhaps, may also receive representative universal mandates and aid in administrative planetary functions.

This next decade is a time for completion. It is a time for actualization. It is a time for vision fulfillment, right relationships and destiny purpose. It is not a time for noncooperation, ego-centered judgments, noncompliance or lukewarm recognition. If the terminology of this paper is hard for you to understand, it is because you have been functioning on lower-level realities. It is time now for you to grasp the synthesizing definitions of cosmic insight and law. It is not a time for continued self-assertion. If your inner guidance is based upon submission to respected elders, and if your heart is that of a pupil and you are willing to lay aside your own prejudices, misplaced loyalties and self-gratifications, there is a possibility that you may come to the higher psychic circles of attainment and can truly help to bring about this transition on Urantia into the pre-stages of light and life with less pain for yourself and your loved ones.

If I were a human personality who spoke these words to you without proper mandate, then you would be in your full right to call me by any of your definitions in the recognition of an arrogant soul. But I am not human. I speak with the full authority of the mandate of the Universe Father, Christ Michael, within the present adjudication by the Bright and Morning Star to be actualized on the planetary level by human mortals appointed as such by Christ Michael

---

[8]At the time of editing this second edition in May, 1995, the only safety area is Planetary Headquarters. The other six areas are not yet secured and may not be until after the year 2000 - 2001.

through the Bright and Morning Star down to Machiventa Melchizedek, the present Planetary Prince. I speak as a finaliter who is here to help regather my own family for whom I am responsible. I am here by choice and by responsibility, and although I have ascended to Havona and Paradise, and have had approximately one million years experience in the superuniverses of time and space, I am yet one under authority; and I have much to learn.

Self-confidence and assuredness of any kind is based upon an inner knowingness of one's capabilities. Usually it is a result of an acquired discipline either in thought or mechanical process. Pride, a small five letter concept in the English language, has created the need for hundreds of universities in the ascension process for the study of its effects on the ascending mortal. Your ability to understand not only the contents of this paper but the contents of this book will designate to us what Divine New Order community you belong in genetically, and more significantly, spiritually. If you presume that a human has written this paper, then you have greatly erred in your analysis. In making this mistake you are not able to recognize the Father/Son circuits of cosmic law of force-energy manifestation and of time-space actualization. The result of such a mistake for a first-time Urantian is one thing, for a second-time Urantian another thing; but for any order of the cosmic starseed, and in particular the cosmic reservists, it can be quite detrimental to yourself and to your fellow brothers and sisters on this planet. If there are parts of this paper you do not understand, my prayer is that before you make jest of it or cynically present it to one of your friends, you take it first to the Father of All and sit silently for a long time in a quiet place and listen to his response.

We give you fair warning. It is a well known fact that God is love, but it is a very ambiguous, misunderstood and forgotten fact that God is also discipline and judgment. It is time on Urantia for the Father circuit to appropriate the judgment, first through the Universe Father, Christ Michael, so that the Earth Mother can begin to manifest herself in all her beauty as a physical form and expression of the Third Source and Center.

All inappropriate attitudes and actions will be dealt with by those Father circuits with swift and decisive action.

Be not deceived; God is not mocked, for whatsoever a man soweth, that shall he also reap. (Gal. 6:7)

We bid all of you meek in spirit, humble and pure in heart, and most of all, loyal to God and to the voice of God within and without, not only to understand this paper but to find your own cosmic family, be it in Sedona first, or wherever your destiny calls you. If you feel that perhaps you have lived before, then for a time your place should be in Sedona, Arizona, U.S.A., for instruction and divine government policy. If you feel you are a first-time Urantian and have reached higher circles, perhaps you also belong in Sedona, Arizona, U.S.A., for a time of instruction, and most likely you will then be sent to your appropriate community as a leader or possibly a founder of that community.

More specifically, Planetary Headquarters in Sedona is a Pleiadean, Ursa Major, and a Centaurian connection. It is also a connection of the highest genetic strains of Adam and Eve, the Material Son and Daughter of Urantia. If you are of the cosmic reserve corps or of the Urantia reserve corps this is where you belong, at least for a time, not less than six months, and most likely for two to three years. For those of you of the First Cosmic Family, you will be asked to remain with your family for the time period remaining in the third dimension, and in the fourth dimension for thirty to forty years into the twenty-first century. After that you will continue in your ascension together in union of souls all the way to Paradise. This is your inheritance. We bid you come. You are needed and you are called.

July 29, 1991

Paladin, Finaliter; by the overcontrol of the Bright and Morning Star and, at the Planetary level, by Machiventa Melchizedek, present Planetary Prince of Urantia; as transmitted through the Audio Fusion Material Complement, Gabriel of Sedona.

PAPER 207

THE REORGANIZATION OF THE COSMIC FAMILIES IN RELATION TO THEIR PARTICULAR ASCENSION STATUS BEFORE THE LUCIFER REBELLION, IN ORDER TO RECAPTURE AND CLAIM THE RESPECTIVE GENETIC INHERITANCE OF THAT PARTICULAR UNIVERSE SOVEREIGN AND MICHAEL SON

Although the circuits were cut off at the time of the Lucifer rebellion in the system of Satania, many of the deceptions of the rebellion continued to traverse time and space through various means of telepathic communication and other mind gravity circuits. Other energy fields were also used to take this rebellion not only to other planets and systems within Nebadon, but to other universes within Orvonton. On a planetary level, the effects of these rebellious messages were never as great outside this system as it was on Urantia or on any of the other fallen planets of Satania. No other Planetary Prince outside Satania fell, nor any other beings of angelic orders, but countless millions of ascending mortals were affected by what they heard and began to function by. Even on planets that had entered the first stages of light and life the effects of the rebellion in Satania in the universe of Nebadon were felt. Many of the concepts of Lucifer were first accepted by the leaders and others of the various families of specific function and administration, both on technical and artistic levels.

On the majority of these planets all of the various endeavors in agriculture, technology, art and science were administered by family units based upon genetic coding of their first and founding fathers and mothers. Within any particular corporate division, there may be upwards to 150,000 descendents of the first ancestor in mortal father form and of the first ancestor in mortal mother form. Usually, but not always, the first mother and father had by now become incarnated finaliters, directing their respective mortal families with the brilliancy of their ascension level. Under their authority were all of their sons and daughters who had ascended to the higher levels of circle attainment based upon the requirements of their particular Michael Son, each universe being different in these ascension requirements.

The scope of this understanding in magnitude is quite beyond the comprehension at this time for those under constellation level ascension status. However, what we can say is that a certain breakdown of authority began to take

97

place. The ancestors were questioned as to their right to rule; and their sons and daughters began to devise their own technologies, artistic attempts, agricultural concepts and many other endeavors based upon individualistic opinion, as opposed to eldership and cosmic perspective. The Planetary Princes of these planets wisely allowed these souls to go their own way, full well knowing that they would become lost in their self-deceptions.

On many of these planets, for hundreds of years, these individuals in rebellion began to set up colonies on satellite worlds, isolated from their home planets, as they were not allowed to present their false teachings to any kind of organizational structure of over one hundred other individuals. When the number of influenced became one hundred, they were immediately and swiftly arrested and sent to a satellite world. The individuals on these satellite worlds grew in number upwards into the millions after a few generations. Never again were they allowed to return to their planet of origin as long as they had not realigned themselves with the cosmic laws of their Universe Creator and the Universal Father.

Upon their death and transcendence, the individuals of these satellite worlds of rebellion were sent to the very place in which their false concepts originated; and that was the system of Satania, under the full approval of that Universe Sovereign Michael, for he felt that these individuals should experience the complete effects of improper thinking on a totally fallen planet and not just on a satellite world. Their memory circuits were cut off when they entered the system of Satania, for they had to abide by the law of that System Sovereign and Universe Father. Upon transcendence, they would also find themselves a mortal on whatever planet of the fallen thirty-seven they had descended to. Many of these, who were at one time very highly technologically advanced, found themselves at the evolutionary stage of post-primitive man. All acquired abilities and knowledge were completely blocked from their perspective, and what remained with them was just enough to allow them to experience the totality of the present mortal experience on their third-dimensional world. In dealing specifically with Urantia, many of the staff of the Caligastia one hundred were in some way related to these repersonalized starseed. The only instinct within all of these repersonalized starseed was the instinct to once again find their cosmic families that they had long lost, now not only by choice but by order of the Ancients of Days.

Presently on Urantia there is a false teaching that is another lie of Lucifer, which says that if you are here on this planet you have chosen to be here, for it is part of your mission. The truth of it is that as of August 5, 1991 there are only fifteen human personalities over the age of 21 on this planet who have chosen to return and they are:

1. Some of the apostles of the first century, excluding Judas and including Paul and Luke. We mention Paul and Luke because they later became apostles and both are second-time Urantians. (Note that all of the apostles are back, some of which are starseed and some of which had to return.)
2. Two other unnamed personalities, male and female.
3. Some of the family of Jesus.
4. Some of the first disciples and women's corps. We are not saying specifically who they are but later transmissions will reveal this more.

Amadon, the human hero of the Lucifer rebellion, is also back on Urantia and is the 3-year old child of the Bright and Morning Star human mandated personalities, Gabriel and Niánn. Other second-time Urantians will continue to come through based upon circumstances unrevealed at this time.

All other personalities who are cosmic starseed of the fourth order would have had to return to one of the fallen thirty-seven worlds of this system. In this sense they have chosen Urantia because it would be easier for them here, because at that point of their decision they had full recognition before the Ancients of Days that their cosmic family was on Urantia and that their finaliter ancestors were in some way in the administration of universe procedure on Urantia, therefore a cosmic connection to their planet of origin. Other starseed of the first and third orders are here because it is part of their ascension process.

Because of the state of their rebellious souls, it has been a very long time for many starseed since they have used their talents and abilities for the true kingdom of God and the Universal Father of all. In their repersonalizations upon Urantia they have, time and time again, rebelled against their cosmic elders whom they did not recognize. In all of these lives they have met their elders at one time or another, but have always managed to do things their own way. Even though they may have loved these elders to some degree, when the elder's higher views went against their lower views, they claimed that they had to follow their own inner guidance, the same inner guidance that first led them to become exiled from their own home planet and cosmic family. They have been allowed in past repersonalizations to become "successful" in power, wealth or whatever pleased their fancy, with the hopes that when they attained these heights of self-grandeur, a realization would come that none of these pursuits brought peace or true fulfillment. Now, on present-day Urantia these starseed have become so-called spiritual persons, disguising their rebellion in spiritual dress, with top hat and cummerbund; and they fool many, even themselves. Now they say they know God and that they themselves are healers and teachers. If this is so, why is it that they do not know who their Universe Father is, let alone where they originated? Why is it that with all of their so-called successes, the majority of them live in fear, anxiety and depression and have many of the physical illnesses of this planet? Why is it that they are not in true, right livelihood? Why are they not matched with complementary polarities (husbands and wives) and close friends of spiritual unity? Why is their friendship based upon the things of the world and not the things of God? Why is it that they're locked into the timetable of Caligastia and have to struggle for their existence and survival? The answer is quite simple. They do not know their Universe Father as well as they think they do. They have forgotten the Michael Sons, and their God has become quite fragmented. The power of God cannot be manifested in their lives, for they are still in a state of rebellion. "Not I," says the New Age networker. "Not I," says the Christian, Buddhist and Muslim fundamentalists.

We are the First Cosmic Family. I, a finaliter of the genetic seed of the Pleiades, call to you who have gone so far astray from the true protection of your God and his representatives who are the hand of love for your guidance. As you have grown quite old in your conceit, you have also grown quite accustomed to turning off the voice of your Universal Father who speaks to you through your cosmic elders in human form, your ancestors. If you cannot hear the voice of God through these individuals, do not claim that you can hear that voice within your own heart, for you are too busy satisfying the lusts and selfish ambitions that you disguise as the call and work of God.

If my words seem strong, they are meant to be. I would much prefer that you come to your cosmic senses now than find yourself upon another third-dimensional world upon transcendence from this one and have to repeat a journey similar to the Urantian one. It is not the time for self-indulgence nor for isolated callings of God. It is the time for the return to your tribe, to the clan, to your cosmic family and its respective eldership and leadership.

The judgment first takes place in the house of God, and it is taking place now. Your decisions will either lead into ascension of Fifth Epochal Revelation understanding or your continual rejection of the government of Machiventa Melchizedek that is being appropriated through your human cosmic ancestors. The result will be your adjudication before your physical transcendence on this planet. This judgement by the Ancients of Days can take place at any time now, on any day, at any moment.

I, as a finaliter with the mandate of Christ Michael, am not here to placate your human egos; nor am I here to win friends and influence people. I am not interested in any of the big names in the spiritual movement. I am only interested in one big name and that is the name of the Creator of this universe, Michael, who came to this planet as Jesus and could return before you even get done with the reading of this paper. When the light is turned on in your room of darkness, the time for apologies will have passed. I speak with the authority of the Father circuits and the mandate of the Creator Son of the universe that you are presently in and, on the planetary level, in liaison with the existing Planetary Prince, Machiventa Melchizedek. I pray that this voice in the wind leads you to the only protective nest that can bring you the first fruits of the first stage of light and life on Urantia. Outside of that nest you will simply have to feed yourself. My tactics are simple. I present to you cosmic fact. So be it.

August 5, 1991

Paladin, Finaliter, in the adjudication by the Bright and Morning Star, in its manifestation on the planetary level in and through the government of Machiventa Melchizedek, present Planetary Prince of Urantia; as transmitted through the Audio Fusion Material Complement, Gabriel of Sedona.

PAPER 208

THE IMPORTANCE OF GENETIC INHERITANCE IN RELATION TO THE CODING OF THE MATERIAL SON AND DAUGHTER, ADAM AND EVE, AND OTHER PERSONALITIES OF THE CALIGASTIA ONE HUNDRED FROM OTHER SYSTEMS AND UNIVERSES — IN PARTICULAR THE THIRD AND FOURTH GENERATION OF ADAMSON AND RATTA AND THEIR PRESENT PROGENY ON URANTIA

This particular paper and many others in the book, *The Cosmic Family*, can best be given to the Urantian mind, including all starseed on Urantia, precept upon precept, first in a somewhat general mode and then gradually into specifics, (as was done with much of the Fifth Epochal Revelation in its beginning stages). As it is now, CFER can best be understood by those on the fourth cosmic circle who are about to enter the third. An older soul, and particularly one with higher genetic coding, can best benefit from circle attainment. First-time Urantians who enter the higher circles can far surpass their planetary human brethren in spiritual comprehension in relation to cosmic reality. If their genetic inheritance is of extra-terrestrial coding, they inherit all that their ancestors have acquired in relation to their ancestors' home planets' ascension status. Therefore, the spiritual maturation process for those who have been genetically linked by the life plasm of extra-terrestrial ancestors, far exceeds the normal evolutionary mindal capacity to comprehend cosmic reality, more than the evolutionary humans who do not have these genetic capabilities. It was the full intention for all upon this planet to have these genetic inheritances. However, because of the default of Adam and Eve, there is only a small percentage on Urantia today who have realized these implanted genetics that more closely link them with cosmic citizenship and universal circuits.

The mating of **Adamson and Ratta** mixed the Material Son genetics with a pure-line descendent of Pleiadian ancestry; and their children's intermarriages with certain Andonites, who had also been given the life plasm of those from the Pleiades, Ursa Major, Centaurus and others, began a restructuring of higher evolutionary genetic strains resulting in higher mindal capacity on Urantia. This information concerning particular planetary and system genetic inheritance by name is now possible because of circuits being reopened, since around 1911, due to the adjudication of the Bright and Morning Star versus Lucifer and now the installation of your Planetary Prince, Machiventa Melchizedek, on Urantia.

The mating of these children of Adamson and Ratta enabled Universe Supervisors to bring into being on Urantia repersonalized starseed and first-time Urantians with higher genetic coding, derived from the ancestors of Adamson, and combined with the higher genetics from other planets, through Ratta. Before this event took place, repersonalization was limited to only a few. The overcontrol in the destiny of these souls and their progeny was quite extensive and all of them were of the reserve corps of their particular generation, up until present-day Urantia. It took several generations for Overcontrol to bring the highest genetic strains together for progeny purposes. The third and fourth generation of Adamson and Ratta consisted of the highest organization of cosmic family ever assembled together for inter-marriage and to create progeny upon this planet. All of the Caligastia one hundred life plasm was represented in genetic coding, as well as the highest genetic strains of Adam and Eve, the first Material Son and Daughter. Within the Caligastia one hundred was also life plasm of other Material Sons and Daughters of other universes. Unlike the universe of Nebadon, Material Sons from other universes often had many wives. Those Material Sons who gave their life plasm to humans gave much of their own reality structure in relation to destiny purpose. The male humans who inherited this plasm were used in seeding many children and have always had a very difficult time in monogamous relationships. Although, in order to comply with universal mandates, at certain times in other repersonalizations they have even been asked by spiritual mandate to become celibate for a time; we will explain more about them in a later paper.

The admixture of the Caligastia one hundred with any of the descendents of evolutionary humans through sexual procedure was never intended. However, since this did take place it was best that an experimental overcontrol be kept on all of these individuals and their progeny for the remainder of the rebellion on Urantia. Now we have close to 200,000 years of experimentation with various interplanetary genetic codings, including interuniversal codings. With the exception of Urantia, these kinds of sexual relationships between distant cosmic relatives are nonexistent on any other third-dimensional world. However, interplanetary marriages between ascending sons and daughters do take place on planets that have not defaulted and are in the higher stages of light and life.

Although it was foreseen that these unions would cause great complexity for these particular individuals as far as being able to fit into their present reality at the time, it was decided almost immediately by Michael that this overcontrol be implemented and that these particular individuals and their progeny become the reservists on Urantia. Not always were the bodies of these reservists perfect in physical structure. This has more to do with DNA and RNA in the blood than it does with the physical body itself; it has to do with the bloodline. Therefore, a soul with very high genetics can be born into a very deformed body, and the mind can be highly evolved and the body physically damaged. Always within these reservists under the supervision of Overcontrol, there is the latent potential for accelerated spiritual growth based upon genetic inheritance. If a first-time Urantian inherits this blood linkage, he or she also has the capacity for accelerated spiritual growth. In the molecular structure of the blood, thousands of circuits can be activated upon universe administration directive.

On Urantia the higher strains of the fourth generation of Adamson and Ratta are located within those people of what is referred to as the Caucasian race, particularly in England, the U.S.A., Canada, Australia, New Zealand and South Africa. You may be of this strain and a first-time Urantian or a repersonalized starseed. The many variables of cosmic identification link you to one particular cosmic family of the Caligastia one hundred.

Throughout the centuries the repersonalized starseed, descended from Adamson and Ratta, have been used to bring continuing revelation of whatever capacity to Urantia in order to usher in various spiritual renaissances. This has come to be known by lower-circle understanding as "the Pleiadian connection," and it *is* very much the Pleiadian connection. I, Paladin, a finaliter originally from the Pleiades, have my own progeny here on Urantia. Ratta was one of the first. It has always been necessary in Overcontrol to bring repersonalized starseed back through certain mated, monogamous relationships because of their genetic linkage to the higher strains. However, on Urantia they have scattered all over the planet. Lesser strains can be found in the Soviet Union, in various parts of Europe (particularly Germany), in Iceland, and in present day Israel. The cosmic family is indeed dispersed. Present-day technology, and an increase in transportation has made it now possible for those repersonalized starseed to find and move to the location where the regathering of their highest cosmic family eldership may be presently located. The regathering of these families is the only thing that can bring individual fulfillment and planetary peace. The United States of America was chosen to become the new Israel, the new world, and the first land of the Divine New Order. The highest of repersonalized starseed were brought through on this particular continent as cosmic reservists several lives before this present one, with the planned purpose in this generation to bring them all together at a point in time at the location, wherever the archangels' headquarters was located. These particular repersonalized cosmic family members have other relatives scattered all over the world who have also had lives in what is now known as the United States of America, and even more specifically at the destined headquarters of the Planetary Prince, Machiventa Melchizedek at Sedona, Arizona, U.S.A. Its cosmic connection is the system of planets your astronomers call the Pleiades.

I, Paladin, in conjunction with Ashtar, also a Pleiadian finaliter, bid that all of you on Urantia resonate with this truth and come to be reconnected with your highest cosmic relatives and find your place in the establishment of the new government on Urantia in the administration of Machiventa Melchizedek and its human representatives, Gabriel, Niánn, and other elders. As Jesus bid his apostles to come and follow him in the first century, he brings you the same message now. We are his voice that aligns with the Spirit of Truth in you. If your allegiance is to that voice, you will understand exactly what I am saying.

August 10, 1991

Paladin, Finaliter; a transmission of Overcontrol by the Bright and Morning Star of Salvington to help implement the Government of Machiventa Melchizedek, the present Planetary Prince on Urantia; as transmitted through the Audio Fusion Material Complement, Gabriel of Sedona.

PAPER 209

DIFFERENTIATION – A COSMIC PERSPECTIVE OF INTERPLANETARY AND INTERDIMENSIONAL TRANSMISSIONS IN RELATION FROM HIGHEST TO LOWEST, I.E. MATERIAL COMPLEMENTS, INTER-PLANETARY RECEIVERS, CHANNELERS, MEDIUMS AND THE DIFFERENCES EXISTENT THEREIN

Throughout the history of Urantia, interdimensional and extraterrestrial communication has always been a part of the spiritual development of this planet. Before the fall of Caligastia many of the staff of the Planetary Prince used interdimensional and extraterrestrial circuits just as easily as you now pick up a telephone and speak to another across the continent. However, the distances were hundreds of thousands of light-years, and more, away. These interplanetary circuits have also been called by other names such as bands, electro-magnetic waves, star routes, portals, link holes, time warps, and anti-gravity locations. In reality, the mode of communication has more to do with the ascending soul and the use of his or her inner circuits that the ancient Tibetans called "chakras."

The staff of Caligastia was highly informed of the thousands of circuits within one's higher bodies that they could tap into at any moment to speak to any other soul anywhere within the superuniverse, in accordance with an overcontrol permission by the Planetary Prince himself. Certain communicative contacts could not exceed limits, and those limits were given to the staff upon its arrival on Urantia. The individual ability of each staff member to personally make circuitry connection within the superuniverse was dependent upon that entity's ascension in spiritual soul status. In a scientific context, the means of communication is much the same throughout the grand universe. The scientific and the artistic fuse, to complement the higher soul in relation to the goal of finality, the attainment of the Paradise personalities. The scope of understanding of this fusion is an eternal quest and so is the understanding of interplanetary and interdimensional communication abilities.

Some on the staff had greater abilities in an interplanetary mode of communication. Even after the circuits were cut off at the time of the rebellion, those of higher mind gravity circuits were able to transmit messages to many of their relatives throughout the grand universe. The implications of this are immense and beyond the scope of this transmission.

106

The highest form of interplanetary and interdimensional communication is the audio fusion material complement. This procedure has to do with Universe Supervisors' administrative decisions, repersonalizations, mandates, and cosmic family regathering. The next highest form of interplanetary and interdimensional communication is the interplanetary receiver, who may also be a material complement, but not necessarily so. Both an audio fusion material complement and an interplanetary receiver need complementary polarities of the opposite mortal sex in order for audio transmission to come through a mandated voice of one of the two. The staff of the Caligastia one hundred, being paired male and female, were complementary in this mode of communication reality. Since the fall of Lucifer, material complements on Urantia have usually been on the fourth psychic circle and above; and all material complements since then have been repersonalized starseed on this planet. None of them have been first-time Urantians.

Before Pentecost, Caligastia and other fallen entities spoke to many humans, which has come to be known as spiritualism and mediumship. Throughout the centuries, certain human personalities with incorrect motives and evil intent have actually contacted Caligastia himself and others closely allied with him. This form of communication is the lowest form of communication, in that the reception of information is for Luciferic purposes. Many times in this process the channeler of such information is in reality contacting his or her lower self and the most iniquitous attitudes and deceptive forms of all of this entity's past repersonalizations, either on this planet or on another. It is possible that if this entity is of the light, to a more balanced degree, he or she can tap into his or her higher self and levels of ascension, and parts of that self and certain memory circuits that she or he may be allowed to remember and transmit on the human plane. Many interplanetary receivers and channelers do this and imagine or fabricate that they are speaking to another entity, but they are not. In cases of evil intent, or even the slightest irrational motive, the forces of the rebellion can actually take over that vessel. The degree of wrong motive either lessens or increases the ability of Caligastia and the rebellious forces to control the moments of transmission. Sometimes the human mind may be speaking from its lowest self, and sometimes it may rise to a higher level and even bring truth to some degree. At other times the mind can tap into its highest self and bring in higher truth.

Those human personalities known as channelers who did receive interdimensional communication, acquired this communication from midwayers. Always they are lower-circuited receivers, usually on the fifth and fourth psychic circles; and always they are matched by similar polarities of male and female complements (husband and wife, or possibly mother and son, daughter and father, but never brother and sister). Usually the process is a relationship of a pair who have in a previous repersonalization, or in this lifetime had children together.

These relationships have to do with certain circuit connections of a scope far beyond the teaching of this paper. The midwayers tried to explain at some level, through information given to all of these channelers, the Lucifer Manifesto and the various distortions stemming from the rebellion in relation to Urantia. Information also dealt with earth changes and evacuation procedures; but higher terminology of Fifth Epochal Revelation concepts was not used, for the vessels themselves would have to be, first, students of *The URANTIA Book*, already in print, and then mandated personalities on the third-to-first circle level, which no channelers who have brought information through by secondary midwayers have reached.

Other personalities who may call themselves channelers should be more appropriately called mediums,* for they indeed receive messages from Caligastia himself or others of his company. This is because these individuals are iniquitous, without exception, regardless of the beauty of their bodies, the persuasiveness of their personalities or the charismatic abilities of their souls. The information at this level is the most dangerous, for it is given by highly iniquitous intelligences and fused with certain cosmic truths which are designed to confound and divide the individual and a certain mass consciousness in various geographical locations on Urantia. Some of the general deceptions will be called by these tags:

1. Right use of will
2. Nonabsolute reality
3. Self-assertion and unbridled liberty
4. God as a force rather than a personality
5. God as an energy rather than a personality
6. The insignificance of the ascension process (all-paths-lead-to-the-same-goal thinking)
7. Dolphin intelligence
8. Misconstrued teachings of Hierarchy
9. The goddess syndrome
10. Inner-guidance-is-all-I-need belief
11. Misunderstanding of visualization and prosperity.

Because of the many voices that speak through these methods, much confusion in the spiritual realm as to cosmic reality has been brought to Urantia, and increasingly so in the last twenty years because Caligastia knew that soon there would possibly be other designated material complements of the very highest order functioning on Urantia with the return of Machiventa Melchizedek and his appointment as the new Planetary Prince of Urantia.[9] What he did not know was that there would be an audio fusion material complement of the highest order who would soon be appropriated on Urantia, an overcontrol complement of the Bright and Morning Star. He was completely oblivious to the mandate of the Bright and Morning Star on this planet and his audio fusion material complement, although he knew of Gabriel of Sedona and of that soul's past repersonalizations during the renaissances of this planet. He was not allowed to see the total plan of Michael, as delegated by the Council of Twenty-Four and Lanaforge, the System Sovereign.

The scope and understanding of all mandates will take many explanatory volumes of procedure. At this point we would like to say that the audio fusion material complement, Gabriel of Sedona, with the mandate of the Bright and Morning Star of overcontrol can actually produce physical manifestations on this planet, manipulating both circumstance and matter if necessary. All mandates have to do with the implementation of the divine government using human personalities. If opposition of certain individuals hinders the structure of this new divine government, they will be either removed from their present circumstances of material comforts or be taken off of the planet altogether; and this will be done quite naturally by them acquiring various diseases, as all divine protection will be eliminated from their daily lives. In this manner the overcontrol of the Bright and Morning Star complements the necessary governmental procedures of Machiventa Melchizedek, the present Planetary Prince. It is a divine response to human disobedience.

As energy follows thought, information given in CFER can only be given at highest levels in specifics to trusted and proven personalities, in this case, the leadership of the Aquarian Concepts Community working in conjunction with the unseen Machiventa Government at Planetary Headquarters in Sedona, Arizona, U.S.A. There are no other audio fusion material complements on Urantia who function at this level of interdimensional reception. As the mandated personalities grow in the understanding of their own mandates, so will the manifestation of power given to them by Christ Michael. CFER can only come through on Urantia in audio form through a personality mandated by the Bright and Morning Star, and even with this mandate it takes five cosmic family members aligned in a union of souls to create an ERC to bring through the Bright and Morning Star of Salvington. There is only one of these mandated persons on any particular planet at one time.

---

[9]See footnote on page 20, and Machiventa's statement on page 22.

I, Paladin, a finaliter, along with others who come from time to time, act as spokesman with the mandate of the Bright and Morning Star in overcontrol to bring CFER. Now on a planetary level Machiventa Melchizedek, along with many of his staff, also bring teachings and instructions. To an audio fusion material complement, the mandate of the Bright and Morning Star is a multidimensional superuniversal circuit linkage, which allows for various personalities of superuniverse level, including the Ancients of Days, to use and speak through if necessary and deemed so by universal supervisors of whatever capacity.[10] No archangels have spoken through lower-circuited channels or interplanetary receivers since the original Urantia Papers. All claims to such are either claims of deception, imagination or sheer ignorance of the fact that it is secondary midwayers who speak to them and cannot tell these people who they are unless they meet certain requirements of soul growth. One requirement is acquiring Fifth Epochal Revelation data within their mindal circuits so that the secondary midwayers can use that data. Even if this does happen, their mandates would only allow indirect audio such as automatic writing or pure impression, which is a form of closer linkage with moment-to-moment divine will. *Since the appointment of Machiventa Melchizedek in December of 1989, all secondary midwayers of the light, who were making contact with lower-circled channels and interplanetary receivers all over Urantia, discontinued contact.* At that point in time and space the functions of the secondary midwayers with these souls were completed at the audio level. Starseed who continue to transmit messages under the assumption that the origin of these messages are extraterrestrial and interdimensional, are in reality experiencing a time-space phenomenon. If these starseed are in the light, they are tapping into their higher selves of a past reality. Never, absolutely never, are they tapping into a future reality of a future self. This is possible, but only through the mandate of the Bright and Morning Star. However, we do not use this process and have never used it with Gabriel of Sedona. Past channels and interplanetary receivers who align themselves with the Machiventa Government and Fifth Epochal Revelation will be used in the cosmic reserve corps at the fourth level. Their memory circuits will be opened as to certain aspects of their planet of origin as given them by Gabriel of Sedona. They themselves will be used to further awaken those of their own genetic linkage and cosmic families presently residing on Urantia, working under direct supervision of the leadership of the First Cosmic Family at Planetary Headquarters in Sedona, Arizona, U.S.A.

---

[10]It takes 100 aligned mortals at the third psychic circle to bring through the Ancients of Days.

The interplanetary receiver who received the Urantia Papers was not an audio fusion material complement, nor was he meant to be a teacher of the revelations; he was a first-time Urantian. CFER comes through the audio fusion material complement and interplanetary receiver, Gabriel of Sedona, in conjunction with the establishment of the Machiventa Government on Urantia and in the development of the Starseed and Urantian Schools of Melchizedek.

In the highest form of interplanetary and interdimensional reception, the fusion material complement of audio transmission is used in a very scientific and technological manner. This has to do with the cosmic laws of physics and other unrevealed cosmic laws that deal with communication circuits in relation to soul ascension. The higher a soul, the more able he or she is to receive communication from distances light years away. This is the same kind of process in regard to visual transfiguration.[11] The accuracy of the audio transmissions of a mandated Bright and Morning Star receiver is of the highest and purest mode and method in any one particular universe, extending in application to one specific superuniverse. Upon certain decisions of superuniverse administration, certain communications can be received within the grand universe using intrasuperuniversal contact bands. In times of planetary emergencies, these may be appropriated when those situations may occur in the future on Urantia. The Bright and Morning Star audio fusion material complement must be highly protected from souls of negative influence within a radius of one acre (Urantian measurement). Noise of any kind can interfere in the reception of superuniversal networks.

Besides being an audio receiver of interplanetary and interdimensional transmissions, the mandate of the Bright and Morning Star also has the full powers of all universe intelligences who can manipulate matter. Since the adjudication by Gabriel versus Lucifer, if necessary, certain circumstances can also be arranged according to the will of Christ Michael in relation to human personalities of negative influence. Even certain wills of iniquity can be superseded by the process called the **will freeze**. The iniquitous souls who intend on coming against the establishment of the Machiventa Government will find themselves helping it instead. They also will find themselves unable to coordinate their own bodily functions and normal mindal abilities until they, as ascending sons or daughters, either align themselves to Christ Michael or completely reveal

---

[11]See footnote on page 20.

to their peers and fellow Urantians the full intent of their iniquitous souls. This division will increasingly manifest itself in clear patterns on Urantia in the years ahead. The Bright and Morning Star mandate can also manifest force fields and can bring about weather changes within a 3000 mile radius surrounding the mandated personality.

It is hoped that several material complements will have the mandate of Machiventa Melchizedek, the present Planetary Prince, by 2040 - 2050 AD, and can be mandated in the establishment of the Machiventa Government in relation to transfiguration of interplanetary and interdimensional personalities, with the purposes of healing the ethereal body so that the physical body can respond.[12] All mandates will be used to contact possible divine government appointees on all continents of Urantia. If those contacted personalities reject the perfect will of the Father and refuse to align with the Machiventa Government, the mandate of the Bright and Morning Star carries the power to remove divine protection from them, which will result in the quicker physical manifestations of their diseases. The authority of all mandates will become increasingly evident to those who receive personal invitations to come to Planetary Headquarters to be taught by its eldership and leadership. Certain starseed personalities in positions of spiritual leadership on Urantia are presently on the fourth psychic circle and are sitting on the cosmic fence between loyalty to man or loyalty to God. They hardly know the difference. A letter to them from any mandated personality should cause them to get off that fence. If they choose correctly, they will come as students. If they choose incorrectly, they will continue in their error and increasingly become more iniquitous. In the future, all self-appointed and false personalities will be contacted by Planetary Headquarters and will be known by the true followers of Christ and it will be obvious who responds positively and who does not.

Several personalities of the mandated positions of the Bright and Morning Star and of many other mandates have also been used on Urantia for other spiritual renaissances in its history. Besides the mandates given to the material complements Gabriel and Niánn of the Bright and Morning Star mandate at this level, there are ten other potential material complements at a second level, all called to be Divine New Order apostles; twelve other potential material complements on a third level, all ascending daughters also called to be Divine New Order apostles; five hundred others in potential on a fourth level mandate;

---

[12]At the time of editing this second edition, May 1995, there were none.

and five thousand others at a fifth level mandate, who are also in potential material complements. All of these mandated personalities will in some way function in a supervisory capacity within the Machiventa Government. All of these personalities will work under the leadership of the First Cosmic Family, consisting of constellation leadership which manifests itself in human personalities presently in physical form in Sedona, Arizona, U.S.A., at Planetary Headquarters in the Aquarian Concepts Community. They will work at six other geographical locations, starting out as communities and expanding into city sectors. After the physical changes on this planet and the evacuation, they will return to set up new administrations in the expanded physical sections where they once started.

Channels, walk-ins, mediums, and those who function under incorrect motive and claim to be cooperating with extraterrestrial intelligence and Hierarchy and use such names as "Intergalactic Confederation" and so on, are in reality either souls of iniquitous and evil intent or souls in error. It is hoped that those in error and under incorrect motive can change their evil ways and come to Planetary Headquarters for instruction. These individuals can be easily discovered, for they are not supported by God or Hierarchy, but are supported by the huge fees that they charge others for spiritual services and information. Much like the Pharisees in the time of Christ, they see themselves as high spiritual leaders, exchanging money in their New Age temples or psychic fairs and giving of themselves to only those who can afford it.

On the other hand, mandated material complements function within the will and blessings of God, within the union of souls and cosmic family relationships, without charging for their time, services, or any other teaching methods that others of wrong intent so easily take advantage of. They are supported by those individuals who connect with the importance of their work and give by free-will choice either materially, financially or in any other way, an offering of love and good will.

The students of today will be the teachers of tomorrow. The givers of material blessings will be the receivers of material blessings. The next nine years on Urantia are a crucial time of discernment as to where and with whom to apply your talents and material resources. This paper is designed in structure to awaken you, first as a possible candidate in one of these mandated positions, and if so, to respond by severing yourself from all other inappropriate information on lower and even iniquitous circles. Once doing so, you can connect yourselves with the Machiventa Government and its overcontrol, the Salvington Circuit. Outside of the first level of mandated material complements and your unalignment to that community, your spiritual growth will be lessened and your value as a worker of the light for Christ Michael will be less significant. This is a statement of cosmic fact.

September 3, 1991

Paladin, Finaliter; in overcontrol with the Bright and Morning Star and in cooperation with Machiventa Melchizedek; as transmitted through the Audio Fusion Material Complement, Gabriel of Sedona, Arizona, U.S.A.

PAPER 210

THE BESTOWAL OF MICHAEL ON URANTIA IN RELATION TO THE GIFT OF THE SPIRIT OF TRUTH AND THE ACTIVATION OF THAT SPIRIT OF TRUTH ON URANTIA. WHAT IS TRUE SPIRITUALITY? DOES IT DIFFER IN THE GRAND UNIVERSE?

One of the reasons why Christ Michael chose Urantia was because of its defaulted condition and his plan of gifting this planet with the Spirit of Truth, a part of his divine Self, which was available on some of his other inhabited worlds in Nebadon, but not yet on Urantia. His divine Self is a dual-origin Paradise Son of the Father/Son circuitry. Now the same Spirit of Truth is available to all planets in Nebadon. Because it was the seventh and final bestowal of Christ Michael on Urantia, a certain cosmic fusion took place that became a birth of the most powerful and cosmic definition of the Spirit of Truth bestowed by the Creator Son himself. Although the spirit of Truth is the same on all planets where it is bestowed, the level and power of its frequency of those various bestowals differs on system and planetary levels. Because of the personal visitation and bestowal of the Spirit of Truth by Michael, Urantia is first in the whole universe of Nebadon in Spirit of Truth personality and force activation, and due to the attention Urantia has received and is receiving since the crucifixion of Christ Michael, is also first in circuitry activation in relation to **Son-circuited** communication networks throughout the grand universe.

On an individual basis, the Spirit of Truth available on Urantia is activated first within the heart circuit. The spirit energy of the Son is an additional vibratory force engulfing and encircuiting all Urantia, and that force, which is dormant Son personality, is a presence which is activated in the heart circuit of an ascending son or daughter based upon certain conditions of that individual's response as an ascending son or daughter in his or her relationship to God the Father. Here, even the person who has accepted a God-presence within his or her reality must begin to closer identify that God in higher cosmic insight and definition. The bestowal of the Creator Son on Urantia is a cosmic fact, an historic event in universe reality. Nonrecognition of a fact of such magnitude at whatever level will keep that person at a lower psychic circle and perhaps on a third-dimensional planet until this cosmic fact is comprehended at a necessary level. In order to tap into existing universe circuits pertaining to memory cycles and cosmic reality, divine law and absolutes, activation must begin within that ovan soul's reality in time and space. This can only be done when the Spirit of Truth is received and activated, particularly on a fallen world such as Urantia.

The ovan soul has to re-receive the Spirit of Truth regardless of whether it has received it in a past repersonalization. If it received the Spirit of Truth in a past repersonalization since Pentecost, certain **Deo-atomic** cells are presently activated within the molecular structure which resonate with higher Deo-atomic reality and Paradise energies from both Upper Paradise and Nether Paradise. Ovan souls who receive the Spirit of Truth most likely have received it once before, and will find themselves uncomfortable in orthodox Christianity and usually will come out of it. If they do remain in it, they will likely become considered by their peers to be nonconformists. Usually they cannot quite fit in with traditional Christian denominations no matter how they try. In observing them for almost two thousand years, it has been noted that, of these ovan souls in various repersonalizations, very few have defaulted by not receiving the Spirit of Truth again, and most of them have been able to either stay away from present-day Christianity or have come out of it. An example of this would be an ovan soul who in a past repersonalization may have been a Christian, perhaps even a priest, and toward the end of his life saw the fallacy of Catholicism but remained in it because he was not strong enough to come out of it for whatever the reason. Now, in this current repersonalization, he may be a Native American and a good person, presented with Christianity by Christian missionaries who try to convert him. Although many within the tribe may convert, this soul is an ovan soul and one who has experienced the fallacy of Christianity once before, and believes in the God of Christianity, but not in the teachings of those who claim to be the messengers of that God. When this soul receives the Spirit of Truth again, it may lead him by pure impression, away from all institutionalized religion, which makes it very difficult for him to earn his livelihood in teaching higher cosmic truths. Usually he has to earn his livelihood in another way, and does not gain the respect of the masses who see him as a renegade. The reality is that those who have not conformed have always been the highest teachers on the planet.

Francis of Assisi discovered in his early forties his error in remaining Catholic. It was not malaria or any other illness that caused his death, but grief when he realized that he did not have to go to the Pope for permission to do God's will, and that he could have been much more successful in his spiritual mission outside of the Catholic church than within it. He realized that if he left the church he would lose those closest to him among the followers in the first order which he founded. He already had experienced one division within his order and he did not want to create another. The Spirit of Truth, with which he was very much in contact, did get through to him in the end but it was too late, for Francis had grown tired and sick.

Present-day Urantia is experiencing confusion as never before among the billions of people on the planet, first-time Urantians and ovan souls alike. It is ever so difficult for the Thought Adjuster and the Spirit of Truth to get through to the mind and heart of an individual. Many millions receive the Spirit of Truth, and then they are gathered by false teachers within the evangelical denominations throughout the world who are themselves deceived. They are then taught the dogmas of man which deactivate the reception of the Spirit of Truth and close the circuits before the Spirit of Truth can truly become activated within the individual. Ovan souls stand a greater chance of escaping the clutches of doctrine and tradition. First-time Urantians presently find it almost impossible to escape traditionalized Christianity. Therefore the Spirit of Truth in these millions and millions of individuals never becomes fully heard. They misinterpret their own desires based upon the teachings of their pastors and their priests, as the Spirit of Truth speaking to them. They go into wrong careers, they marry incorrectly and live their complete lives as Christians in a lower reality, and a false one at that, never reaching the third circle of attainment. Therefore they are open candidates for every disease known on Urantia to afflict them. This is all caused by incorrect thinking, false obligations and misplaced loyalties. Those who do come out of the Christian churches who have seen the fallacies within them, usually have no place to go and so they fall into other entrapments. Some leave the Christian faith altogether and become Buddhists or Muslims or perhaps identify themselves with the present New Age, which contains much evolutionary superstition and borderline black magic.

Up until the Fifth Epochal Revelation and its publication in 1955, in reality there was no place for these souls to go. The Urantia movement was the beginning of a plan by Celestial Overcontrol to lead all these individuals, first in the United States, and then in other countries around the world, to small groups of higher circle attainers who could receive the Spirit of Truth at a higher level of activation. As of 1967 they could have also received an additional gift of the Holy Spirit to further help them understand higher revelation. (See PAPER 213.) Unfortunately, as happens in institutions, many of the Urantia study group meetings lost the concept of interpreting the papers with the gift of the Spirit of Truth. They read about it. Some even asked to receive it, and then they made a similar mistake that the born-again Christians make. They looked to Chicago for the answers and not within to the Spirit of Truth or the Thought Adjuster. They were not even aware that the Holy Spirit had become available to them at a higher activation; and perhaps they are still unaware, all because the interpreters of the Fifth Epochal Revelation became man, and when man interprets God's absolutes, it usually manifests itself in either relative or fundamentalist thinking. In this case, within the Urantia movement, readers old and new alike became Urantian fundamentalists. Presently on Urantia, thousands of them are stuck in this static spirituality. And so the question arises:

WHAT IS SPIRITUALITY?

First of all, we will tell you what it isn't. It isn't a dress code. No form of dress makes a man holy or wise or indeed spiritual, not robes, not collars, not turbans. It is not the way a person walks. It is not their height or their weight. It is not in their ability to speak, nor their intellectual acquirements. No degree given to man or woman can make them spiritual. No university on this planet can proclaim in their schools of theology that a person is now spiritual. No fasting over a period of time or sacrifice can make a person spiritual. Neither can the diet of certain foods or vegetarianism as opposed to meat eating make a person spiritual. No substance found in the earth and ingested can make a person spiritual. No modern chemical injected can produce a spiritual personality. No amount of wealth, fame or prestige can bring spirituality to a person. No appointment of position by man to man in any capacity can make a person spiritual. No self-sacrifice, no matter how great, alone can make a person spiritual; not the giving of a son or daughter or their rightful husband or wife to God, nor the giving of one's income, nor the continued public announcement to others that you are God's chosen. No amount of adulation of man for man can make another spiritual.

True spirituality or virtue is a process that begins based upon certain universe laws and procedures. True spirituality cannot be defined so simply. For example, even those who appear to present the fruits of the spirit may not be so spiritual at all. The virtues said to bring about the fruits of the spirit can be disguised at various levels of deception in the third dimension. It is not so simple, and many factors have to be taken into consideration. Virtue for an ascending son or daughter is an acquired thing. It is learned over a period of time and that time may be hundreds, thousands and indeed, millions of years. It does not come upon you as the Baptists and Pentecostals say, in a moment of time upon the reception of the Spirit of Truth, making you perfect. It is an eternal process. When you reach finality you can begin to say that you are spiritual. Throughout the grand universe the degree to which you are truly spiritual is the degree of your own individual blessedness. Blessedness is the beginning of individual happiness; but blessedness is higher than happiness, for one can be happy in sin.

For too long on Urantia Lucifer has tried to replace spirituality with other things, thereby decreasing happiness for so many millions at whatever level they could acquire happiness. Whatever level your spirituality is, it creates the reality in which you find yourself and what you have and what you have not. It separates that which you desire from that which you will get. As your spirituality increases, your desires that are based upon the desires of God will become manifest. The Spirit of Truth is the beginning of higher spirituality on Urantia; and the hearing of it, moment to moment above all else, is the activation of that spirituality which leads to your individual happiness and fulfillment. Spirituality is a golden box and within it can be found treasures; treasures that cannot be bought by ascending sons and daughters, for this golden box is owned by the Supreme Deity; and its gifts are bestowed based upon each individual's willingness to seek his or her God in whatever way one can, based upon that search and knocking on the door of the heart of God, and then the golden box begins to be filled. As you become honest, the gift of honesty is given. As you become patient, the gift of patience is given. As you become giving, the gift of things are given to you. As you seek wisdom over pride, wisdom is given; and the golden box begins to shine with the light of God, and we shall call this box the heart circuit. Wisdom, which increases one's spirituality, cannot be purchased. Even when written, words of wisdom may not be understood, for wisdom is given in and through the Holy Spirit to those who put others first above their own selves, for it is written that love should not seek its own welfare but the welfare of others.

Motives, in harmony with divine ordinance, increase spirituality and bring the body into higher morontia realities and above. Individuals, who are trapped in third-dimensional patterns in regard to religious thinking and even livelihood, cannot even begin to reach the higher motives, for the higher motives deal with others outside of one's own nuclear family, where most of the people of Urantia are presently obligated. Even worse than that, millions do not even have concern for their own families, but only concern for themselves as individuals. The more people whom you can place into the sphere of your responsibility, the higher your spirituality. This is a divine thing, and it is divinely understood at different levels; and at whatever level you can now begin to grasp it, it is given to your planet. Certain spiritual leaders of the past have understood this, but it is available for all to understand; and when the mass consciousness of a planet can realize that we are each others' keeper, the suffering of that planet will end. Words can be written and taught but little understood. For thousands of years, philosophers have philosophized upon very high spiritual statements written by prophets and wise men of God, but few manifest the power of those words within their own realities for the benefit of the planet as a whole. At certain periods on Urantia at the time of certain renaissances, many ovan souls who had once come to the realization of selfless service to mankind were again brought to this planet and repersonalized as contemporaries, sometimes together and sometimes in other countries. It has been necessary on Urantia for these ovan souls to come back, for they have been the only voices to cry out against the established way of Caligastia.

What is spirituality? Many may think it is rebellion; and indeed it is. It is rebellion against Caligastia; it is rebellion against Luciferic reality; it is rebellion against evil, sin and iniquity. Jesus was a rebel who came against the established norm. Today on Urantia the Spirit of Truth is even more so a rebel. Today the societies of the planet are much worse than they were even in Jesus' time. Then, the people suffered in slavery and poverty. Today the people are also blinded because of materialism and foolish self-pursuit. Spirituality is faith. The faith to be humble, the faith to give of one's talents and abilities to the true spiritual teachers and elders on this planet when they can be found and recognized. Spirituality is gentle when it has to be and forceful when it has to be. It is Father-Mother. It is not just Mother nor can it be just Father; and when the son/daughter is in balance with both, spirituality can be perfected, for the fusion of childish youth then is incorporated with maturated age; and a liveliness of spirit presents itself instead of rigidity and inflexibility. Spirituality enjoys a good laugh, and some of the most highly spiritual personalities of time and space are great comedians. But the comedy is pure and is based upon cosmic fact of the relationships of the evolutionary process which is most humorous on the higher levels. Spirituality is discipline. Discipline and perfection are wonderful as long as within this perfection one does not become so stagnant that one cannot change when necessary. Spirituality to those who recognize it commands authority, and we bow to those of higher spirituality because of that spirituality in relation to the God of all. Spirituality and authority cannot be escaped, neither can spirituality and responsibility. Many refuse to become spiritual because they realize, even at a lower level, that they cannot escape responsibility for themselves or for others. Spirituality begins in knowing one's place with God at any particular moment in an individual's existence. The saints of the past may be spiritual, but as they ascended to the higher mansion worlds and above, their spirituality increased, as it does with ovan souls who return to this planet, and others, and who do not default in their reasons for being on Urantia or on their missions if they are cosmic reservists. Spirituality is strong character; and strong character is the fusion of the Universal Father, the Eternal Son and the Infinite Spirit in mortal likeness.

On some planets there are beings whom you would consider quite obese, but in comparison to any spiritual Urantian mortals at this time they would be like one with a Ph.D compared to a kindergarten child in terms of their spirituality. It is because spirituality is a nontangible thing. You cannot touch spirituality, nor can you always judge it by appearance, and when you do you have erred greatly. On some planets, those who are highly spiritual may be in a body form that would be so different from yours that they would actually frighten you. But those of us who have ascended high enough to sense the essence of God within them, once again, bow to their spirituality at whatever level they have attained it. Spirituality cannot be technically acquired or scientifically produced. It can be scientifically analyzed in accordance with higher understanding and Ascension Sci analysis, but it cannot be programmed, for only

God can create a perfect being and the Creator Sons are the only ones given this power.

There is a difference between courage and foolishness. True courage demands some form of spiritual attainment. The more courageous one becomes in true spiritual alignment, the more one will accomplish for the benefit of all on a particular planet. Spirituality is colorful and creates in the astral realms the purest perceptions of divine colors that can resonate around any one particular individual personality. These colors in turn manifest healing to that individual and to those who are blessed to be near them. On Urantia, the highest spiritual personalities most often become drained of energy, for so many others unknowingly draw from their life force. True spirituality is fragrant with odors that higher celestial personalities can distinguish. This is why, sometimes around high spiritual personalities, flower essences are recognized even by humans. These things, such as color and smell, are a science in themselves and we are just beginning to touch on the subject. The higher the spiritual personality, the more in control of one's self in all respects one needs to become. It is increasingly easier to take into account many wrongs suffered without justifying oneself, for one begins to realize that justification is not necessary and it is only pride that wishes to make itself correct. It is one thing to correct a person's wrong thinking. It is another thing to do it when it is either out of pride or not necessary. The line is so thin that it may take thousands and thousands of years to come to the place of accuracy. Higher spirituality is knowing the difference. Spirituality is knowledge fused with wisdom and applied with experiential reality in the evolutionary worlds and above. It is applied existential and experiential reality in relation to God and to others of God's creation.

Higher spiritual personalities are social creatures. They are not isolationists. Solitude, although not only a temporal reality, can become a damaging thing when the spiritual personality begins to self-contemplate to the point of misaligning with higher authority or one's peers at any level. Social communication with colleagues within the same realm of spiritual ascension is medicine for the ovan soul. It is within the union of souls that higher spirituality can be manifested and actualized by ascending beings. Higher spirituality in the company of one's elders knows when to voice an opinion and when not to, and higher spiritual teachers know when to ask of those individuals their opinions and when not to. Higher spiritual personalities are ever so absolute. There is no question once they have presented their opinion based upon absolute reality as they know it. If question arises, it is in the misinterpretation of what the lower individual heard them say, and this is so throughout the ascension process. Truth is often misinterpreted, for it is heard at the level of one's own spirituality and no more. The problem always arises, how does a higher ovan soul or being communicate with a lower one? Thus, spirituality is the ability to descend to a lower level and make one's self understood at that level of communication. For if you are not understood at any level, you have no value as a teacher of cosmic reality. You may do well in the solitude of the libraries of time and space, but in practical application to the rest of creation you could become a worthless individualist, and at the point where this begins to happen, the personality begins to default. Always in these cases, lack of patience is found in these individuals; and so it is increasingly important that the art of communication to lower- circle individuals be learned and acquired; and it begins in the personality when one begins to look at one's own impatience and inflexibility. These tendencies are common to mortals of time and space void of the higher reception of the Holy Spirit, particularly in stronger Father-circuited personalities. In my own ascension to Paradise as a finaliter, it was one of my faults hardest to overcome. It is not in the text of this transmission to give the solutions to the preceding statement, I can only state the possible problem.

A person with higher spirituality is not envious or jealous of those who have acquired what he has not, either materially or nonmaterially. Envy and jealousy are two of the most difficult things to recognize in one's self. It can take thousands of years within the growth of an ovan soul before the degrees of envy and jealousy of an individual can be recognized. These faults of character are again, lengthy in concept to describe. These unfortunate traits were found in Lucifer, and we have found that it is ever so difficult to open the eyes of those who have followed in his footsteps and acquired these unfortunate traits. Justification of one's own jealousy and envy is quite a thing to measure on our side. There are volumes written on these subjects in the higher schools on the satellite worlds, so it is not a subject you just touch on. One thing that we have found where envy and jealousy continues to exist in personalities is a decrease in their clairvoyant perceptions and of course the reception from their own Thought Adjuster, depending upon the spiritual acquiescence and other attributes of those individuals that determine the many things pertinent to their present reality and certain mandates given them. Mandates can be given to individuals who have traces of envy and jealousy, as mandates can be given to those with other bad habits. It is true, God is the judge of these things; and it should be left to the Creator Son and personalities of Paradise origin to decide these things and contemplate upon them. We at lower levels can discuss these things and contemplate as to why mandates are given to the imperfect, but it is much easier for us to do so, for our memory circuits are more open at higher levels, and we remember our imperfect selves more clearly. It is written that ascending mortals at times often think too highly of themselves. Spirituality and humility are siblings. They balance each other out and indeed are from the same parents. Humility cannot be known unless some form of spirituality exists, but spirituality can exist at a lower level where no humility at all exists. Spirituality comes first; humility follows and grows and grows and grows. Throughout eternity humility is a learning process which increases one's spirituality.

Spirituality is visionary. It is not crippled by fear. It is prophetic and finds its purpose in the recognition of the divine purposes of others as well as of oneself. The more one can recognize the function of others in the divine plan and can recognize another's individual placement in the timetable of the divine clock, the higher the spirituality within the personality. Spirituality is adventurous. It begins to take risks because of its increased faith, not only on the defaulted worlds of time and space, but in relation to other unknowns of time and space higher spirituality begins to build. It first learns to plant the seeds; then it learns to find the correct soils and what seeds to plant for the various beings of time and space; it learns the particular foods that need to be digested in body, mind and spirit. Spirituality does not always feel good to the individual, who learns to do what feels good to God, and learns to recognize that one's own feelings may interfere with the perfect will of God. A person learns to separate one's likes and dislikes for the higher good of all. Higher spirituality is not based upon always catering to your feelings; it discerns the will of God upon the combination of mind and heart fused with the mandated purposes of God as given first through the Thought Adjuster, Spirit of Truth and Holy Spirit within, and agreed upon then by Celestial Overcontrol at various levels, and on evolutionary worlds, by mortal eldership. Higher spirituality learns not only to listen to the inner self but to the inner selves of others who are their spiritual elders, human or celestial personalities who are all together hearing the same divine mind. Higher spirituality understands the difference between rest and slothfulness and can discern the same in others and can make use of idle time for the purposes of God wherever it may find itself. Moment to moment, it is always useful to God, even in periods of rest and relaxation it is in divine will. Higher spirituality does not overwork itself to the point of indifference to family, social or union-of-soul responsibility. Whatever it does, its purpose is within the divine will; and it has learned to accept each moment as a gift of divine origin and looks upon the moment as a continuing learning experience.

The previous comments on spirituality are just a beginning of the comments that could be made and is not complete by any standard of time and space. They are presented here to clarify some misconceptions on Urantia of who and what is spiritual; but before you can begin to understand any of this at the level necessary, I suggest that you turn your life over completely to God and request the Holy Spirit to make itself known within you, and this begins by accepting Christ Michael, your Universe Father, who became Jesus and left behind his Spirit of Truth for your education. Begin your registration now at the University of

Salvington so that your circuits can be opened to the capital of this universe of Nebadon, and align yourselves properly with the absolute truths which are the foundation and stepping stones to Paradise. If you have not taken this first step, please do.

February 6, 1992

Paladin, Chief of Finaliters; in cooperation with Christ Michael, Creator Son of Nebadon; in the adjudication by the Bright and Morning Star vs Lucifer for the implementation of the Planetary Prince, Machiventa Melchizedek, and his government on Urantia; as transmitted through the Audio Fusion Material Complement, Gabriel of Sedona.

PAPER 211

PROPER RESPONSE IN RELATION TO MANDATED PERSONALITIES, SPIRITUAL ELDERS, COSMIC PARENTS; AND CLARIFICATION AS TO MISPLACED LOYALTIES AND THE POWER ONE GIVES TO NONSPIRITUAL ENTITIES AND OTHER SELF-PURSUITS OF EGO-CENTERED PASSIONS, EITHER TANGIBLE, NONTANGIBLE OR ABSTRACT

Throughout the grand universe of nondefaulted evolutionary inhabited planets, with populations consisting of thousands of varieties of personality bestowal and ascension acquiescence, including nonmaterial and spirit personalities, those with authority of God-force are easily recognized and most respectfully responded to. On the defaulted worlds of time and space like Urantia, where self has become the center of the universe and the acquisition of power and materialistic possessions deaden the true light force of souls, it is almost impossible for a personality of pure motive and Godliness to be understood. It is also almost impossible for that God force personality to influence and appropriate true change by programmatic procedure in relation to helping individuals use their talents for the kingdom of God and helping others find their latent abilities, dormant because of the many problems on this defaulted world.

There is a saying among the prideful souls on Urantia, "I must be careful not to give my power away." Yet this same soul will daily give his or her power away to many nonspiritual individuals who are most often iniquitous. You make heroes out of spiritually dead movie stars, athletes, published authors, television personalities, musicians, and politicians. You will pay huge sums of money to go see these personalities in your public auditoriums and civic arenas, even though you are not even able to get within a distance to really see what these personalities look like and seldom get an opportunity to speak to them personally. When many eyes are fixed upon one personality in any particular geographic place, depending upon the reasons their eyes are fixed upon that person, all of those individuals are giving some of their power away to that popular personality. These personalities are those who affect how you think and respond to your life situations. These personalities also determine how you respond to the voice of God and to his will. They are instruments in the hands of Caligastia and the rebellious forces. You vote for them. You ask them for loans. You pay them for their standardized educational teachings of nonspiritual reality. You read their books and magazines. In your youth you try to look and be like them. You pursue careers to try to become just like them. You spend your recreational time watching them in films and television where they tell you what your life should be like in relation to their values and thinking processes, most of which are void of the will of God and the language of God. However, you understand their language well; it is a part of your reality. You were brought up to succeed in this language.

With the authority of Christ Michael, I, the present Planetary Prince of Urantia, tell you who read this transmission that this is not the language of the Universal Father. It is the language of the Lucifer rebellion as presented in form, structure, vocabulary and logical thought with materialistic values and self-seeking realities. In the present world that you now find yourself, you are not happy or fulfilled, yet you struggle to obtain that which others, when obtaining these very things, are also not happy with or fulfilled in. You remain in antiquated religious institutions, or perhaps you adopt fundamentalistic and dogmatic views of higher revelation that you have received, for you have become intellectually stimulated but are spiritually dead. You pride yourself on mind, yet you avoid sincerity and heart. You speak of love, yet you control and manipulate others based upon your own desire for self-assertion and freedom. True freedom you know very little about. The freedom that you do know is the freedom to do your own thing that you consider your personal right.

If you were one of the starseed who lived on this planet at the time of Michael, in Jerusalem you cried out at the top of your lungs, "Give us Barabbas!" "If you are really the Son of God, save yourself." You who had two donkeys in your stable, owned property and had fine clothes and food on your table shouted the loudest to have him crucified, for you thought, in your pride and arrogance, "If this one is really the Son of God, he should be dressed in fine linen and with a crown of gold and the authority of Caesar."

Those who saw differently were stoned to death. They starved. They were imprisoned and tortured and eventually thrown to wild beasts, animal and human. Yet today you same starseed, all 170 million of you worldwide, still give your allegiance to Caesar and to the many false gods that this world has to offer. All of them are much more pleasing to you than God the Father, for with these other gods you can do your own thing and get away with it. You can lend your talents to this god who is just as vain as you. Or perhaps you choose to deny God altogether, as you are still looking for the easy way out, as when you expected Jesus to come down from the cross. It was the wills of men and women who put him on that cross, and it is that same mass consciousness that causes all of the present suffering on Urantia. It is that same mass consciousness that keeps the rich in material wealth while billions struggle for their existence. It is that same mass consciousness that does not recognize true spirituality. It is that mass consciousness that looks for its religious leaders in robes of righteousness, with crowns of gold or television ministries. It is that same mass consciousness that looks for spiritual leaders to flash the credit cards of social acceptance and success. You buy the newspapers that make heroes out of iniquitous souls. You purchase the magazines and books that promote degradation and moral decay. You buy your children books which promote violence and inhumanity to each other. You do all of this in the name of the great American dream which has now reached the four corners of Urantia, and now on every continent most wish to obtain this American dream. You wave the flag while bombing innocent people, and you consider yourself a good and patriotic citizen of the world. You put individuals in power who only proclaim God in their speeches, but who in their lives and actions deny the very existence of God. Yes, you give your power away to all of these souls by misplaced loyalties and pursuits. You have no idea of what you really need or who you really are.

Perhaps you have adopted the belief that money makes the world go round. It is God who makes the world go round. It is he who gives you the next heartbeat. It is his grace which allows you to go your own way in pride, arrogance and ignorance. It is love that is needed to make this world go round. Talents that an individual may have are parts of God that need to be given freely for a common purpose, this common purpose being the implementation of the kingdom of God throughout time and space. On a world where love is the force energy of individuals, there is no need for capital or currency of any kind. The uniqueness of each individual is clearly seen by all, and talents and energies are given for the common good of their local family, which is an extended family of both cosmic and native origin, incorporating diverse careers of artistic, scientific and philosophic natures. The foundation of happiness is the fatherhood of God and the brotherhood of man. Beyond all else, the spirituality of each individual soul is recognized, and the most powerful souls on these worlds of light and life are those of the highest love and spiritual ascension.

Urantia is in need of a complete revision in all of its structures, institutions and, in particular, religious reality. It is time for all the people of the earth to come out of the systems and out of the jobs that grant you livelihood and find your proper eldership and spiritual representatives of the Machiventa Government presently implemented on Urantia. It is time to give your talents to these communities, your families and your genetic ancestors. If you cannot see the light of these words it is because you are blinded by your own selfish pursuits and vain ways. If you choose spiritual teachers who agree with your own confused and deceived thinking of reality, then so be it. You have chosen your destiny.

A loving father makes provisions for his children, has a plan for his children and wishes for those children to be everything they can be and to experience daily the wonderfulness of the moment. A true father will discipline the child of disobedience so that the child does not become rebellious, disrespectful and ungrateful. If you cannot receive instruction at the level needed for true change of your soul, you are in danger of continued childishness. Even though you may consider yourself "spiritual," you are void of true spirituality, for true spirituality places itself under the authority of those of higher status. There is wisdom in the counsel of the elders, yet you find yourself outside of this counsel. Your lives lack the wisdom that is available from your God, for God speaks to you through mandated and appointed personalities who you can touch and see. God is ever present in many forms. All of these forms together represent all that God is, at whatever finite level your soul may find itself. One soul alone, even a mandated personality, cannot represent all that God is; but the combined council of elders can more potently represent the Paradise reality in the lower evolutionary worlds of time and space. Existent within the First Cosmic Family will be that representation. Those wise enough and spiritually in tune enough to come into the presence of these elders will greatly benefit themselves, and furthermore one day become elders themselves so that the kingdom of God will manifest on all of the continents of Urantia, before and after the change point.

The Salvington Circuit, a direct link to the universe capital and the Creator Son, is more strongly felt and recognized through those personalities mandated by the Bright and Morning Star and myself, Machiventa Melchizedek. Pontius Pilate who said, "What is truth?" tried to deny the truth that he saw stand and speak before him. Washing his hands of his own guilt, he placed the blame on the mass consciousness of others. I ask you who read these words, how often do you wash your own hands of self-guilt? To become truly great, one must become totally immersed in the divine will of God the Father. It is better to labor in the fields of toil in the will of God than to eat the fruits of selfishness and dwell in the mansions of prideful opulence. Be it not denied that "whatsoever a man soweth he also shall reap." The government of Machiventa is looking for laborers of the harvest. The Bridegroom says, "Come, do not look backward but forward; do not try to build your reality in an old order that is presently passing away. Lend your eyes and give your hearts to those of gentle persuasion. Join the mandated communities of love and your cosmic or Urantian family of origin. Find yourself, your God and the representation of your Creator, in the reflections of those souls who have ascended closest to the likeness of Paradise harmony, and are the voice to Urantia at this hour."

September 15, 1991

Machiventa Melchizedek, present Planetary Prince of Urantia; in cooperation with the Bright and Morning Star and in coordination with the Midwayer Commission of Urantia; as transmitted through the Audio Fusion Material Complement, Gabriel of Sedona.

PAPER 212

A BEGINNING THESIS AS TO THE COORDINATION OF CERTAIN CELESTIAL PERSONALITIES, IN RELATION TO THE ADJUDICATION BY THE BRIGHT AND MORNING STAR VS LUCIFER AND THE IMPLEMENTATION THEREOF THROUGH THE MACHIVENTA MELCHIZEDEK GOVERNMENT AND MORE SPECIFICALLY, THE MASTER SERAPHIM OF PLANETARY SUPERVISION AND DESIGNATED MANDATED HUMAN PERSONALITIES

Now working with each of the twelve groups of master seraphim,* are assigned pairs of seraphim, cherubim, sanobim and midwayers as well as finaliters such as myself, designated more specifically as a genetic gatherer in relation to the specific cosmic families of various universe orders on Urantia. Frequently, previously unrevealed personalities are also designated to certain cosmic reservists and Urantian reservists alike, for purposes of destiny alignment. Many of these unrevealed personalities and their functions, point of origin and certain other information that can be revealed about them, will be revealed in a correlated paper pertaining to this particular thesis. The coordination of these celestial personalities in relation to reservists has been implemented by Machiventa Melchizedek to upstep the process between dimensions, so that these previously unrevealed personalities can more easily interact in the world of the third dimension without being seen and can remain invisible, yet interact with physical matter when and if necessary. Increasingly, the use of these orders will become ever more important as continued chaos and natural disasters increase on Urantia. Reservists, cosmic and Urantian alike, who have aligned themselves with the First Cosmic Family and the Machiventa Government at Planetary Headquarters, will be assigned one or several of these personalities to aid in the protection of those individuals from the forces of Caligastia and other negative influences that take form in human rebellion, and to take action against those reservists who will not align themselves, and do indeed oppose those who do.

1. THE EPOCHAL ANGELS

The epochal angels will now be assigned specifically to spiritual leaders of all religions, and in particular those entrusted with the Fifth Epochal Revelation that is already in print, to bring all of these, the leaders of many thousands and millions of souls, to the place where they will be willing to accept CFER. If they do not, they will suffer the consequences of their continued obstinacy and rebellious tendencies to the true purposes of their Creator Sovereign, Michael of Nebadon. The epochal angels will work with the physical in correlation with those personalities previously mentioned. Those who continue to follow the path that is right in their own eyes will no longer be protected from the forces of Caligastia in the physical.

2. THE PROGRESS ANGELS

The progress angels will now work specifically with those leaders involved in the education of all the races on the planet, who should be teaching higher spiritual principles, as opposed to the secular philosophies and intellectual propensities which lead hundreds of thousands to materialistic pursuits instead of a natural spiritual evolutionary progress in the ascension of the sons and daughters on this planet. Those leaders who do not align themselves with the purposes of the Machiventa Government will also no longer be protected from the full force of Caligastia's control. Those who do align themselves and recognize the spirit of God within and outside of them, will give their talent to the schools of education in the Starseed and Urantian Schools of Melchizedek, first as students themselves and then as instructors of CFER.

3. THE RELIGIOUS GUARDIANS

It has been determined during the centuries of rebellion on Urantia, that gradual change, although necessary and functional, has become increasingly difficult on Urantia due to the controlling methods of starseed who have been able to place themselves in positions of power and influence in their many repersonalizations on Urantia. Therefore, the religious guardians will also take away their protective hand from the various religious institutions and allow the full force of Caligastia's influence to have its day. The repercussions will be massive within all religious institutions and spiritual organizations which proclaim to be the keepers of divine truth on Urantia. Their full force of authority will be only to withhold or uphold CFER and those spiritual human personalities and elders within the Machiventa Government who have aligned themselves to the purposes of Christ Michael and the Bright and Morning Star in the adjudication process.

4. THE ANGELS OF NATION LIFE

This group will take away all stabilization of human personalities in control of human government, which of course will cause increasing confusion and political upheaval, and will cause fear in leaders because their own people will increasingly turn against them, so that the leaders will have to align themselves with other, more iniquitous forces, in order to remain in power. This will be made to appear as peace initiatives to the general public, but in reality, it is an international control by a few iniquitous personalities and families. Increased police control over the peoples of this planet and suppression as to travel rights, material goods to buy, food to eat, and the ever increasing need for pure water to drink will become paramount. Those in power will tighten the reins because they fear the unknown forces, which now are becoming more noticeable in their attempts to unseat them from power. They will feel there are revolutionary forces organized, presenting them with problems they cannot control, and they will take it out on the working class. The reality is that the spiritual forces are working on every soul on the planet to have those souls choose between the divine government and the human leaders appointed within it, or the governments of rebellion and the forces of Caligastia that control them.

5. THE ANGELS OF THE RACES

This group is specifically designated to cosmic reservists and Urantian reservists for the purposes of their coming together within their original cosmic family linkage. All overcontrol and supervision that had previously been appropriated for proper breeding and genetic linkage to the other races of mankind have now been eliminated. This process will cause continued problems in many areas such as overpopulation, the mixing of lower genetics with higher genetics, dysfunctional personalities, spiritually inept personalities and physically deformed personalities. Only those souls who have aligned themselves with the purposes of the Machiventa Government will be able to find their complementary polarities of the opposite sex and procreate normal children, and indeed, higher orders of genetic linkage to Material Sons and Daughters of Nebadon and other universes. Starchildren at the age of twelve and thirteen will increasingly rebel against their human parents and thousands of starseed will become runaways, adding to the already overloaded problem of the homeless young. These young starseed need to be found by the Machiventa Government and educated in CFER. Their human parents will not be able to control them. Their cosmic parents, if not aligned with the Machiventa Government, will find themselves being taught by these children, but many parents' own pride will not allow them to listen.

6. THE ANGELS OF THE FUTURE

All those in the various religions particularly the highest of these, Christianity, (because of the higher truth of Christ Michael within it) will find themselves increasingly fearful of the future because of outward circumstances that they can no longer control. Those who have attained the partial activation of the Spirit of Truth through Christ Michael, with gifts such as the word of knowledge, discerning of spirits, prophecy and visions, will no longer receive the manifestation of these gifts unless they leave the institutions in control and seek the higher spiritual revelations that exist in the Fifth Epochal Revelation and CFER, and in particular, come within the jurisdiction of the Machiventa Government. All supernatural reception in these areas will be pointed towards the Fifth Epochal Revelation and CFER. It will not be speaking of the building of huge new churches, of printing bibles in various languages, of the salvation of souls through the "born again" experience, for even though a great truth exists in this reality, the methods used have become iniquitous, and the churches themselves have become the strongholds of Caligastia. New terminology and higher revelation must be used to bring people to Jesus and God the Father. They must begin to understand the cosmology of the master universe and Urantia's proper place within that great scheme in the mind of God. All supernatural healing through the ministry of the laying on of hands will be withheld, even from those of pure motive within the Christian world, until those individuals remove themselves from those institutions and hear what the true Spirit of God is saying to the churches. The lives and true identity of those false ministers and prophets will continue to be revealed in the light, and they will lose the control that they wield over the masses and their own congregations. This will take place in all the religions on the planet.

7. THE ANGELS OF ENLIGHTENMENT

Because of the extreme importance of the little time that is left on Urantia for the gathering of the reservists, both cosmic and Urantian, all angels of enlightenment will work specifically at Planetary Headquarters in coordination with those other angels of enlightenment who have already been assigned to those who have reached the third psychic circle and aligned themselves with the Aquarian Concepts Community at Planetary Headquarters where the purposes of Machiventa and his government are outworking in human personalities. They no longer will be allowed to visit some areas of this planet, until certain human personalities of specific families of various Material Sons and Daughters group together in designated areas protected by Celestial Overcontrol. For the time being, these angels of enlightenment will work specifically to reach their human counterparts through the means of literature such as this paper and other literature from the Aquarian Concepts Community. Also, they will use word of mouth, for the purposes of the establishment of the Machiventa Government, first at Planetary Headquarters in Sedona, Arizona, U.S.A., and then in various other parts of the world. It will become increasingly more difficult to reach the third psychic circle outside of the first protected area in Sedona, Arizona, U.S.A., and alignment with the eldership of that community. Those who have received an angel of enlightenment and reached the third circle and still refuse to align themselves, will drop back to the fourth circle and lose the angel of enlightenment formerly assigned to them. Those with spiritual observation ability will see the change in these individuals, and particularly this will take place within the Urantia movement.

8. THE ANGELS OF HEALTH

Since the adjudication has begun on this planet in various stages, the beginning of which was the first contact with the vessel who was used to bring the first part of the Fifth Epochal Revelation, there has been an increase in the various diseases which affect mankind. Since the appointment of the Planetary Prince of this planet, all the celestial overcontrol that has formerly held back various viruses from taking their full course in the events of mankind and in the individual physical body, will no longer act to prevent their full reign of devastation. Plagues of various kinds will increase and only those who have come out of their political and religious entrapments and have aligned themselves with the purposes of Christ Michael and the Machiventa Government will be protected from fatal viruses. All of the health guardians of spiritual orders are concentrated now at Planetary Headquarters and will be assigned to various other areas of the planet when representatives are sent out to those designated areas upon first being educated at the Starseed and Urantian Schools of Melchizedek in Sedona, Arizona, U.S.A. Even old diseases that have long been cured by medical technology will return to Urantia, along with viruses that modern science will be far from understanding and hundreds of years away from curing under its present consciousness. Any healing of fatal diseases that does take place, will first happen at the Planetary Headquarters of the present Planetary Prince and the headquarters of the archangels. This is an example of divine construction, in which the Creator Son first creates his capital world and administrative government and then proceeds outward. His example is the example for the establishment of the pre-stages of light and life upon this planet to bring about the first stage. Healers of all kinds will be called to Planetary Headquarters and will be assigned specific health guardians, as well as angels of enlightenment when they reach the third psychic circle. This will enable them to understand the higher concepts of health and healing even on a morontia level, so that this mota can be applied to present-day Urantia for the ultimate in healing procedure as applied to mortals in transition from one dimension to the next. It is mind and will in cooperation with heart, in alignment with divine mind, will and heart, working with appointed human leaders and other celestial counterparts, that will bring true healing to this planet.

9. THE HOME SERAPHIM

This group will now work specifically to help bring together the First Cosmic Family and those complementary polarities for the future appropriation to this planet of higher Urantians and starseed. It is in the context of genetic inheritance and in the regathering of the higher genetic strains of the Material Sons and Daughters of this planet and of others, that necessitates this regathering process. In particular, those Urantian and cosmic reservists who need to be properly mated must be brought together by Overcontrol, but this can only be done upon the freewill choices of those reservists in relation to the divine purposes of the first perfect mind of the Universal Father, and in the perspective of the adjudication by the Bright and Morning Star vs. Lucifer, for each reservist has the capability within them to become either an instrument of light or an instrument of darkness. At this time on Urantia, the lukewarm will no longer be allowed to sit on the cosmic fence of indecision and complacency. If they choose incorrectly they will remain in the families of rebellion and will not be placed with or meet their families with higher genetics and spiritual-ascension origin.

10. THE ANGELS OF INDUSTRY

All technological and industrial progress on Urantia will cease until the adjudication is completed. Inventions of major significance by enlightened individuals will be experienced only within the geographic location and context of the designated areas within the Machiventa Government. Minds of inventive design who have not aligned themselves to the higher principles of their Creator will become distorted and delusioned. Confusion within the scientific world outside of the Machiventa Government will add to the increase in instability among the intellectual elite on Urantia, causing continued anarchy within the arena of the universities and corporate research laboratories until such time that individuals come out of those systems and institutions and give their talents to the true purposes of God, to their true leaders at Planetary Headquarters in Sedona, Arizona, U.S.A., or they will suffer the consequences that their own inventions have brought to Urantia.

11. THE ANGELS OF DIVERSION

This group now is assigned only to the purposes of the Machiventa Government at Planetary Headquarters. Their function on Urantia in the next eight years or so will be strictly to the Divine New Order communities of the Machiventa Government. Millions of others will find themselves unable to take advantage of vacation periods for one reason or another because of the various circumstances of chaos on Urantia. They will find no safe havens of peace and tranquility, as many of the known vacation areas will become increasingly confused and violent and the energies there will be far from tranquil, with increased crime and political upheaval. Those iniquitous individuals in the music and film industry will continue to produce Luciferic concepts and visual manifestations of rebellious personalities, so that any form of home recreation that is not chosen by the divine mind, will bring to them emotional and psychological trauma as a result of these recreational devices. Other forms of recreation will begin to be invented by Luciferic minds which will further cause the human user hallucinogenic responses to normal mind wave decisions which will make them unable to conduct normal lives. Games of chance will be developed so that individuals will continually adhere to practices of self-assertion and unbridled liberty as opposed to providential guidance and faith principles based upon a relationship with a personal God and Creator. Ever increasing leisure will slow the mind and bring thousands of individuals to mononucleosis, and laziness will take the place of motivation, and the continued increase of drug abuse will add to the deterioration of the human mind, particularly in Western civilization and in places all over the planet where the capitalistic and materialistic dream has taken root. Instant gratification and mindal recreation of distortion will bring about in teenage populations almost clone-like and robotic tendencies and attitudes of personality, physical body movements and psychological reaction to the normal processes of thought life. This is already taking place among the young in many parts of the planet under the influence of distorted patterns of music which have helped to cause psychological distortions in the personalities of the young. Music, which can be used in divine healing, can also be greatly used by the forces of Caligastia for the continued purposes of rebellion, not only on this planet but on all the planets fallen in the system of Satania. Only in the safe and protected areas on this planet under proper eldership and control, will individuals find true recreation and leisure.

12. THE ANGELS OF SUPERHUMAN MINISTRY

Since most angelic overcontrol has been removed from certain areas where large populations reside, it has caused the mass consciousness to become increasingly distorted. Sanobim and cherubim as well as seraphim are all located at one geographic location on the planet and that is Planetary Headquarters, where the archangels and the Planetary Prince have their headquarters. At this time all ERCs, where angelic personalities enter by seraphic transport* or other means of universe travel, are located only at Planetary Headquarters. Increasingly, it will become more difficult for guardian angels to travel from their headquarters on this planet to other points on the planet because of the continued distortion of the world. Therefore, all celestial personalities will find themselves more rooted at Planetary Headquarters than they have been in the last 200,000 years of rebellion on this planet. Their ministry to one another will be in context of the present adjudication and re-establishment of the Machiventa Government.

Particular specific procedures will be withheld from CFER until certain eldership reaches the level where they can understand higher celestial ministry and union of souls in relation to the ascension process. These procedures appropriated by Machiventa Melchizedek in accordance with the seraphim of master control on Urantia are in many ways unique to the universe of Nebadon, but in other ways they are similar to those applied to any particular planet when it comes to an adjudication of the rebellion process. Overcontrol policies provide for compliance with the sometimes hundreds and thousands of circumstances based upon that individual world and the complete trust in the appointed Planetary Prince who has had personal experience in the dimensional frame of personality contact with mortals, so that experiential knowledge replaces cosmic analysis. The close cooperation of mandated human personalities and all aligned cosmic family, further aid the Planetary Prince in uniting both human perspectives and overcontrol procedure so that correct and more perfect decisions can be instantaneously made by the Planetary Prince and his staff in regard to the adjudication, and in the separating of those rebellious personalities and those billions of others who, unexpectedly perhaps, are caught in the grasp of the Lucifer rebellion as perpetrated by the Caligastia forces on this planet. The union of souls is a team effort of various orders and personalities of the divine mind on lower worlds of time and space, designed to produce a true harmonic convergence of divine appropriation resonant upon immediate action, to bring joy, fulfillment and divine purpose to each individual team. From one dimension to another, from the nonmaterial to the material, from all levels of the morontial to the physical, we are joined in cosmic effort to bring about the purposes of the Universe Sovereign of Nebadon and the Universal Father of Paradise. All together we form a divine team at various levels and a created team of the divine to harmonize and cooperate in the adventure of eternity within time and space. As the ascending sons and daughters develop their spiritual minds, they begin to grasp the union of souls, at all levels, who are always geographically present in their own reality in one way or another. Increasingly, you will become more aware of the friendships of first dozens, then hundreds, then thousands, then millions, then trillions, ad infinitum, all joined together at specific moments of divine ordinance in relation to the outworking of the Master Plan of the First Source and Center, unseen perhaps, but yet ever so close to your personal reality. Each cosmic family represents a link in the divine chain of mortal genetic inheritance and divine Deo-atomic structure, all working together to stabilize and bring about the higher stages of light and life within the context of superuniverse divine characteristics. The authority of God exists in orders of beings created by the Universal Father and Creator Sons in the universes of time and space. Divine love is represented in this authority. You cannot separate one from the other. It is the proper balance of these two aspects of divine personality that all mortals and nonmaterial beings must evaluate, recognize and adhere to in the cooperation of their own individual destinies and in the purposes of the outworking of all life that has received the fragment of the Father or individualization of the Son or the Infinite Spirit in the worlds of time and space. It is in this context that CFER is now being presented to the people of Urantia, both cosmic and native.

All of these directives have now taken effect as of January 1, 1991, and will continue to increase as of January 11, 1992, and so on, each year, coordinate with numerological sequence in relation to the alignment of Urantia with planets in light and life within the system of Satania.

November 12, 1991

Paladin, Finaliter; in cooperation with the Bright and Morning Star; and at the planetary level, in compliance with the appropriation of Machiventa Melchizedek, present Planetary Prince, to bring about the upstepped adjudication of the Lucifer rebellion on Urantia; as transmitted through the Audio Fusion Material Complement, Gabriel of Sedona.

PAPER 213

THE ADJUDICATION BY THE BRIGHT AND MORNING STAR VERSUS LUCIFER, THE ESTABLISHMENT OF THE GOVERNMENT OF THE PLANETARY PRINCE USING HUMAN PERSONALITIES AND THE ANNOUNCEMENT OF MACHIVENTA MELCHIZEDEK AS THAT PLANETARY PRINCE OF URANTIA

My adjudication began in the earth time, approximately 1911. This occurrence had been prophesied through other prophets. It began with the beginning of the Fifth Epochal Revelation and slowly, throughout the years, with representatives of my government, under the mandate of Christ Michael, our Universe Sovereign, rematerializing on Urantia. In 1934 and 1935 a higher vibratory frequency was established. In 1955 an even higher vibratory frequency was established. In, 1967, quite unknown to the Urantia movement, another vibratory frequency was established. By this time the Urantia movement had fallen from the clear reception of their Thought Adjusters and the Spirit of Truth within them. Had they been open to the voice of God, many of them, and so many other millions, would have received the baptism of the Holy Spirit of my Divine Mother, the Universe Mother Spirit, and would have manifested the gifts of her Spirit. It would have enabled them to receive and understand CFER now being given through the mandated personality, Gabriel of Sedona. Many Protestants and Catholics alike received these gifts. If the obstinate *URANTIA Book* readers had asked for it, they too would have received the manifestations of the Mother circuits and could have been an aid to those Protestants and Catholics to help them in the understanding of the Fifth Epochal Revelation. I call upon all *URANTIA Book* readers to receive the baptism of the Universe Mother Spirit and humble themselves and seek learning from God and CFER which the Spirit of God is pouring out upon this planet for all who have ears to hear. It is her last gift before her rebirth. It is a complement to the Thought Adjuster and the Spirit of Truth within. It is the dance of the renaissance. It is the fruit of the tree of life. It is the cleansing water of the soul. It is the mirror of complacency and pride. It is the fire for the slothful. It is milk from the breast of the Mother for the obstinate, and the final covering of the divine hand from our Paradise Father. It is the awakening light in the eyes of all souls who receive her, the essence of true respect and submission to the Father and all personalities that are elders within the Father circuits of time and space, particularly to those who are mandated within the Government of Machiventa Melchizedek, the present Planetary Prince of Urantia.

It is not within the text of this paper to define the mandate of the Bright and Morning Star, given to Gabriel of Sedona, or the mandate of Machiventa Melchizedek given to other future ambassadors. However, what I do give is for you who are chosen to read this paper to activate that which is within you as reservists and awaken you to your proper destinies and soul urges. It is the mandate of the Bright and Morning Star, given to Gabriel of Sedona, to manifest to all of the vast cosmic family, quite real physical blessings, to change circumstances and to come against any of the evil forces on behalf of any of those cosmic family members who wish to align themselves with the First Cosmic Family and the establishment of the Machiventa Government upon this planet. It is a mandate that brings the highest love mates together, their highest spiritual complements. It is a mandate of fulfillment to individual personalities and souls. It is a mandate of perfection which comes from the overcontrol of thousands of unseen celestials on this planet. It is a mandate of universe administration unified on a third-dimensional plane upon entering the fourth dimension. It is a mandate of interdimensional and interplanetary communication. It is the reopening of the circuits of Nebadon and Orvonton with your world, Urantia. There is only one personality on any one planet that can have my mandate, co-shared by his highest spiritual complement. It is a mandate of healing of the soul, astral body, and all other bodies which you will come to learn about including the physical Urantian one. It is a time-and-space-warp mandate that knows no boundaries within its universe of existence, that being Nebadon. The past, present and future are coexistent within this mandate.

You will come to learn of these things since you have this personality with you and I am with you; Gabriel of Sedona being the audio fusion material complement for me. Until your planet has entered the first stages of light and life, a process that is being greatly accelerated by this adjudication and within the government of Machiventa Melchizedek, I, the Bright and Morning Star, take personal representation and overcontrol. All those within the First Cosmic Family who align themselves perfectly with their God, first-time Urantians and those from other universes and particularly those of **Avalon,** to some degree can manifest the power, harmony and love of this mandate. I bid you all come from the four corners of this planet, who are to be part of this great work and manifest destiny. The harvest is ripe but the harvesters are few.

October 9, 1991

In servitude and eternal loyalty and love to my Father Christ Michael of Nebadon, the Bright and Morning Star of Salvington; as transmitted through the Audio Fusion Material Complement, Gabriel of Sedona.

PAPER 214

HOLOGRAM APPEARANCE OF MACHIVENTA MELCHIZEDEK TO ONE OF HIS POTENTIAL MATERIAL COMPLEMENTS AND POTENTIAL VICEGERENT FIRST AMBASSADORS, WITH THE ANNOUNCEMENT OF HIS ELEVATION TO THE OFFICE OF PLANETARY PRINCE OF URANTIA; CLARIFICATION OF THE TITLE OF THE PLANETARY PRINCE; WARNING TO CALIGASTIA REGARDING PROTECTION AND SAFE PASSAGE FOR ALL THOSE CALLED TO THE STARSEED AND URANTIAN SCHOOLS OF MELCHIZEDEK AT PLANETARY HEADQUARTERS IN SEDONA, ARIZONA, U.S.A.

It was decided by Christ Michael, the Bright and Morning Star, the Acting Governor General of Urantia, and the Chief of Seraphim that it was time that I announce to human personalities the reestablishment of the seat of the Planetary Prince on Urantia. It happened on December 9, 1989, in Santa Fe, New Mexico, U.S.A., an area very close to several ERCs near the Four Corners area in which hundreds of celestial visitations had been made by physical spacecraft and seraphic transport alike, an area that had slowly deteriorated in mass consciousness from the spiritual position it had been designated to obtain. We had previously found our audio receiver in 1987, and he was given the complete mandate of the Bright and Morning Star and all that went with it. Now it was time to appoint the first two[13] of the potential hologram receivers, who would act as a representative of myself after 2040 - 2050 AD. Other celestial personalities would form images of themselves through the light body of all future Vicegerent First Ambassadors. They were appointed to be the first two to

---

[13]Note: Because there will eventually be other Vicegerent First Ambassadors, we prefer not to use the names of the first two, as all future stabilized First Ambassadors will share this mandate. For approximately 40 years they will be tried and tested before they become actual full stabilized third-to-first-circle First Ambassadors. When the mandate of the Bright and Morning Star leaves the planet, the ambassadors and all mandated personalities of the 12 World Councils will still have to be accountable to the overcontrol of the Bright and Morning Star mandate and the then Gabriel of Satania, which Gabriel of Sedona will become. Their individual godly authority will depend upon their loyalty to Christ Michael and the Universal Father and the love of God in their hearts.

serve Gabriel of Sedona and Niánn, with the mandate of the Bright and Morning Star. These two potential **Vicegerent Ambassadors** were apostles of Jesus in the first century. Far from saints, they still had much spiritual growth to obtain. It was decided that my announcement would first be made to these two as they had the higher mindal ability to comprehend and follow up with an announcement of my appointment to the rest of the world. Now in this century the virtue of their heart would have to match their mind. They would be given the opportunity to complement the virtue of Gabriel and Niánn and the mandate of the Bright and Morning Star. Several others[14] had been contacted but failed to step completely out of the Caligastia system and make my announcement public.

Caligastia was told many things that I cannot give in this transmission, but what I can say is, that he was not allowed to try to take their lives or cause any physical accidents to the first two potential Vicegerent First Ambassadors, or any others in the future; also upon their leaving, neither he nor any of his representatives would be allowed within a five-mile radius of their physical bodies. A half dozen angelic beings were assigned to protect this radius until these two would eventually come to the protected area at Planetary Headquarters in Sedona, Arizona. The reason I give this information is because those who read this transmission and know you are also supposed to be in Sedona, Arizona, might wonder if Caligastia could try to do the same thing to you. Fear not, for if your alignment is in the will of the Father, you will have that same protection until you reach your destination within the Aquarian Concepts Community at Planetary Headquarters in Sedona, Arizona, U.S.A. What these two did not know then is that my government would be established in Sedona; and I physically would live there, although unseen at this time, but ever present within the same five-mile radius of Gabriel and Niánn, and other family members. This first community will be the prototype for the first cities of the Divine New Order. It is not just a government of human beings but a government with divine overcontrol and design, using mortals to exemplify the administration of divine projections within a lower world framework.

The signature of any mandated elder to the mandate of the Bright and Morning Star carries with it a warning to those who assume to be spiritual teachers but whose motives are far from divine. It is a warning to those who call themselves messengers of the brotherhood of light, channellers of archangels or even of Michael or whomever they claim to be contacting, that they must humble themselves and become students at the Starseed and Urantian Schools

---

[14]Before December 1989 certain prospective reservists and Vicegerent First Ambassadors were contacted by the Midwayer Commission and Machiventa in Toronto, Ont. Canada, and other energy reflective circuits.

of Melchizedek. They first must find their true God and the Creator Son of that God, the ruler of their universe of Nebadon, Christ Michael, and then submit to his appointed and mandated human personalities. The first of these is Gabriel of Sedona and the second, the Liaison Ministers and all other elders, men and women alike, who have first aligned themselves with their complementary polarities and cosmic ancestors at Planetary Headquarters. If they refuse to heed the request of these mandated elders then they have refused me, for their signature carries the complete authority of the Office of the Planetary Prince of Urantia just as Gabriel's name carries the complete authority of the Office of the Bright and Morning Star of Salvington. Each of them will come to learn of the complexities of their own mandates in the years ahead, and so will all of Urantia. We suggest to those who are interested in the healing of their physical bodies that you request PAPER 205 of *The Cosmic Family, Vol. I*, for Gabriel works within the astral, and **Tron therapists** and stabilized third-circle Vicegerent First Ambassadors with the etheric.[15]

"**Sananda**" was the title of Christ Michael on another planet when he took the office of Planetary Prince in one of his bestowals. It is not the name of Christ Michael and never has been, not on this planet or any other. If you receive a personal letter of request from either Gabriel or other personalities of the Divine Government, I pray that you treat it with the utmost respect, for any reason they would have to contact you is in accordance with the true spiritual government of this universe and the lines of communication therein, starting with Christ Michael and proceeding from the Bright and Morning Star to myself, Machiventa Melchizedek, on Urantia. We have at our fingertips thousands of supermortal and celestial personalities to see to it that you begin to respect their requests, for this indeed is the adjudication of Urantia. Truly, let the love of God brighten your horizons. Let the discipline of God guide your thoughts and let godlike humility direct your decisions.

October 9, 1991

Machiventa Melchizedek, Planetary Prince of Urantia; in cooperation with the Bright and Morning Star of Salvington; as transmitted through the Audio Fusion Material Complement, Gabriel of Sedona.

---

[15]At the time of editing this second edition, July, 1995, no potential Vicegerent First Ambassador had stabilized on the third psychic circle. Five former apostles of the first century, James, John, Luke, Matthew and Paul, which include the two mentioned, have been unable to so far. James is the closest candidate. Santeen who has a higher mandate as a Liaison Minister is the only example of the office of Vicegerent First Ambassador functioning the way it should under the mandate of the Bright and Morning Star.

PAPER 215

DELUSION ENERGY FREQUENCIES, DISTORTION WAVES AND DISTORTION SOUND WAVES IN RELATION TO THE ADJUDICATION OF URANTIA, IMPLEMENTED BY MACHIVENTA MELCHIZEDEK, PRESENT PLANETARY PRINCE OF URANTIA

On October 11, 1991 certain physical energies, as a result of planetary alignment to other planets within the system of Satania, began to cause harmonic patterns to be implemented on this planet. On a normal planet, this series of events would be good for all inhabitants, but on a planet such as Urantia, that has defaulted in its dispensational revelations by higher personalities, entrusted to teach the evolutionary races, and because the evolutionary races themselves in their failure to truly find their God and Creator Father, I have decided to take the force of these energies and use it in separating the good seed from the bad seed. The implementation of my mandate is international in scope Urantia and will affect all of the citizens on this planet. This time-space reality was foreseen by John the Revelator, and it is in this context that I am about to present the manifestation of my decision.

First, the **delusion energy frequencies** are sent specifically to particular individuals whose imbalances are such that they no longer are candidates for the first mansion world, and have been chosen for extinction by the Ancients of Days. Crimes of murder, rape and inhumanity to man of all kinds will increase on Urantia. Terrorism and torture will become commonplace, to the extent that it will bring dread to millions, and many will fear for their lives. Insanity will increase and so will the symptoms of secular psychological illnesses — the disunion of mental and emotional harmony — such as schizophrenia, psychopathic tendencies, sociopathic behavior and mania. Those who have not taken the first steps in their own consciousness as to the reception and activation of the Thought Adjuster within and to the reception of the Spirit of Truth, will become completely controlled by the delusion frequencies that they themselves have chosen to receive by cause and effect. Many innocent will suffer. In reality, transition of the innocent by physical death is a transition for them to a higher reality and in a sense an escape from the tribulation to come upon Urantia. It is hoped that the loved ones of those afflicted innocent can begin to hear the Spirit of Truth that stands at the door of their hearts and knocks. All on Urantia must leave the institutions that further these delusions.

Distortion waves will affect every major city on the planet with a population over 20,000. With the exception of the protected areas, distortion waves will cause the breakdown of equilibrium in the physical body and certain thought patterns. The physical energies of mortals will increasingly lessen, and their minds will not be able to organize thoughts. Many will be romanced by their own distorted realities which they will begin to further hallucinate upon as they go about their daily work schedules. This will begin to induce accidents at all levels in the work force, causing many deaths because of human mistakes. Many of these human mistakes will be blamed on the machinery. Many in the fields of media and communication, such as authors and journalists, will begin to increasingly corrupt the minds of their readers, listeners and viewers. They will do this because they themselves will become increasingly corrupt and distorted. Hospital surgeons and anesthesiologists will increasingly make fatal mistakes, causing the deaths of their patients. Those in positions of responsibility, such as pilots, bus drivers and railroad engineers will find themselves daydreaming upon their delusions, which will cause accidents that affect the lives of hundreds and even thousands.

Sound distortion frequencies are also appropriated on a mass level and will affect all population centers of over 20,000. These frequencies will cause all animal life that have the ability to hear the sounds of these frequencies to become more aggressive. These frequencies will also cause machinery of all kinds to break down, which will increase the probability of accidents and deaths. Only those individuals who are in the perfect will of God will be protected in air flight or whatever means of transportation they choose to use. All others will be open to the effects of all accidents due to sound frequencies.

Protected areas and those within them will be safe. Those within protected areas who are not yet aligned to the eldership of the appointed, mandated personalities within them, will be protected up to a time in the near future by the grace of Christ Michael. At a certain time in the future, they will be forced to leave these protected areas. At that point, the first two energies mentioned, delusion and distortion energy frequencies, will be directed to certain individuals. It will become increasingly clear to those who understand the effects of these energies upon individuals as to exactly what is happening. Sometimes distortion energy frequencies will be specifically assigned to those of the light, with the hope of trying to get them out of a particular geographic location where they no longer belong. They will find that it will be impossible to live without complete alignment with the purposes of Christ Michael and the government of Machiventa Melchizedek now being appropriated on Urantia. They will be led by these distortion energies and delusion energies to the Starseed and Urantian Schools of Melchizedek in Sedona, Arizona, U.S.A. Many of these individuals who do not understand what is happening to them will seek advice from psychiatrists, doctors, clergy and even fortune tellers; but they will not be healed from the effects of these energies until they align themselves with the purposes of the implementation of the Machiventa Government upon this planet.

This procedure I have implemented, is because of the unwillingness of those in the Urantia movement to totally accept and align themselves with CFER and the implementation of my government at Planetary Headquarters to which many of them are asked to come. We are not interested in your degrees, in your bank accounts, or in your status positions. We are interested in your love and loyalty to Christ Michael and the Universal Father. We look upon your dogmatic views of the Fifth Epochal Revelation as childish and dangerous; dangerous to the cause of true growth and ascension. We pity your smugness and pray for the end of your obstinacy. It is because of the consciousness in the Urantia movement that I have had to implement these delusion and distortion frequencies, with the hopes that many of you will awaken. If you cannot understand the love of God in the work and lives of those mandated personalities, some of whom you have already met, then perhaps you can better understand another side of God that you will begin to see shortly.

October 18, 1991

Machiventa Melchizedek, Planetary Prince of Urantia; in cooperation with the Bright and Morning Star of Salvington in overcontrol of my implementation; as transmitted through the Audio Fusion Material Complement, Gabriel of Sedona.

The following Papers 216 to 222 are co-authored by the **Race Commissioners** on Urantia in cooperation with interuniversal personalities under the direction of the Bright and Morning Star of Salvington, the Bright and Morning Star of Avalon, the Bright and Morning Star of Wolvering and the Bright and Morning Star of Fanoving.

PAPER 216

ATAVISM[16]* IN RELATION TO THE VARIOUS COSMIC FAMILIES ON URANTIA AND TO THE URANTIAN STRAIN AND LINKAGE TO THE MATERIAL SON AND DAUGHTER, ADAM AND EVE, ON URANTIA

Modern science has increasingly discovered characteristic traits in the physical strains of certain genealogies; the obvious of these have been color and texture of hair, nose and other body formations, height and bone structures. It is becoming increasingly obvious to those in the fields of science that sociological and cultural influences cannot account for similarity in certain physical traits. With the use of fact-finding and computer technology it has also become increasingly obvious that certain habitual personality characteristics are not caused by social consciousness nor the family traditions of a present lifetime. Present-day nationalistic races can be quite distinct from a neighbor even though, geographically, they may inhabit the same environment, have similar religious beliefs, similar cultural habits, similar means of acquiring knowledge, careers, transportation and leisure. Ethnocentric modes of thinking can cause divisions within peoples of very similar culture which has little or nothing to do with lack of education, social justice or equality.

In regard to various problems of modern societies in Western civilization, observations and assumptions of the scientific researchers are based upon conclusions that have no basis in the criteria of cosmic fact and reality. Conclusions drawn in the observance of humans supposedly of the same culture do not take into consideration those individuals' original genetic inheritance, let alone their cosmic inheritance, which modern science knows nothing about. The strongest genes of the human physical body alone will make that individual a unique variety pattern of that human ancestry. Something unmeasured by modern researchers, either in sociology or psychology, are the variables of 170 million starseed intermingled on this planet, all over the age of twelve years, and of the millions of starseed under the age of twelve. This presents quite a problem in

---

[16]*Atavism:* "Appearance in an individual of some characteristic found in a remote ancestor but not in nearer ancestors." *(Webster's New World Dictionary)*

recognizing, coordinating, counseling, educating and raising all of these diversified and unique souls that present-day Urantia has incorporated upon this planet. The 170 million starseed are designated by universe registry in a different category than the millions of starseed on Urantia under the age of twelve. For those under the age of five years old, there is a different universe registry pertaining to the various orders of starseed presently repersonalizing on Urantia from various systems and universes outside of Satania and Nebadon. As of this writing, under twenty individuals over twelve years of age presently on Urantia have chosen to be here. All of these starseed and all of the other 170 million are in the process of their own ascension in relation to the mandates of their respective Creator Sons and to the Creator Son and Father of this universe, which they are presently very much a part of, regardless of their point of origin and the ascension process of their original Michael Son. Unique to each of these individuals are dozens of supermortal characteristics that have been suppressed from their repersonalizations within Nebadon and more specifically the system of Satania, due to:

1. The mandate of Christ Michael to cut their circuits off at the time of their rebellion.
2. Their unwillingness to align themselves with cosmic truth and law pertaining to all of the universes of time and space.

It is known by some in the higher spiritual arenas on your planet that the circuits of the body are connected to certain glands and other physical parts and elements. What is not understood is that incorrect thinking, cosmic misbehavior and indeed, evil, sin and iniquity will, without question, cause the functioning of the physical body and certain other mindal malfunctioning which leads to psychological and emotional disturbances. Starseed on Urantia who are beginning to realign themselves with cosmic truth — the first and foremost being the foundation of the fatherhood of God and the brotherhood of man — are beginning to create a more open flow between the circuits in their body, which is an actual linkage between a higher planet of light and their own body functions, and which activates a hopeful quest for divine purposes to be fulfilled within their thinking. Starseed who have taken another step and have come into the Fifth Epochal Revelation, have activated even higher circuits within themselves, connecting to higher educational and administrational planets which should, even on the third-dimensional plane, bring them continued physical health and spiritual prosperity as long as it is a heart experience in a relationship with and love for a personal God and Creator. Those starseed who find themselves obtaining CFER will be activating additional circuits and stronger open frequencies of even higher worlds, and in particular the one of the capital of Nebadon, the Salvington circuit. This activation in each individual will begin the process of the reappearance of atavistic characteristics of a past reality of fourth-dimensional ascension and higher, which that soul has obtained previous to the fallen third-dimensional reality in which he or she finds him or herself on Urantia.

As the new morontia (light) body begins to create itself within the framework of the lower body, a great friction will occur, creating physical, psychological, emotional and perhaps spiritual conflict. Only upon receiving CFER will individuals be able to create for themselves their long-lost morontia, or higher body, within the framework of the present adjudication of Urantia in which they find themselves. Interests will change, likes and dislikes will fluctuate; old habits will cease and new habits will begin; cultural and traditional viewpoints, even those once molded to the very character fiber of those individuals, will become trite and even embarrassing to persons rediscovering themselves. Inner conflicts based upon cosmic insight versus cultural programming, especially concerning human family ties, will increasingly cause psychological turmoil to starseed at every level of psychic-circle attainment, particularly from the age of twelve years throughout the teen years. In trying to discover who they are, they will no longer be satisfied with the answers their human parents, clergy, teachers or counselors of any kind will give them, as their memory circuits are being opened to the higher realities they once had before their fallen states. Many will find themselves, at these very young ages, with great intuition and abilities but will not be able to actualize them because of the restraints put upon them by their parents and educational authorities. Many formerly unrealized inventions, higher political and cultural systems, and agricultural and dietary laws will continue to be born within the minds of these individuals, yet also be continually suppressed by those who either do not understand these young starseed because they are not capable to do so, or because they simply refuse to, due to their own pride and desire for power. Starseed over the age of thirty will find it more difficult to overcome their lower selves and to accept what their higher selves are telling them.

Chronological maturation has a standard mean of calculation on any one planet and it can be measured regardless of the ascension of one's soul and the respective plane that one may find himself on. There is another variable, quite unmeasurable by human standards; it is called **cosmologic vibration pattern**. Cosmologic vibration pattern pertains to the normal pattern which resonates among the unfallen planets in any universe. This also has to do with a person on any one particular planet in rebellion who fluctuates between right and wrong thinking or desire. For fallen starseed to attain cosmologic vibration pattern, they must begin a process of spiritual growth that separates them from the norms of the various nonspiritual institutions in which they may find themselves. When a person begins to choose correctly over evil, sin and iniquity, they come under another measurement which has to do with their alignment with the cosmologic vibration pattern. On Urantia this has been possible only by the complete escape from all social systems into either a monastic or an isolated life of some kind which, in reality, cannot solve the problem of planetary rebellion to the degree necessary to actualize a real change on the planet. Individuals themselves may grow to a certain level of spiritual achievement, but they cannot make much of a change in the mass consciousness in the surrounding cities nearby, nor can they dent the planetary problem in any way. This became quite obvious in some of the greatest renaissances of light such as the Franciscan movement of Francis of Assisi and others like it. Enlightened people must be completely divorced in every aspect from the old order.

The use of the human brain is so far from actualization in regard to its full potential that it can be compared to the difference between the brains of an ant and those of a dolphin. Those forgotten properties that the children of complementary polarities and their parents will now begin to have, will create divine realities on Urantia in every field of human experience: in education, in the use of talents and abilities, in agriculture, in all the various art forms, and particularly in all of the physical sciences which also will begin to align with what has previously been called the supernatural. Deo-atomic reality (atomic structure in alignment with God) will become synonymous with cosmic science, as man will discover that true science is of divine origin and cannot be separated from the fact of God-reality.

Physical bodies of starseed of various chronological ages on this planet, and of different soul ages and ascension orders, will begin to align with point of origin in relation to the Creator Son of Nebadon and to other Michael Sons and their respective universes. Characteristic universe traits will begin to become recognizable by enlightened students of CFER through observation of those bodies and of thought patterns. Even the observation of the digestion of foods on Urantia will help to further analyze characteristic traits of diversified starseed. Many starseed on Urantia will find that Urantian food of all kinds, plant and animal, will become increasingly unpleasant. This is because the memory circuits are being opened to what their genetic inheritance calls for and is coded for in regard to digestion of matter within matter. What may be the norm in regard to eating within one universe, may be completely different in another. Moreover, a standard set by Material Sons and Daughters in this universe may conflict with what is set as the ideals of another universe, not only in foods digested, but in the basic structures of family life, procreation and social administration. Starseed who find themselves at Planetary Headquarters and properly aligned with the eldership so that they can benefit in the spiritual ascension process, should find themselves at war with their lower natures and in discomforts of all sorts with their physical bodies, unless of course, they have already become perfect, and, as of this date, we have found no one on Urantia who meets this criteria, with the exception of Michael, 2,000 years ago. Therefore, as you begin, with increased insight, to discover your potential and strive for that actualization, increased pain and suffering in your present body will be your reality as your old self dies and your new self becomes born.

Introspection should increasingly become cosmic in nature, and any insight as to higher spiritual purpose must be linked to respective celestial personalities in positions of overcontrol within the system of Satania and the universe of Nebadon. Just as you have a desire to learn of human corporate structure if you are hired as a new employee, you should have a greater desire to learn cosmic corporate structure in relation to divine purpose, with which your soul at this present hour should have aligned itself. Past traits and abilities, far beyond even your own imagination to conceive, are awaiting your arrival into the recognition of:

1. Cosmic and human authority in relation to divine administration.
2. CFER in relation to the adjudication on Urantia by the Bright and Morning Star.
3. Your point of origin and your genetic inheritance in relation to your cosmic family.
4. Your destiny purpose in relation to that cosmic family within the government of Machiventa Melchizedek before the change point and perhaps fifty years beyond it.
5. Ascension position in relation to the universe mandate that you receive upon transition from Urantia to the next assignment.
6. Transcendence into morontia (light) body, at a specified time in accordance with your will in alignment with divine will so that the process of physical death will not be your reality.

Unbalanced personalities who become famous from exhibiting seemingly supermortal talents or abilities in one area often can obtain unwarranted influence in unrelated areas. Mozart and other artists who excelled far beyond their peers were quite incompetent in other areas, which not only caused them and their families grief, but affected mass populations when these individuals obtained power they were not ready for. Today on Urantia, particularly in the United States, sports heroes and movie stars have been put into positions by unscrupulous and iniquitous individuals for the purposes of greed and power. Because of this fact, starseed of spiritual purposes have been protected by Celestial Overcontrol by not being allowed the recognition of the world, so that they would only be recognized by those of the true spirit of God, the Universal Father and First Source and Center. Increasingly on Urantia, those spiritual leaders mandated as such by Celestial Overcontrol, will be recognized by those starseed who are first realizing their own ancestral inheritances which connect them with interuniversal reality which far exceeds planetary appetites. As true mandated human personalities begin to be recognized, the beginning stages of true freedom, divine government and individual fulfillment will first begin to be actualized within the context of the First Cosmic Family at Planetary Headquarters in Sedona, Arizona, U.S.A., and then proceed outward to other locations on the planet where other cosmic families will be brought together and formed. Those with various atavistic characteristics in relation to their unique genetic inheritance, cosmic or Urantian, will first be brought together at Planetary Headquarters, trained, and then sent as leaders to regather those with similar atavistic traits in relation to their respective cosmic inheritance. Every person on Urantia who is truly looking to serve their God and their fellow man, can only do so when they first find themselves. Those reservists, both cosmic and Urantian, who call themselves such, are commanded by their Universe Sovereign, Christ Michael, to be trained at the Starseed and Urantian Schools of Melchizedek under the direction of the present Planetary Prince, Machiventa Melchizedek, to whom they may give recognition, in order to truly find themselves and their own respective cosmic family.

The First Cosmic Family is the organizing vehicle of all the others and is the beginning melting pot which will always contain a mixture of the other six cosmic families that have existed on Urantia since the combining of human genetics with the Caligastia one hundred, and more specifically, in the intermarriage of many of the Caligastia one hundred with the evolutionary races of this planet. The proper procedure in rediscovering who you are in relation to the open circuits within your central circuit that connect to higher universe administration and planets, can and will be discovered only within that First Cosmic Family and its authority structure, human and nonhuman alike. All isolated starseed and Urantian reservists who claim such self-discovery are in continued rebellion to the mandates of Christ Michael and the Ancients of Days who have appropriated for this planet the safety that checks and balances can have for you within the framework of the human eldership of your own individual cosmic or Urantian ancestry. Within the context of proper authority and cosmic ancestry you will realize your fullest potential, for the structure within and outside, will begin to manifest for you as you recognize your elders and other cosmic relatives, and they recognize you. This mutual response resonates and activates latent potentials, traits and characteristics that only can be activated by mutual consent within the context of love, respect and loyalty to each other, to Christ Michael, the Universe Father and to the Universal Father of All, the originator of this plan of reflective recognition.

November 18, 1991

   Paladin, Finaliter; in cooperation with the Bright and Morning Star; your Planetary Prince, Machiventa Melchizedek, and the twelve Master Seraphim assigned specifically to actualize this paper; as transmitted through the Audio Fusion Material Complement, Gabriel of Sedona.

PAPER 217

DEO-ATOMIC TRIADS IN NUCLEAR STRUCTURE WITHIN THE ULTIMATON IN RELATION TO CELLULAR PHYSIOLOGICAL GENETICS INHERENT IN SOULS WHO ARE IN HARMONY WITH COSMOLOGIC VIBRATION PATTERN

This paper is an attempt to offer scientific analysis of certain physical cosmic facts as to force-energies of Paradise origin in fusion with cosmic anthropology within the structure of the union of souls and the various cosmic families from other universes now resident on Urantia. Within sociology on Urantia, and more particularly anthropology, the term nuclear family has come to be known as mother, father and children, and even some of the extended family who are closer to the first nuclear family have come to be included as part of it. The unseen but ever present ultimatons,* atoms and molecules function in a vast network of organization based upon the same criteria that on your human side you base your relationships, one to another. Those of you who flow best with one another are those who have like patterns of thinking and are more kindred of spirit in the ways in which you react to certain circumstances and other life situations. On a fallen world like Urantia, which has been so divided by corporate institutions, both religious and secular, oneness among individuals is based upon association due to outside circumstances and influences that have nothing to do with the divine mind. As you incorporate patterns of thinking within yourself, these energy patterns create messages within your physical body that either respond to a cosmologic vibration pattern within the divine mind or to confusion, nondivine pattern, disharmony and self-assertion. If they respond to the cosmologic vibration pattern, they begin to create within the ultimaton, a Deo-atomic structure which is, in itself, part of the divine Paradise Triad, of either the Father, the Son or the Infinite Spirit. Deo-atomic cells combat in many ways negative influences within the physical body, such as the digestion of poisons, the breathing of toxic air and viruses that attack your body inhibiting you from fulfilling the will of God that day. The more Deo-atomic cells that you have within your physical body, the more prepared you are to combat the forces of destruction against the will of God that confront your body daily. These Deo-atomic cells are created by will and thought. They are the unseen healers that come against all disease within the human body. They are as yet unmeasured by Urantian scientists, but quite observable on certain worlds of the morontia levels. They are so measurable that they can be captured one at a time or several hundred thousand at a time. They can be "packaged" and they can be artificially injected into even an unsuspecting life form. This has nothing to do with the reception of the Thought Adjuster. **Deo-atomic triads** become increasingly a part of the make-up of the morontia body and the first light body. First-time Urantians who attain the first mansion world bring with them only that part of themselves that has become Deo-atomic. As that person ascends, the Deo-atomic cells increase. As they increase, the body becomes less physical and more spiritual. They do not come easily. Even the highest ascending souls on Urantia, starseed and Urantians alike, decrease and completely annihilate these Deo-atomic triad cells whenever they begin to think improperly within the alignment of the Luciferic teachings or when they express attitudes or actions other than divine. A fit of inappropriate rage or anger can completely annihilate hundreds of Deo-atomic triads that perhaps you have attained in your total ascension process at any one time or on any one planet. Then it takes several days, or several weeks of Urantia time for realignment to cosmologic vibration patterns to recreate those Deo-atomic triads. Literally billions of Deo-atomic triads can inhabit the physical body at any one time. Each psychic circle you have attained and can remain on, brings to the chemistry of your body several million new Deo-atomic triad cells. Dozens can be added daily, reaching a maximum of one hundred a day, based upon a combination of will, mind and heart circuits in relation to the cosmologic vibration pattern of your universe, your Creator Son, and your higher comprehension of a universe spiritual science, which in the morontia worlds is called Ascension Science (Sci).

Ascension Sci is an understanding of your soul's relationship, first to your God and then to those of your genetic inheritance. Your physical reaction on any level, until you are pure spirit, affects the good of the whole nucleus (nuclear family), meaning your first mortal cosmic parents and your first mortal cosmic family. If you are an evolutionary mortal, your Ascension Sci genetics are based upon your relationships within that cosmic nuclear family and the Deo-atomic triad genetics that you have attained in relationship to both your God and the cosmic family in which God has placed you. You are who you are, based upon your Deo-atomic inheritance, as an atom is what it is, based upon its electrons and their velocity. If you misuse your talents and abilities outside of your cosmic family, which should be the nucleus of your reality, you become as an isolated amoeba needing again to rebuild the old atomic reality within yourself. That part of your ancestral genetic inheritance which remains in rebellion may only be enough to sustain your life form in subdued existence, but not in divine fulfillment. This is the state of most souls on Urantia, including the majority of the 170,000,000 starseed. To begin to recreate the Deo-atomic triad structure, one must begin to flow within the concept of Ascension Sci in relation to one's nuclear cosmic family.

Physical genetics, that which can be measured by known science, has nothing to do with the genetics of Ascension Si. This can only be measured by the higher order of Celestial Overcontrol, and these genetic inheritances are given under the criteria designated by the Life Carriers presently remaining on Urantia and the Chief of Seraphim coordinating with the other groups, of seraphim designations. That is why a first-time Urantian set of parents may have a starseed offspring. Everything which that offspring is in relation to Deo-atomic reality has nothing to do with the genetic inheritance of either parent. That which the child seems to incorporate within himself in thinking and action has more to do with sociological behavior and little to do with physical genetics. Physical genetics will have more to do with the physiological functions of the body itself and its reactions to foods and diet, and that is all. A starseed soul entering the womb of a mother who may be a new soul herself can be completely different, even in body form, from either mother or father if Universe Supervisors deem it so, and you may find that to be observable on Urantia. The union of male sperm and female egg to create life has nothing to do with the inheritance of Deo-atomic triad life. This inheritance is strictly obtained by souls themselves in their alignment to their God and to the cosmic family and union of souls with which they belong.

> *Nucleus*[17] (of cell): The large body embedded in the cytoplasm of all plant and animal cells (but not bacterial cells) that contains the genetic material DNA. The nucleus functions as the control center of the cell....

In order for individuals to find their nucleus, their center, their divine purpose, and also to inherit the genetic characteristics of their Deo-atomic ancestors' ascension, they must begin to align themselves in Ascension Sci fusion within their cosmic family.

> *Nuclear fusion*: A type of nuclear reaction in which atomic nuclei of low atomic number fuse to form a heavier nucleus with the release of large amounts of energy....

From the very beginning, it has been measured on all the rebellious planets of time and space that individual fulfillment for fallen entities can only come when they connect with Ascension Sci protoplasm. This begins creation, within the soul, of the Deo-atomic triads to combat deceptions and physical disease. The more individuals who do so on a mass level, the more the planet begins to come into the pre-stages of light and life within certain time periods. This may be a very slow process for the planet as a whole, taking thousands of years before the citizens of a planet reach the third psychic circle.

---

[17]Definitions are from *Concise Science Dictionary*.

Protoplasm: The granular material comprising the living contents of a cell, i.e. all the substances in a cell except large vacuoles and material recently ingested or to be excreted. It consists of a nucleus embedded in a jelly-like cytoplasm....

The same principle is at work in the Deo-atomic protoplasmic structure within the morontia body. It is just as measurable as the molecules within the blood system, and again, can only be obtained by right relationship with cosmic origin and ancestry. On twentieth-century Urantia, the majority of individuals find themselves in occupational positions based upon survival and materialistic endeavors. These positions, in which they spend at least eight hours a day of endeavor for at least five or six days a week, may increase their prestige, power, various lusts of the flesh, and even their pocketbooks, but for many millions, it can at best keep a roof over their heads and food on their tables. However, the misuse of their abilities in structures based upon greed and power cannot build the Deo-atomic triad cells within their higher bodies that are necessary to begin their Ascension Sci process of understanding on this planet. They are open to all the diseases on the planet that cause them severe pain and suffering. They place themselves in circumstances where they are caught in the tragedy of wars, famines and natural disasters. They, as individuals, cannot create within themselves that which is necessary for Ascension Sci to take place. (Please refer to nuclear fusion.)

Cosmic family and nuclear fusion in the Ascension Sci process is a power of light that can change the destiny of whole planets as to the reality of those planets, and upstep the evolutionary process of those planets by millions of years. Loyalty of light-workers cannot be bought for any price. It comes through the proper understanding of their place and destiny purpose within the ancestral family in which their Creator Son has placed them. The significance of Deo-atomic triad cells, pertaining to various universes in the incorporation of one particular third-dimensional body and fourth-dimensional morontia body and upwards, is immense in scope. The cosmic family that is functioning in complete harmony within a universe cosmologic vibration pattern can attain several million members at any one particular time, working together as one single unit. On older planets where progressive enlightenment has reached the first stages of light and life hundreds of millions of years ago, administration and family unity is beyond your scope of understanding. Slowly, as CFER comes to Urantia, you will begin to see the immensity of genetic inheritance and cosmic family structure within one nuclear cosmic family. At any one time, all of those millions of family members can be transported from a planet of light and life to a fallen world to work within the Divine Government to help stabilize that world and bring its rebellious inhabitants into the cosmologic vibration pattern of their particular universe. This can be done in a very physical manner, with the inhabitants of that world fully seeing the millions that have just been brought to govern. This procedure has taken place thousands of times throughout the seven superuniverses of time and space. Other ramifications of this process will be given in later papers. Deo-atomic triad cells which these individual beings have incorporated within themselves are at various levels in regard to morontia bodies within the universe of Nebadon. On Urantia, where the whole process of Ascension Sci and Deo-atomic reality are beginning to become known now, only a handful of humans benefit from this knowledge; but they can create within themselves the nucleus that can cause a fusion which can bring Deo-atomic realities to hundreds, thousands, and perhaps millions before the change point takes place, thereby easing the sufferings of all of them and even escaping the death process itself. When individuals become aware of Deo-atomic reality within themselves, those cells which they have already created by their own alignment with divine mind, become stronger, creating a synergy that connects with the Deo-atomic triad cells of those around them and closest to them in any one particular radius of one acre, one mile, three miles and five miles. Physical healings can take place increasingly on a third-dimensional world where diseases still exist, and these aligned individuals themselves create a form of protection, even outside of Celestial Overcontrol. They create a cosmic nuclear fusion which is quite real and physical, and the force energy that it puts out is an auhter energy which has now become measurable on Urantia because of the beginning alignment of the First Cosmic Family and the members therein. It is a fusion of the Deo-atomic structure of Father circuits, Son circuits and circuits of the Infinite Spirit on the level of the evolutionary worlds in the relationship of mortal to mortal as they find themselves within their respective cosmic families.

December 3, 1991

Paladin, Finaliter; in cooperation with the Life Carriers present on Urantia and visiting Life Carriers from several universes, primarily Avalon, who made this paper possible; in cooperation with Machiventa Melchizedek, present Planetary Prince; as transmitted through the Audio Fusion Material Complement, Gabriel of Sedona.

PAPER 218

APOSTLESHIP, DISCIPLESHIP AND FAITH BELIEVERS IN RELATION TO THE PRE-STAGES OF LIGHT AND LIFE AND THE ESTABLISHMENT OF THE MACHIVENTA GOVERNMENT USING HUMAN PERSONALITIES WITHIN RESPECTIVE MANDATES AS CHANGE AGENTS, AMBASSADORS, ASSISTANTS, WATCHERS AND CIRCLE GUARDIANS

Since the coming of starseed upon this planet, the use of them has been basically as reservists in some category in relation to their own ascension level and circle attainment. These reservists were both students and teachers of their fellow Urantians. Many of them, because of their soul growth, were able to reach high levels of leadership in the social and political structures of this planet, even though they were within their own modes of default, and didn't attain the spiritual status that they were capable of in any one particular repersonalization. When a fourth-circle attainment was reached, many of these starseed and first-time Urantians alike were able then to be designated under a certain category of kingdom usage; some as apostles, some as evangelists, some as teachers, some as pastors and some as elders, for the total edification of all those who in some way had connected with the Bestowal Son's Spirit of Truth on Urantia. Before Pentecost only limited appointments of titles were able to be given to certain starseed and Urantians. The first-century apostles (including Matthias and Paul) were a mixed group of starseed and Urantians. There were seven starseed and seven Urantians. Jesus himself picked six starseed first. The seventh starseed was not necessarily chosen for apostleship by divine mandate, but was accepted into such a category by the relegation of this appointment by Jesus to the other apostles, as was the case with the other six. In this manner, divine mandates can be chosen by man if power of choice is given by Overcontrol. In the case of the apostles, it was Michael himself who gave the other six apostles this authority. One of these apostles, Judas Iscariot, defaulted completely. Others had varying levels of imperfection. None of the twelve reached the human perfection of the Master. The seven starseed have been back on this planet several times as apostles, ambassadors, teachers, pastors and evangelists. They were used time and time again in different centuries, to be leaders within the ecclesia of Christ. Paul was chosen by divine mandate and was a Urantian. The apostles with Jesus who were first-time Urantians have come to Urantia again since 1934. In this century, the starseed apostles have repersonalized since the adjudication began in 1911.

160

Within the kingdom of God, when an ovan soul comes in through an apostle father, the son or daughter automatically receives apostleship status if this son or daughter does not default in his or her sojourn and destiny purpose. Apostleship is now more appropriately designated as "change agent." Change agents all have mandates of varying degrees and function in relation to the establishment of divine government principles on third-dimensional worlds moving into fourth-dimensional realities. On Urantia, where the consciousness of the masses is so divided in relation to the spiritual, the power of mandated change agents is limited to those who recognize who they are at the level necessary to create physical change through circumstance by the manipulation of matter, and by their soul growth and mental growth in relation to the Fifth Epochal Revelation. When the unseen Overcontrol Administration becomes visible, of course the human mandated personalities will become much more powerful in regard to obedience of human to human. Due to Luciferic reality, authority on Urantia is held by power and wealth, popularity or hero worship. In many cases throughout the worlds of time and space, divine authority is given according to the progression of souls in mutual understanding of reflectivity of higher spirit entities, and their own likeness to the perception of their God-reality. To a primitive man a first-century man may seem a god. To a first-century man, a fifteenth-century man may seem a god. What one perceives to be god-like, one worships, right or wrong.

Unfortunately, on Urantia incorrect perceptions give improper respect to nonmandated, self-appointed or man-appointed spiritual leaders. The status in the title of Change Agent or Divine New Order Apostle comes to those individuals who have earned it through trials and tribulations, not only in one lifetime perhaps, but in many repersonalizations. Older souls who are starseed and have been granted change agent status are souls of high authority in the kingdom, but it will only be after the change point that many of these change agents will totally realize the full power of their mandates. Change agents are pioneers. Pioneers are seldom understood by the masses. They are the beginning builders of the new epochal revelations, and usually they are persecuted by the very descendents who will later call them saints. In any one lifetime where the potential change agent and his or her cosmic family together have not reached the third psychic circle, even though they have been working together as apostles in the renaissances of Urantia or any other planet, the degree of power within that mandate is equal only to the degree that each potential change agent understands cosmic fact, truth and reality. When apostles reach the third circle together at any one time they become change agents. If this occurs with two brothers or more, then the stronger Father circuits can begin to be established through them to others, therefore, establishing on that planet of default an adjudication process at a more rapid rate and increasing soul-ascension teachings to those previously stuck in static spirituality. Also, ERCs are reestablished or stabilized so that cosmic ancestry can also communicate to whomever can bring in audio reception based upon that ovan soul's ascension and opposite sex polarity complements (which can be one or more within one particular lifetime). Complementary polarities of brother to brother can establish transfiguration circuits of visual rematerialization of cosmic ancestry and others, to certain degrees.

The apostle must first become a student of the walk of faith. The right livelihood of an apostle is first and foremost in bringing the kingdom of God and spiritual teachings therein to one's fellow mortals, on whatever world of the fallen thirty-seven where that person may be sojourning. That apostle will be provided for by Overcontrol and will not cease to exist from starvation or the elements unless that person defaults. That apostle may find him or herself in very unpleasant situations time and time again, lifetime after lifetime, until other members of his or her genetic heritage ascend together to the third circle and higher and they can be geographically joined together in the union of souls. Change agents will find their own destiny purpose very interrelated to their cosmic relatives. The physical circumstances of their lives will slowly become more pleasurable; and certain unused talents, abilities and wishes will begin to be actualized increasingly until all of the planet is in light and life.

The first one draws the second, the second the third, the third the fourth and so on, until dozens and then hundreds are drawn together, first in twos then in small groups in various locations on the planet. These small groups will then be drawn to the higher groups and will usually move to where their eldership and cosmic relatives are geographically located. If a Trinity Teacher Son* bestows on a planet where this has not begun to take place on any level, within a period of three to six weeks, one hundred fifty thousand to two hundred thousand genetically related souls will be joined geographically in any one particular sector on that planet. This was foreseen by John the Revelator, when he mentioned the number 144,000. He saw the coming together, not of the tribes of Israel, but of the First Cosmic Family and other families. Basically, these cosmic families are pilgrims from other universes who have found themselves repersonalized many times on Urantia for one reason or another. Some of these worlds are the Ursa Major, Centaurian and Pleiadian worlds. More correctly, they are the universes of Avalon, Fanoving and Wolvering. The appropriate match-up cannot be given at this time.

Those who function as disciples can be found in all walks of life on Urantia and usually have had to earn their living working in the Caligastia system, while they simultaneously function in some capacity to bring the message of Jesus as they know it. Many millions of disciples today are trapped in Christianity and in the Caligastia system, which limits the power of their individual mandates. If they could come out of their false churches they would find their right livelihood, whatever that may be, in the true ecclesia of their Divine New Order family of cosmic heritage, genetic linkage, or spiritual relationship. Disciples find themselves and their fulfillment and right livelihood because of the change agents who have gone before them and paved the way. If they cannot recognize these change agents (apostles), they will not find their destiny purpose and will have to transcend this planet by physical death. Many of these disciples, who do recognize these change agents and join their respective cosmic families, will become assistants, **watchers** and **circle guardians** and will no longer have to earn their living in the Caligastia system, even before the change point.

The wheel of Ezekiel is interrelated with the hierarchy that exists in the physical, morontial and spiritual. When ovan souls of fallen worlds begin to see true spiritual hierarchy and higher cosmic truth, their physical eyesight and clairvoyant perception can also see physical spacecraft and nonphysical beings if Overcontrol wishes them to be visible. In the later 1990's these phenomena will begin to take place at a more rapid rate for those who have the ears to hear what the Spirit of God is saying to the true ecclesia, and the eyes to see the spiritual kingdom of God being physically represented and set up by mandated human personalities. Then these mandated human personalities will be recognized by hundreds of thousands of the Divine New Order who have finally seen through the falsehoods of the chains with which others have bound them.

Millions on Urantia claim to follow Christ. Let those who read this paper and who make that claim follow the true Christ, Michael of Nebadon, above all else, and then you too can be chosen by Overcontrol to become the change agents, ambassadors, assistants, watchers and circle guardians necessary to bring true change on Urantia, and the establishment of the New Jerusalem in which the Divine Government can come through myself, Machiventa Melchizedek, and which will function for all the seeds of Urantia, and from other planets. If you call yourself an ambassador, then you must choose your ambassadorship based upon the laws of Christ Michael and the Universal Father instead of the interpretation of those laws by man. True ambassadorship is for divine purpose and no man can place you in this position of divine function. In the Divine New Order you will find this ambassadorship within the cosmic family of your genetic inheritance. Outside of this ancestry you are a rebel, and the time has come on Urantia that all rebels will suffer the consequences of their arrogance and pride. As all higher spiritual unions are in complement to one another, the appointment of Machiventa Melchizedek in the human personality is in complement with that of the Bright and Morning Star, with cosmic brother to brother, cosmic sister to sister, cosmic father to son, cosmic mother to daughter, cosmic uncle to nephew, cosmic aunt to niece and on down the line, respective of that individual's ascension status and title earned. It is the way of reality on all the worlds of time and space.

If you do not understand much of what has been said in this paper, you are then quite outside of the reality in which you should be. If you are beginning to understand this paper at some level, you are beginning to walk into a reality that is necessary for your next level of attainment and prospective mansion world assignment. If you come to the conclusion that any of this paper is foolishness, then you are in grave danger; and I pray that you humble yourself and truly seek your God above man and man's social badge of acceptance, for you may soon meet the Ancients of Days who will personally read this paper to you and remind you of the very moment in time when you rejected it! The divine Father/God and his hand can be very sensitive and soothing, gentle and caressing. It can also be quite disciplinary when you need it. It is your choice. Choose wisely.

December 23, 1991

Machiventa Melchizedek, present Planetary Prince of Urantia; in cooperation with the Bright and Morning Star in the adjudication process on Urantia; as transmitted through the Audio Fusion Material Complement, Gabriel of Sedona.

PAPER 219

PRE-THOUGHT-ADJUSTER FUSION AND POST-SOUL AND SPIRIT FUSION IN RELATION TO SOUL IDENTITY FUNCTION IN RESPECT TO UNIVERSE OF ORIGIN AND COORDINATING DEO-ATOMIC ANCESTRAL INHERITANCE

In each universe of time and space where a new soul has reached the equivalent of the first mansion world of Nebadon in accordance with the ascension process of that Creator Son, personality coordinated with spirit and soul reflects a certain identity function corresponding to the Paradise Trinity* in Deo-atomic reflectivity. The soul itself becomes an ovan. An ovan soul is a soul which has reached survival status from any preceding evolutionary world or dimension in which it has experienced its first existence. It may have physically gained an ascending son or an ascending daughter status, and depending upon the ovan Deo-atomic inheritance of what it has incorporated of the threefold Paradise circuit in its understanding of God, that soul will be identified on the first mansion world as to its beginning ovan circuitry to the Paradise origin. The designation of an ovan soul's body form in relationship to physical male or female reproductive organs will also depend upon its universe of origin. In some universes an ovan soul has the ability to be reproductive, although it always remains either an ascending son or an ascending daughter. The classification of its ovan status has nothing to do with the physical body given to that ovan. Each universe is unique, and within any one particular universe the identity function of a particular soul is measured, not upon the creative abilities of the Creator Son and that Creator Son's creation, but upon the Eternal Son and the circuits that the individual ovan soul has to the Eternal Son circuit which is spirit identification. Thus we speak of every surviving mortal as an ovan soul, who has become linked more closely with either the Universal Father, the Eternal Son or the Infinite Spirit by free-will choice and gained a personal understanding of his or her Creator.

Where procreation ceases on beginning mansion worlds, organs of identification in the physical body of its previous existence are removed. The **uniform** body remains very visibly male or female in the ascension process as does the ovan soul in its repersonalizations. However, the ovan soul may more functionally be connected to a particular circuit because of Deo-atomic inheritance which does not fully resonate with its repersonalized body form or organ reality. On many planets an imbalance between ovan reality and the proper relationship with physical reality creates a race of uni-form personalities who are not properly matched with the original purpose of each individual soul within the master plan of the First Creator and Eternal Father. Where ovan souls have found themselves on such planets, they have a difficult time in normal male and female relationships on third-dimensional worlds as ascending sons or daughters. Only when the Eternal Son can be more properly identified within the ascending mortal son, through the bestowal of The Comforter within that ovan soul, or the circuitry connection of the ascending daughter with the Infinite Spirit circuit, can the actual representation of proper Deo-atomic cellular structure be implanted within that ovan soul in balance. Full well knowing the Deo-atomic structure of ovan souls, Lucifer created a conceptual disharmony, misunderstanding and imbalance on the thirty-seven worlds of Satania which spread to other isolated planets in Nebadon and to other planets in other universes closely associated in interplanetary marriage among ascending mortals who do procreate in their higher body forms.

The 170 million starseed on Urantia have ovan identification. This identity function began with individuals when survivor status was granted to them regardless of their rebellious nature. Because of their ancestral genetic inheritance, their molecular physical make-up far surpasses the lower strains of the evolutionary races on Urantia.

That which the body is composed of on Urantia is a product of that which is available to the physical controllers and certain archangels, and designates the height, metabolism, skin color and certain diseases which individuals may develop within their normal life span on Urantia. If certain other Deo-atomic cells are not incorporated within that body to counterbalance the unseen disease viruses that are not detected by modern science, that body will inherit the diseases of its ancestors. That is why the Bible states that the sins of the fathers are inherited from one generation to another up to the third and fourth generation, and that is why some innocent children are born with defective bodies. The soul within the body may be an ovan soul and a starseed. These souls within bodies of such deformity are, of course, brought into this planet for special purposes; either for the ovan soul itself which is quite iniquitous or near extinction, or just the opposite, where, in many cases, the soul is allowed to come into such a body so that it can in some way minister to the human parents, brothers, sisters or guardians. Where the parents of deformed babies are completely out of the will of God in their individual lives, it will be determined at one point in the pregnancy if that child will be an ovan soul who will be more closely linked with one or the other of the parents, or if that child will be a first-time Urantian and inherit the deformed body that its human parents have designed for it because of their rebellion to God and to the principles of absolute truth. The variables involved as to the choice of what ovan soul will be given or if the child will be a first-time Urantian are of great magnitude. The race commissioners, in relationship with soul progressors and the Bright and Morning Star himself, make a decision and bring their decisions to Christ Michael, who either agrees or disagrees. An ovan soul who may be quite pleasant in personality may be quite out of balance in identity function in relation to its own status as an ascending son or daughter. A certain number, upwards at times of one hundred thousand to a half million, within a twenty-five year Urantian time period, may repersonalize into deformed bodies so that they can gain ovan identity as to their origin status as an ascending son or daughter. A life of seeming trial, tribulation and pain on Urantia, which may be from five to twenty-five or more years on average, can elevate that ovan soul to the seventh-stage morontia worlds of Nebadon, bypassing several hundred years of Urantia time, of ovan growth. At a point in the morontia progression which is unrevealed at this time, an ovan soul can decide on that particular course of ascension growth, not only for its own rapid ascension but for the sake of others that it will influence. As with many ovan souls, some memory circuits are blocked and previous abilities are forgotten, but in some instances, seeming miracles occur where former artists, who in this particular lifetime do not have the use of their hands, can paint a masterpiece using their mouth or their feet, or can learn to play a complicated instrument such as a violin, with little dexterity of fingers, or with missing or deformed fingers. It is the ovan soul's ability to remember its higher capabilities and use existing body parts, which proves to the keen observer of ascension processes, that spiritual cellular reality and Deo-atomic inheritance transform and manipulate physical handicaps in the third dimension. Moving into the first stages of light and life, many ovan souls and first-time Urantian souls alike, who begin to understand the reasons why they are in a deformed body, can create within themselves the morontia light body which can completely heal them of their physical diseases. This is possible now on Urantia because universe and superuniverse circuits are now responding to the ovan souls on Urantia who have realigned themselves with the purposes of the Universe Father of Nebadon and the Eternal Father of All, and the cosmic laws of their respective universes of sojourn.

When the establishment of the First Cosmic Family becomes a reality on any fallen planet, great administrative changes by Celestial Overcontrol begin to be administered to that planet. Thus on Urantia, the mandate of the Bright and Morning Star was given to an ovan soul who has proven himself in other repersonalizations and has been used in previous spiritual renaissances of Urantia. The cosmic brothers, sisters, sons and daughters of that soul, who have also proven themselves loyal to Christ Michael and the purposes of the Universal Father, will also be given mandates of the Bright and Morning Star. The identification of these souls in ovan identity function to the Father/Mother circuits, establishes a closer link with Urantia and Salvington, the capital of Nebadon. Because of the ascension of these individuals and others of the First

Cosmic Family to fourth-dimensional realities and CFER, they have established the reconnection of universe circuits and have enabled the return of Machiventa Melchizedek and the overcontrol of the Bright and Morning Star, with personal visitations from the Bright and Morning Star in executive capacity with the Planetary Prince in a frequency of visitation which has previously been unheard of. In the universe of Nebadon, the Bright and Morning Star seldom visits evolutionary worlds in this capacity. Because of the personal visitations of the Bright and Morning Star, and the present alignment of five or more ovan souls representative of the First Cosmic Family, an ERC has been established that is a transport circuit and a broadcast circuit, not only from Salvington to Urantia; but at a point in time if all the first-century apostles of Michael have regathered and stabilized on the first psychic circle, or 12 others on the first psychic circle, besides Gabriel of Sedona, or 100 others on the third circle, it will be a broadcast link from Uversa direct to Urantia. At that time one of the Ancients of Days will be able to speak directly through Gabriel of Sedona, who has the mandate of the Bright and Morning Star. We, at our level, pray for this event and look forward to the opening of these circuits.

As it is in the outworking of the master plan of the Eternal Father, it is always he who supplies the canvas, the Michael Son who supplies the paint and the Universe Mother who supplies the brushes; but it is the free-will choice of those aligned with the eternal purposes of the Father of All that creates the masterpiece and the reality. Individual ovan souls who have reached the higher circles of attainment as to their own identity function and destiny purpose, create the auhter energy that will draw the other higher ovan souls who may presently be quite unsuspectingly attracting a portion of the Lucifer manifesto that they themselves think they are not a part of. They have been allowed to fall into these hidden entrapments up until now, for they have to see just how easy it is to be deceived and just how powerful Lucifer is in his distortions of cosmic reality and how easy it is for people to be right in their own eyes and comfortable in their own view of spiritual reality. What is truth? Perhaps it can be more properly identified as an ever expanding elastic band which can stretch even into the outer levels of the master universe, but which begins its stretching process in the palms of the hands of an individual ovan soul who has first discovered God, or rediscovered him, on a defaulted and backward world such as Urantia.

December 30, 1991

Paladin, Finaliter; in cooperation with a Divine Counselor for the adjudication of Urantia; and in cooperation with Machiventa Melchizedek, present Planetary Prince; as transmitted through the Audio Fusion Material Complement, Gabriel of Sedona.

PAPER 220

THE COSMIC FAMILY IN RELATION TO GENETIC INHERITANCE IN RESPECT TO THE MALE AND HIS VARIOUS FEMALE COMPLEMENTS IN PROCREATION WHICH INFLUENCES THE UNION OF SOULS AND GROUP DYNAMICS, CREATING AUHTER ENERGIES WHICH TRANSCEND NEGATIVE INFLUENCES CAUSED BY REBELLION AND LOWER-CIRCLE CONSCIOUSNESS IN THE ASCENSION PROCESS TO PARADISE

On Urantia there is a saying, "Birds of a feather flock together." It is understood by the students of nature, and in particular of insect and animal life, that the group colonies corporately, can miraculously overcome great obstacles and perform seeming miracles, whereas they, as individuals have little or no power or even high intelligence. The ant seems to function in a higher vibration of intelligence when it is connected to its colony and has found its own individual place within it. These individuals together function as a single unit, and if dispersed by unnatural circumstances, the sole objective of each individual is to find its respective place within the particular function of the colony that has just been disrupted. If the complete function has been disrupted then a second sensor is activated and that directs it to find its queen. If it can, it would then be balanced enough to find itself again in its destiny purpose for that level of the evolutionary process. Many of the creatures of the air find themselves quite naturally in flight together at certain seasons. There seems to be something that calls each individual to join its own kind and to go in a certain direction. Scientists have long sought to discover why, and to measure these things. Various theories have developed as they have also tried to measure sea life and the very same instinctual habits exhibited therein. In the evolution of these animals, at what point were certain patterns set in motion? Has it always been so? Or are certain patterns of behavior brought about by the need for survival of the species; and if so, if survival is based upon group compatibility and cooperation, what is it in the human family which presents quite a different sense of corporate dependency? Is the instinct of an animal the same as that of a clairvoyant or the extrasensory perception of an individual?

Taking into consideration the normal evolutionary process of a planet within a particular system, constellation, universe, minor or major sector of a superuniverse that has not fallen to a rebellion of any kind, under the particular mandates of that particular Creator Son, a certain Deo-atomic coding is inherited from an evolutionary male mortal, through the sperm entering the egg of the female and then mixed with that of the female, based upon her Deo-atomic structure, her universe of origin, and her ascension level, which then creates the fetus. If the soul is an ovan soul it brings with it the Deo-atomic structures of its cosmic parents. If the soul is a brand new one it inherits, at that very moment, the Deo-atomic structure of its first cosmic family. Each time an ovan soul is repersonalized through a different mother or father who are not of its original cosmic parents, it inherits the positive Deo-atomic genetics of its new parents. It also inherits negative malfunctioning **diotribes** which are the opposite of the Deo-atomic cells in relation to Paradise Trinity personality. A personality bestowal of the Father is a fusion of the Universal Father, Eternal Son and Infinite Spirit consisting of Deo-atomic molecular structure. The complete activation of this personality bestowal in the actualization of the ascension process is an eternal quest, not finding its actualization until finality status. So when, on a lower evolutionary world, you speak of a mature personality you are, in fact, speaking of an infantile fusion of personality and soul. The cosmic maturation process is dependent upon:

1. The individual's first cosmic parents and their ascension status.
2. The ascension status of each parent of the repersonalized ovan soul.
3. The ovan soul's individualized ascension status.
4. The genetics and the Deo-atomic inheritance of various wives or husbands with whom each individual has procreated.
5. Continued sexual union of male and female procreation with either a higher complementary polarity or one influenced by lower diotribes.
6. The holistic health of the individual body, mind and spirit.

All children are the eternal responsibilities of the first cosmic parents, regardless of their many repersonalizations; and they are furthermore the first responsibility of the cosmic father over and above that of the mother, who has a certain set of responsibilities which will be further discussed in upcoming transmissions. Depending upon the female complementary polarity, the seed of that couple are designated in **pair-unit classifications**. Each of these children will inherit a particular original personality and form based on the first cosmic parents, which reflects the Universal Father, Eternal Son and Infinite Spirit at that particular moment in time in which he or she first became a potential mortal soul within the womb of a mortal mother, an ascending daughter. There are many ovan souls who look alike in some way and have the same personality traits but may be from different nationalities, even different races. Human genetics alone do not account for these similarities. It is entirely the result of the Deo-atomic inheritance in relation to their first cosmic family parents.

One of the reasons why supermortals are not to procreate with evolutionary mortals is that a personality can be so opposite in polarity that a child can become a genius in one area and quite retarded in another. On Urantia this has been the case because of the default of Adam and Eve and the fall of the previous Caligastia sixty. The higher Deo-atomic cells will create the astral body, which will in turn create, in the fetus and throughout the early formative years, its physical features in the third-dimensional body and, even furthermore, into the morontial levels of bodies. Therefore, those individuals who come to discern Deo-atomic physical structures and even diotribe physical structures will be able to ascertain with a higher capability certain universe-origin races and certain rebellious races and each level of their individual ascension/birth status, based solely upon certain present personality features and the higher understanding of the status of their original cosmic parents, with the full knowledge of each parent's total personality status upon that child's moment of birth.

On Urantia, if the soul is of the evolutionary mortals alone and has not repersonalized and ascended to the first mansion world or above, it was born in either the pre-Planetary Prince era, the Planetary Prince era, the postrebellion era, the Adam and Eve era, the post-default era of Adam and Eve, the Melchizedek era, or the post-Bestowal Son era in relation to the reception of his Spirit of Truth. Each era is significant on this planet in that the parents of the child born will give that child Deo-atomic inheritance based upon their understanding of the higher spirit realities recognized at the particular time of the child's birth. On planets where rebellion has not occurred, dispensational eras flow quite naturally into the stages of light and life and so does the personality bestowal of the Eternal Father. The acquisition of higher personality attainment on these planets far surpasses what has been available on Urantia, with the exception of the starseed personalities who have procreated with cosmic wives or husbands time and time again, for these cosmic mates have always been reservists and always have been destined to meet, mate and procreate. For many reasons, all too complicated to get into at this time, the majority of them have not been able to stay together, and divorce has been commonplace among starseed as well as first-time Urantians. Many of the starseed males in other universes have had many wives with whom they have procreated. On these planets it is the norm, and marriage as it is known on Urantia, as well as child raising, is quite different. Child raising there is the responsibility of the group and not just the parents. Urantia, being a planet of mixed starseed from other systems and universes as well as Urantians, has had a very difficult time in its social structures and family units. The various races are mixed with higher starseed Deo-atomic structures within individuals who try to fit into the lower evolutionary realities which their cosmic ancestors had long since outgrown. Therefore, they find themselves in a constant battle between what they desire and what they have to live with within the present set of circumstances in which, in most cases, they have found themselves to be a victim. At this time on Urantia, it is impossible for the higher starseed personalities to realize the total actualizations of their personality bestowals, their latent abilities and their higher mindal capacities. Therefore, they live in every day conflict and unfulfillment.

Within the stages of light and life it is prearranged, first by the Eternal Father and then by his personality creations at various levels, that certain groups and cosmic family members find themselves within sector governments and corporate families, functioning for the total good of that colony or sector tribe. On planets where default has not occurred, these sector tribes consist of the first cosmic parents and anywhere from 100,000 to 500,000 of their offspring. Small cities consist of one cosmic extended family, each individual knowing his or her inheritance, place and destiny within that sector government and corporate family; and most importantly, there is a union of souls within the overall corporate plan of the Divine Mind and Eternal Father. Within these sector tribes there are groups within groups, with heads of groups. The designation of the function of these groups is dependent upon the individual planets within each individual system and universe; but no matter what superuniverse or universe you are from, there is always a commonality. This commonality is an inward reality based upon the bestowal personality of the Eternal Father and each individual's acquiescence to that personality, and the group consciousness which precedes any individual's relationship. Group policy, group compatibility, group functioning, group dependency, group identification, group activation and even group diversification depends upon the totality of that group in relation to the personality of the Eternal Father. This higher energy field created by the joining or rejoining of families or groups is called auhter energy and is quite measurable by higher beings. Each group within the sector tribe is appointed by Overcontrol to have a certain administrative authority based upon that group's connection to the Father circuits, Eternal Son circuits and the Infinite Spirit circuits, based upon the first Eternal Father's personality bestowal. In this kind of reality among ascending sons and daughters a Paradise Son, such as Immanuel, can become a personal counselor and liaison minister, using as a contact personality the first cosmic ascending son who would always have the mandate of the Bright and Morning Star, and would also be able to visualize through a full First Ambassador with the mandate of Machiventa Melchizedek.[18] If, at some point in time and space, Machiventa Melchizedek would become visible to certain mortals, then Immanuel may choose to visualize and even rematerialize in some form himself at any one moment in time in order to counsel with the eldership. He may choose then to transfigure through the Planetary Prince himself, which would be a stronger materialization of his spirit presence rather than using an evolutionary mortal with that mandate.[19]

In order for this kind of Paradise visitation to actualize, the group reality would have obtained twelve members of the First Cosmic Family on the first psychic circle and seventy-two individual offspring in any relationship with the First Cosmic Family or any cosmic families, all together within a radius of five miles. The seventy-two must all be on the third circle. On planets that are in the first stages of light and life and above, this is the reality. On Urantia it is the goal. Universe differences are always superseded by superuniverse commonality of Havona reality and Paradise absolutes.

On Urantia one of the greatest problems in relation to the attainment of absolute truth, which is Paradise reality, is the relationships of men and women in spiritual unions, marriage and procreation. One of the primary reasons for giving CFER on Urantia now and on into the twenty-first century is for the awakening of interuniversal cultures to be appropriated on this decimal planet. It must begin first with a certain group of individuals who have reached the higher circles of attainment in mind, in Deo-atomic molecular structure in ovan souls and in the fusion of these personalities within the first sector tribe (which is presently on Urantia) within the government of the present Planetary Prince, Machiventa Melchizedek, geographically located at Planetary Headquarters on Urantia, where he resides. Furthermore, there are human personalities who are mandated by Celestial Overcontrol to organize the regathering of the First Cosmic Family so that the other cosmic families can be found, organized and trained in order to become functional on this planet. Each cosmic family has a job to do and each cosmic family is dependent upon the First Cosmic Family to succeed and not default.

If you, who read this paper understand its contents at a level high enough to cause a stir within your soul, then perhaps there is an activation of higher circuits happening within you, circuits that have been closed perhaps since the Caligastia rebellion. The universe circuits are opened first to individuals and to ovan souls like yourself and the other 170,000,000 ovan souls upon this planet who CFER is meant to reach prior to the change point. At whatever level you do comprehend part of this paper, you can be led into a higher destiny purpose for the good of all mankind on Urantia. There are many groups on this planet with which you can choose to unite, according to the level of your spiritual

---

[18]As of this date June 22, 1995, Amadon is the leading candidate to become a full First Ambassador.

[19]At the time of editing this second edition, July, 1995, no evolutionary mortal has that mandate.

acquiescence, the level of your personality attainment and your relationship to the Eternal Father. So be it!

January 13, 1992

Paladin, Chief of Finaliters on Urantia; in cooperation with Life Carriers of Nebadon, Avalon, Wolvering and Fanoving in the adjudication of Urantia; in cooperation with Machiventa Melchizedek, the present Planetary Prince of Urantia; as transmitted through the Audio Fusion Material Complement, Gabriel of Sedona.

PAPER 221

MORTAL PAIR-UNIT CLASSIFICATION IN RELATION TO PROCREATION IN ANCESTRAL LINKAGE TO MATERIAL SONS AND DAUGHTERS OR OTHER UNREVEALED BREEDING PERSONALITIES AND THEIR PLANETARY ADMINISTRATIVE FUNCTIONS IN DIVINE GOVERNMENT ADMINISTRATION

Mortal pair-unit classification is a classification of ascending sons and daughters who are complementary polarities and mating pairs and is divided into three divisions with eleven subdivisions. Division one has four subdivisions, division two has two, and division three has five. The status of a couple's pair-unit classification is always in relationship to the ascending son and it is outlined accordingly with three divisions, which are:

1. Time-space location
2. Reality level
3. Ovan soul ascension level

In classification these three divisions are to be abbreviated in relation to respective interuniversal language. Urantian English may differ with morontia mota language, but conceptual understanding is the same. Let's take time-space location, using as an example, Amadon and Teantra. Before we give classification to this pair unit we will now give the eleven subdivisions. Abbreviations are given in parenthesis.

DIVISION I: Time-space Location

Superuniverse	(SU)
Universe	(U)
System	(S)
Planet[20]	(P)

---

[20]This is always the male's planet of origin unless otherwise noted on the right of the planet's name.

175

DIVISION II: Reality Level
    Light and Life Stages/Planetary Epochs   (LL/PE)
    Dimension   (D)

DIVISION III: Ovan Soul Ascension Level
    Survival Status   (SS)
    Psychic Circle   (PC)
    Spiritual   (S)

    Emotional   (E)
    Physical   (P)

Amadon and Teantra   Teantra (separated unit)
    (**R**epersonalizations **T**ogether) RT-0

DIVISION I: Time-space Location
    SU Orvonton   "
    U   Nebadon   "
    S   Satania   "
    P   Urantia   "

DIVISION II: Reality Level
    PE Planetary Prince   "
    D   3rd   "

DIVISION III: Ovan soul ascension level
    SS Thought Adjuster   "
    PC 3rd (upon meeting)   4th (ending)
    S   2nd stage of 4th dimension   "
    E   Bonded   "
    P   Children 16 R.P.E.   "
    (All will be **R**epersonalizing in **P**resent **E**ra on Urantia)

Classification of other mortal pair units with differences in many subdivisions:

Gabron and Neese (pronounced Nee-see) Neese (separated unit) RT-6

DIVISION I
SU	Orvonton	"
U	Avalon	Fanoving
S	Chocca	Unrevealed
P	Valmar Minor (upon meeting)	Valmar Minor

DIVISION II
LL	Pre-stages of Light & Life	"
D	4th	"

DIVISION III
SS	Thought Adjuster	"
PC	1st (upon mating)	"
S	4th stage, 4th dimension	"
E	Bonded	"
P	Children 25 (by 6th repersonalization)	"
	4 R.P.E. (**R**epersonalized, Urantia, **P**resent **E**ra)	

Manto and Beea   Beea (separated unit) RT-7

DIVISION I
SU	Orvonton	"
U	Wolvering	Avalon
S	Laconis	Tasmania
P	Loor (met in Centaurian system)	Spinx

DIVISION II
LL	Pre-stages of Light & Life	"
D	3rd	"

DIVISION III
SS	Thought Adjuster	"
PC	5th (upon meeting)	4th
S	7th stage, 3rd dimension	"
E	Bonded	"
P	Children 62 (by 7th repersonalization)	"
	5 R.P.E.	

Depending on the variations within Division I in time-space location, the cultural differences of inherent Deo-atomic reality, and in many cases physical coordination in respect to body form, physical appetites and visual preferences can be vast. On a planet like Urantia, where the evolutionary races of one human mortal species have developed the physical aspect of relationships of pair-unit classification, this is both instinctual and learned. On worlds where different body forms are integrated among ascending mortals and where there may be mortals of different species, human and nonhuman, the visual coordination with physical likes and dislikes is triggered in the nervous system in relation to learned behavior respective of that ovan soul's point of origin. On some planets you would be quite surprised at pair relationships in different physical structures. As long as procreation is a physical reality on these planets, body preference is a nonemotional thing. Spiritual compatibility usually is not evident until the pre-stages of light and life; and within the third dimension and above, it does not become quite evident in relationships until the seventh stage of the third dimension. Higher emotional bonding between pair units is indigenous to worlds where the Thought Adjuster, the Spirit of Truth and the Holy Spirit are coordinated within the individual ovan soul or first-time personality. Primitive humans in pre-Thought Adjuster reality mate and procreate based strictly upon instinctual and survival reality. Spiritual and emotional reality is void in their thinking process. On other planets where the intellectual has reached the higher stages of development, but spiritual attainment is not evident, emotional bonding is an unknown factor. In some Centaurian worlds emotional relationships are unknown. In the master plan of the Divine Mind we can only speculate as to this phenomenon, and within this speculation, now in my own process, there are volumes written by ones like myself, as to when the Spirit of Truth will be given to Centaurian candidates who have not left their point of origin.

There is also much speculation regarding the higher activation of the bestowal of the Infinite Spirit by the Universe Mother Spirit, when this bestowal will be given to a world which does not have it, and perhaps why it is activated in a person who has the Thought Adjuster fragment but who does not have the Spirit of Truth. Here we have an individual and a world connected to the Father and Infinite Spirit circuits of Paradise origin without the circuit of the Son. On worlds where this is commonplace, and there are millions, this situation will determine the physical development of a third-dimensional body or below. This does not hinder mindal development as one might think, but it does change the personality quotas in relation to the Paradise Absolute. In these cases, the reality is sub-absolute and the sub-absolute is a becoming absolute in physical body form; and in Nebadon, and particularly in Satania, it is to become a morontia body, which is the standard body form because of the Satania **oversoul** body classification in biped construction. The term oversoul in this context means a similarity within morontia physics, in relation to the ovan soul in semi-physical form relating to every ascending son or daughter from the first mansion world body to the last morontia body. It is visibly identified and mathematically precise. Therefore, what you know as human mortal form, even in the higher stages of spirit acquiescence, continues to be your body form and structure, although devoid in these stages of all procreative organs. It is commonplace when ascending sons or daughters reach a certain spiritual status within the ovan soul, having been in several time-and-space locations other than Nebadon (and even in Nebadon, upon approval of the System Sovereign), that they can very easily transform their body reality to any body form lower than their present earned ascension status. Therefore, in cases of educational, or certain training assignments, they can interact on interplanetary worlds quite easily without being recognized if they choose not to be or, if ordered not to be. As long as their material bodies have sex organs, they can and do procreate with other planetary species upon the need of that planet for these relationships to take place within interplanetary citizenship. This is all based upon the state of the planet and its evolutionary process and its respective ascension process correlated with the Creator Son.

The variables involved in the molecular cellular structure within the Ascension Sci process when these interplanetary marriages take place, is a science called **interplanetary decimal mating**. On Urantia it is done in a physical manner in the normal process of dispensational evolutionary schedules with the offspring of the Material Son and Daughter. On other planets and other universes it is done with other unrevealed personalities having the same function as Material Sons and Daughters. Some of these personalities are human mortals, others are not. Present on Urantia, in human mortal bodies, are an unrevealed number of these personalities consisting of both men and women. All of them are the offspring of certain mortal pair units who are their cosmic parents of origin, and who may or may not be with them on Urantia at this time. The repersonalization of these unrevealed personalities on Urantia throughout the last 200,000 years has helped to keep the Deo-atomic coding of the higher strains of the interuniversal and intrauniversal Material Sons and Daughters and other mating personalities together and balanced in coordination, so that higher mindal capabilities and spiritual acquiescence can be accomplished on Urantia, all under the supervision of the race commissioners, and the Chief of Seraphim, and certain finaliters, including myself. Although marriages on the emotional level are not made in heaven, genetic relationships are indeed the design of these higher celestial personalities and within the divine plan of the Divine Mind, which then creates spiritual mating complements.

When the sperm of any male is received by a female there is a chemical reaction and a cellular transference which can be a healing process to both, or it can be just the opposite. This is based upon Division III ovan soul ascension status. On the physical level, when the two individual personalities are basically on survival status alone, procreation is a necessity for race survival and no damage is done to the soul nor to the mind. But, in higher levels where the emotional bonding takes place and spiritual bonding is at levels necessary for Deo-atomic inheritance, sexual cohabitation can result in the receiving of diotribes which, if sexual cohabitation is a continuing thing, will result in a confused equilibrium within the physical, emotional and spiritual bodies. An ovan soul who cohabits with a primitive human can bring healing to that primitive individual in many ways. It can also so restructure the cellular patterns of the personality that it can actually kill. This is why cohabitation by higher personalities is strictly warned against in visitations to certain planets. Where cohabitation is based upon physical preferences alone on a third-dimensional level lower than the sixth stage, both of these individuals will suffer, and in reality be trapped into stagnant spirituality; and it is unlikely that either individual will enter the fourth dimension unless a change in relationship occurs. Upon the reception of certain diotribes from the more negative individual, diseases will manifest in the physical body. This is why, on Urantia, many physical diseases cannot be totally cured as long as Urantians and ovan souls remain in relationships of inappropriate pair-unit classification. On Urantia, where the 170 million starseed exist in various pair-unit classifications, and they have not come into their own individual highest reality in Division III classification status, disease is prevalent.

When divine government begins to manifest upon a planet and the first stages of light and life become a reality, the first thing that is done by divine mandate is the separation of mortal personalities, male and female, who are not classified equally. To the extent that spiritual differences exist in ovan reality, so does disease exist within the spiritual and physical body, and an individual cannot be cured completely until such separation takes place, so that the one cannot receive diotribes from the other. If individuals in improper pair-unit classifications are alive on planet Urantia, they are then sent directly to planets of like classification. Those awakened from the sleep state at the time of the adjudication of the sleeping survivors will also be sent to their respective classification planet. The thirty-six other fallen planets of Satania are not the only planets where these classifications exist, there are several thousand other planets in other universes that have not reached the stages of light and life as a system, where these ovan souls can be sent. Again, we are not talking about first-time Urantians, although we may be talking about second-time Urantians because of the adjudication process of Urantia since 1911.

Just as the Deo-atomic cells vibrate and resonate with Paradise circuits, diotribe cells resonate with Luciferic reality. Luciferic reality has no place in the first stages of light and life. Any diotribe cells among the perhaps billions of cells within one body can be easily detected by the race commissioners and seraphim. Upon the physical manifestation of Divine Government upon any planet where this occurs, we cannot take the cell out of that individual but must take that individual out of the planet. Your free will allows that cell to remain there, and just one diotribe within the individual, consisting of several billion cells, will prevent that individual from entering the first stages of light and life on that planet. Thus it is their own individual free-will choice in time-and-space lag and time-space reality level, which will remove them from the physical location of their presently earned physical body. The rest of the planet, and the individuals on it, will inherit morontia bodies devoid of any diotribe cells. Personalities who have continued in sinful and iniquitous ways may perhaps have hundreds of thousands of diotribes within them. Just one of these diotribes can cause any number of physical diseases and stop certain brain mechanisms from working. The relation of the central nervous system to cellular structure and brain wave patterns is pertinent to spiritual ascension at the third psychic circle and above when we speak of full brain capacity. The full use of the brain is prohibited by improper spiritual thinking in relation to cosmic fact and cosmic law. It is written, "You are what you think." It is not just written in the books of Urantia per se, but in the books of Paradise. The mercy ministers function in time and space based upon dispensational schedules and the time lag of justice. On Urantia the mercy dispensation is the ending of an era. Any diotribe cells that are found at any time-space location out of the trillions and trillions that may be found in any individual, will cause that person to be removed at a certain predesignated time. It begins when an adjudication takes place between the head administrator of any one particular universe and those rebelling forces who started the diotribe reality, and it ends in an instant of time in accordance with the schedule of time-lag mercy justice. On Urantia it began in 1911. The ending may be sooner than you think, and when it ends it will do just that, END. If there is one diotribe cell found within the billions of cells in your body, you will be removed from this planet.

Higher celestial personalities can enter a third-dimensional plane through an ERC where Deo-atomic cells are resonating together and which can be seen hundreds of thousands of light years away by ascending mortals using higher technological telescopes. The auhter energy produced by these Deo-atomic unions can also be seen by higher celestial personalities as flashes of white light millions of light years away, even in Havona. This auhter energy is now beginning to be seen on Urantia because of the gathering of the First Cosmic Family, who are beginning to find their pair-unit classification with one another, and because of their gathering together in one physical geographic location, which creates doorways from that dimension to ours. It creates interplanetary audio and visual communication, and soon it will also create physical manifestations of us. When enough members of the cosmic family are gathered in any one physical location geographically, we can and do materialize. This can, and hopefully will happen, before the adjudication ends and the change point begins.

In future papers we wish to talk more of the negative repercussions of inappropriate sexual unions between ovan souls. In this context, an ovan soul is one who has repersonalized one or more times on Urantia or on other planets. Pair-unit classification in relationship to administrative functions on a planetary level is always in relationship to coordinating celestial personalities and their function and administrative position. Therefore, mortal pair units will represent celestial units and will vibrate and resonate with their unseen but yet personalized celestial overcontrol team. Together they act as complements in the implementation of Divine Government within certain mandates that the mortals themselves inherit. The mortal pair unit receives certain universe ascension status and the powers thereof from their team celestial personalities who are coordinated with their own ascension status. Therefore, a pair unit can have the full authority of seraphim, cherubim and sanobim, and begin to function and realize that power of the light, light in this sense referring to the Machiventa Melchizedek Government as mandated by Christ Michael, the Universe Father. In the CFER to come, the various acquired power-force energies in which these higher celestial personalities function will be given so that mortal pair-unit classification teams can begin to resonate with that higher reality, and latent abilities, that they had once attained as a pair unit in a higher dimension, can again become activated and actualized. On a planet where this is taking place with first dozens of individuals and then greater numbers, it can change not only weather patterns but the physical geographic reality itself. As the earth itself responds to that auhter energy, so that energy can also manifest itself in what is called the will-freeze process, causing rebellious individuals to either respond to the higher truth of the auhter energy created by these pair units en masse, or those rebellious individuals will not be able to remain in that specific location. This is already happening at Planetary Headquarters, at the Archangels' Headquarters and where the Machiventa Government resides in Sedona, Arizona, U.S.A. It will continue to happen at an increasing rate, and within the one mile radius of the higher Deo-atomic reality, few individuals will be able to remain and will be removed by their own free-will choices, which will no longer resonate in that area, or by disease which their rebellious attitudes will cause them. Heart attacks will be on the increase in these areas. This will not only be the quickest way for Celestial Overcontrol to remove an ovan soul, but will actually be the most merciful.

If you who are destined to read these words can understand them at the level necessary, you will not only have to move your soul and heart into ascension, but most likely also have to move yourself physically to Planetary Headquarters in order to be trained in CFER. CFER responds not only to a mass consciousness, but to the individual in their moment-to-moment decisions and their relation to Christ Michael, the Universe Father. CFER is also a part of the adjudication process. These papers will be used not only on this planet to realign rebellious personalities and other personalities in error, but will be used on other planets. It is hoped that you can understand these writings while still on this planet so that you will not have to study them on another planet. But if you do read these again on another planet, it will mean that you have missed them the first time when you should have read, and had the opportunity to understand them. These papers will also be studied after the change point on this planet by those who are destined to work with Celestial Overcontrol on other rebellious planets and into the outer levels of the master universe in future eras.

January 17, 1992

Paladin, Chief of Finaliters on Urantia; in cooperation with the adjudication process of the Bright and Morning Star; working directly with the Chief of Seraphim of Urantia; and in liaison with Machiventa Melchizedek, present Planetary Prince; as transmitted through the Audio Fusion Material Complement, Gabriel of Sedona.

PAPER 222

PHYSICAL THIRD-DIMENSIONAL BODY TYPES, IN THIS CASE THOSE OF HUMAN MORTAL ASCENDERS, IN RELATION TO MORTAL PAIR UNITS, AND THE OVAN SOUL'S ETHERIC BODY AND MORONTIA BODY IN RELATION TO DEO-ATOMIC INHERITANCE

On the worlds of time and space, cohabitation is necessary in the procreation process, and on those planets where emotional bonding is unknown, races with high technology are developed by mortal direction without communication with spiritual overcontrol, and, in its end result, that particular planet is peopled with races of almost robotic body forms and movements. The athletic ability of these races is quite limited, it is much easier for a primitive man to become an athletic type than it is for a highly advanced technological mortal. Because of these factors, many of these races become, in body form, quite unlike human mortals. The middle torso becomes very round, the legs become bowed and small, and the head also becomes smaller. The height of such a race is seldom above five feet, five inches, and these races that still digest foods of any substance become increasingly slow in movement. This creates a culture whose people are very interdependent upon one another and live in close quarters with one another, even though transportation methods are available. The designation of what type of flesh body these races may have depends upon the evolutionary process and origin of these mortals. Because of interplanetary amalgamation in procreation, various body types in relation to human mortals have developed.

On a decimal planet like Urantia life implantation cells that are mixed genetically with interuniversal diotribe **intraction cells** and with intrauniversal diotribe cells, you have various degrees of body realities forming and growing.

Diotribes: Cells within the body which are out of alignment with Deo-atomic reality due to Luciferic or rebellious thought forms manifested in cellular reality.

Diotribe intraction cells: Diotribe cells from other universes that have found themselves in material or semi-material individuals who have aligned themselves to Luciferic thinking and/or rebellious thinking created by thought processes other than Deo-atomic interuniversal procedures and alignments coordinating with individuals.

On a third-dimensional world, and in this case one that has defaulted in its epochal revelation dispensations, you also have, along with other variables, digestion of certain foods within these bodies which causes their inability to shape themselves into their natural form, based upon the strongest cells which resonate with other variables mostly related to the planet of origin and universe of origin. Basically, the present Urantian vegetables and fruits are not functional for the necessities of interuniversal mortals. The process regarding digestion has little to do with the spiritual. However, the spiritual does have much to do with the shape of the body and certain other features, particularly in the morontia worlds and here on Urantia for those individuals moving into fourth-dimensional reality. More will be given on this subject in other papers. It is all related to physiological and universal physics about which earth scientists as yet know nothing, which is Ascension Sci reality.

If one could look within the molecular structure of ovan souls on Urantia, one would find interuniversal cells which are indigenous to specific planets, systems and universes. Genetic and cellular scientists in the higher morontia worlds and above can collect these cells from the body, work on each cell individually, and reimplant each cell into the body or into another body, all based upon various factors. These cells are grouped and categorized. Deo-atomic cells and diotribe cells have a certain classification. Within the spiritual classification, thousands of other cells have other classifications strictly based upon physical matter that can be detected and measured within the higher levels of scientific analysis. This is why upon Urantia the metabolisms of individuals within the same parental unit may differ so much. Three children may tend toward obesity while a fourth who eats the same quantity and quality of foods may tend to be slender. On Urantia you have tried to explain these situations with moral judgments which may or may not be appropriate. The three who tend to be obese may not have developed negative habits at all, but just have to eat much less than their brother or sister who remains slim and yet eats the same foods and perhaps is even less active. In another family you may have children with blonde, red or black hair, all by the same set of brown-haired parents. One child may be tall and thin, one may be short and stout, and one may also have a completely different bodily structure from the other two; yet all three have grown up on the same foods and have the same food habits. All three may look completely different. One may have thin lips, one thick; one may be dark skinned, the other light skinned; one may have long legs, the other short; one may be bow legged, the other not; one may have long arms and the other one short arms; one may have long fingers, the other one not. What are the phenomena which cause these physical differences among these children of the same nuclear family?

In the area of the mind, a child of twelve may seem to be much more mature than another child of twelve who seems to be what on your planet is considered the normal twelve year old. One child may seem at times to be quite specifically different in the way in which he or she can manipulate his or her peers, while another child the same age can hardly communicate with them. One may excel in mathematics while the other can't even add two and two. One may speak philosophic words of great wisdom whereas the other wishes to play childish games. What is the uniqueness in the personalities of these individuals? Why do they differ so in intellectual, physical and social maturation? The answer to this lies in interuniversal and intersystem genetics.

On a decimal planet like Urantia where this is a universal fact, ovan souls and those pair units, who have met in other systems and have procreated in other universes, have become co-creators of certain classifications of human mortal, specific characteristic body forms in the third dimension, which then become the precedent for their descendents from then on throughout the worlds of time and space.

On planets which have not fallen in rebellion, there is a strong correlation between the etheric and morontia body and the way the soul within the body responds to its spiritual ascension, which creates the outer body and forms a mechanized and spiritualized movement. This body movement is called **famotor movement.** This movement is a recognized movement by those of higher discernment as to the offspring of mortal pair-unit classification. Famotor movement usually dictates to the body its physical form in the long run. It may take many repersonalizations before the physical body, at any level of dimension, will correctly conform to famotor movement, but it can be recognized in even the lesser bodies and distinguishes itself from other pair-unit classification origins. This is not only a measurable classification among ascending human mortals, but famotor movement is also measurable among nonhuman mortals who are ascending sons and daughters of time and space. Famotor movement recognition may be observable in human mortals, and has nothing to do with the height or weight of the body; it is within the movement of the body and the body's response to its own thought processes, its reality level and its reality view.

The recognition of famotor movement first begins within the mandate of the Bright and Morning Star, and within members of the First Cosmic Family on any particular planet that is coming into the first stages of light and life. One of the reasons is that Celestial Overcontrol, with the direct help of the Midwayer Commission of that planet, sees to it that these genetic ancestors will meet, and that those who connect at the highest spiritual levels remain with each other. The more you are familiar with each other's famotor movements, the more you begin to recognize others with the same interuniversal inheritance. It will always be the mandated Bright and Morning Star personality who will have the highest perception in this recognition. After that, some of the eldership may begin to notice famotor movement. Many times starseed and ovan souls who are unfamiliar with the concept of cosmic family, but recognize famotor movement in a person of the opposite sex, may confuse the reason he or she likes that individual and may think it is strictly a physical preference and sexual attraction, but in reality has nothing to do with physical likes or dislikes at all. Because it is not understood, one may think that she or he lusts after certain ones of the opposite sex because of the sex-drive within the human mortal race. On Urantia it is quite difficult to separate the two.

Male and female pair units who have procreated in past realities on other planets may meet again, and those who have paired as complementary polarities usually unite at another point in time to procreate. This is particularly true on planets that need higher genetic strains. On Urantia, where the marriage and mating process is not based upon interuniversal standards of the morontia levels, where procreation still exists within fourth, fifth and higher dimension realities, it is almost impossible for these pair units, to be reunited, and usually they end up in inappropriate relationships and give birth to inappropriate offspring. Here on Urantia where the cultural norm is monogamy, pair units, where several females should be paired with the same husband, is almost unheard of, with the exception of lower levels of religious groupings. Where the imbalance with the higher reality becomes commonplace, such as in certain Muslim cultures and in certain aspects of Mormonism, it results in static spirituality because these individuals are responding to their interuniversal instincts but do not respond to higher levels of spiritual ascension, and they become trapped in lower-evolutionary religious practices.

On planets where there have been no defaults affecting the evolutionary process, monogamous reality in relationships can become quite adequate in the evolutionary process of mating and procreation for the breeding of higher races. If Urantia had not defaulted twice, first in the rebellion of its Planetary Prince and then in the default of its Material Son and Daughter, Adam and Eve, monogamous pair-unit classification could have been the norm, and repersonalization on Urantia most likely would not have taken place. On planets, particularly decimal planets, where experimentation has occurred along with several defaults, monogamous pair marriage, particularly between the higher strains of interuniversal genetic ancestry, is not beneficial to the planet nor to the individuals who find themselves unfulfilled in those relationships and will continue to do so until they are reunited with their higher ascending procreation units of the opposite sex in which they have their original famotor movement reality.

On Urantia, where the emotional aspect of the personality is particularly prevalent in ascending daughters, it would be more difficult for them to come into alignment with these cosmic absolutes in relationship to their own destiny purpose and individual peace and fulfillment. Some of these ovan soul ascending daughters may also wish to have several male counterparts. This can function normally as long as those pair units are not:

1. Cosmically related, i.e. brother/sister,[21] father/daughter, mother/son; as these relationships would be interuniversal incest.
2. Offspring and/or a genetic link of a monogamous Material Son and Daughter as the pair-unit classification of that planet in relation to famotor movement seed of that couple.
3. In any sexual cohabitation where the ascension level of each individual is not the same in the ovan soul, which has to do with the inheritance of diotribes.
4. A nonmortal personality with a mortal personality, unless it is done with the offspring of that pair.
5. One in which the cosmic mother and father of an ascending daughter were monogamous at her point of origin, in which case, her Deo-atomic inheritance as an ascending daughter is to mate with only one ascending son at any one moment of time and space.

In relation to number five above, if a daughter is born to a cosmic mother who has several husbands, she will inherit the pluralistic reality within her Deo-atomic structure if that planet is in the first stage of light and life or above. If it is in the pre-stages of light and life, she inherits the instinct but in an unnatural mode. This will result in many variables of emotional trauma, psychological trauma and in some cases reality bewilderment, basically because her cosmic parents practiced pluralistic relationships in procreation without the higher spiritual cohesiveness, themselves being in error, sin, and in some cases, possibly iniquity. Females procreated in those circumstances on this planet or on any other, will choose to become a mortal pair classification unit based upon their own individual acceptance of whatever procreation reality and relationship reality they choose, as long as their spiritual ascension as ascending daughters does not interfere with their relationships to ascending sons and the ascending sons' authority over them in other areas where it is necessary for ascending sons to exhibit Father-circuited decisions and attitude responses in a moment-to-moment relationship to them, and others around them, at any one particular time when this may happen. These individual daughters, at any one point of time in the pre-stages of light and life, will find their happiness in monogamous

---

[21]Occasionally, under certain circumstances, a brother and sister can become pair units within God's will. This is explained in later volumes.

relationships with their highest ascending spiritual complementary male polarity. He, however, may be of a pluralistic interuniverse mating reality. Always, even in the other universes where pluralistic marriage is the spiritual norm, it will be in the pre-stages of light and life, just before the change point or beyond, where the cosmic family is beginning to organize, and all ascenders, male and female, will need to have reached the third circle or higher before they can be mated properly in a spiritual, emotional and physical union. On Urantia, with the First Cosmic Family, now and after the change point, this also has to be the standard. This spiritual ascension is the prerequisite for opposite-sex relationships to procreate higher offspring of genetic linkage, and without the spiritual alignment, even if one of the two wishes a relationship with the other, it is cosmically prohibited by Celestial Overcontrol and is registered as iniquitous when the guilty party joins intimately without the spiritual alignment which is the prerequisite to destiny purpose and individual actualization and fulfillment.

January 20, 1992

Paladin, Chief of Finaliters on Urantia; in cooperation with the Life Carriers on Urantia and other visiting interuniverse Life Carriers, and in particular the Avalon Commission Life Carriers, in relation to the implementation of the Machiventa Government; and in cooperation with Lanaforge and Machiventa Melchizedek, present Planetary Prince; as transmitted through the Audio Fusion Material Complement, Gabriel of Sedona.

PAPER 223

THE INFUSION OF INTERUNIVERSAL DIOTRIBE INTRACTION CELLS WITH INTRAUNIVERSAL DIOTRIBES IN RELATION TO THE LUCIFER REBELLION, AND THE MANIFESTATION OF THESE UNIONS RESULTING IN INTRACTION COSMIC LANGUAGE, WHICH IS AN INHARMONIC PATTERN THAT DISORGANIZES FREQUENCY CIRCUITS FROM VARIOUS HEADQUARTERS WORLDS WHERE THESE BROADCASTS ORIGINATE, AND ARE RECEIVED ON URANTIA BY MINDAL PROCESS REFLECTIVITY AND OTHER SENSORY RECEPTORS INNATE IN CERTAIN ORDERS OF ASCENDING AND DESCENDING BEINGS

On the evolutionary worlds of time and space, on morontia worlds and higher, upward and inward to Paradise, wherever language is used as a means of communication, cosmic truth resonates with a force power in conjunction with Paradise authority when that language is fused with cosmic absolutes and resonates in vibratory patterns with certain frequencies that would be referred to on Urantia as musical in sound, and which create, in the earlier stages of development, the beginning of the higher bodies. It was said of Christ Michael that he was one who spoke with authority, and when he spoke certain words in alignment with the Paradise Father's will, seeming miracles took place. In actuality, this was a demonstration of the fusion of **Deo-atomic famotor language** frequencies as sound connected to Paradise circuits, erasing all intraction cells or intrauniversal diotribes from present body units. In cases where the individual was in agreement with what Michael was saying by any adherence to faith practice, these diotribes, which had been intractioned and had upset the harmony within the body, would be permanently removed, or only temporarily removed in cases where the hearers of these words were not in alignment to universal principles and cosmic law.

On a planet where the natural evolutionary process has not been retarded because of default in relation to genetic and spiritual inheritance, the mortals of that realm benefit from languages which are more highly resonant with constellation level and higher reality. This creates on that planet certain sound frequencies which can be measured, captured and used in many ways in the areas of heart, particularly in music composition and sound, and in the area of higher healing where disease may still exist in certain forms on such a planet. On other planets these captured and reproduced sound frequencies are most likely to be used where disease is more prevalent, and where interplanetary circuits and travel are commonplace, particularly on lower evolutionary worlds. In **Dalamatia**, prior to the Caligastia rebellion, this science was beginning to be used in many areas of Dalamatian life. The use of these sound waves can also actually heal the earth itself, and is used in agriculture, botany and in geological sciences where the healing and the changing of the earth itself is called for.

In relation to **intraction language** on a one to one basis between individuals, this creates a certain energy which has many implications in the natural realm, resulting in uneasiness to the ears, even though the sound itself may not be heard. Sometimes the ear may ring. Earth scientists have been unable to determine why this happens. In many cases, what is happening is that intraction cells have created a disturbance within the vibratory reality of your hearing, which then creates a sound that your ear can and does pick up. In times of tragedy, or in other cases of disruption, iniquitous behavior creates such disturbance that machinery can actually be affected, and even weather patterns changed. Because of the increase in iniquity that has continued on Urantia for such a long time, and the continued use of intraction language by individuals who may not be iniquitous but simply in error, great earth changes are now beginning to take place on Urantia and will increase until the first stages of light and life are actualized.

On an individual level, where a person has diotribe cells in large quantities within his or her molecular structure, which may be caused by ignorance of higher truth and cosmic law, and he or she continues to speak in error with opinionated and incorrect speech, the very air itself becomes inharmonic with divine harmony. The sound at that geographic location becomes more distorted by that individual, and can be increasingly distorted by others of incorrect speech to such a degree that midwayers and other lower angelic personalities cannot even inhabit the same space or dimension. Where hundreds or thousands with inappropriate speech or behavior patterns are gathered, angelic personalities are unable to prevent natural disasters from occurring, nor can they help the Thought Adjuster to communicate the perfect will of the Father to an individual. In cases where intraction energies are such because of the more iniquitous interuniversal intraction cells located in any one particular geographic location, certain superstitions and myths have arisen where it was thought that evil could be collected in certain objects. Such ideas have their origin in the cosmic fact that diotribe cells, and in particular, intraction diotribe cells from other universes, when leaving a certain body, at times, because of that ovan soul's momentarily or permanently coming into a higher alignment with universal principles, can be found themselves temporarily in an inanimate object until those cells are drawn toward another rebellious or ignorant individual by free-will choice. This is the reason prophets of old and other spiritual teachers sensed that certain objects or places seemed to be unclean. In a real cosmic sense this could have been true at the moment the seer sensed or felt the object, but in most cases these diotribes can only remain in the object at the most for a few hours before they are drawn into an unsuspecting mortal by the free-will choice of that mortal through ignorance, or possibly a rebellious attitude toward cosmic absolutes and facts.

To the higher circle ascender and sensitive on the morontia level and above, intraction language waves are felt before they are heard, and at times they may be felt and not heard at all. This is due to the picking up of the movement of intraction cells based upon the neurological movement of these cells because of improper thinking even without speech. This is why it was stated by Christ Michael that he who has thought of doing wrong has already committed the act. To the degree of the implementation of incorrect thinking, is the degree of cause and effect. This is why sensitives, empaths and other clairvoyant personalities find it difficult to live in surroundings of loud noises or around individuals who are not of higher Deo-atomic reality. Iniquitous sensitives can more easily exist in noisy or populated locations because they are attuned to intraction realities, and they perceive and accept certain sound vibrations resonant with specific diotribe and intraction cells based upon Luciferic reality. This is why those who have been called the saints of the past have usually had to separate themselves from the rest of society in monasteries or retreat areas permanently or at least temporarily at times. The higher the ovan souls and of course, celestial personalities, the less they can inhabit the same space where intraction occurs. The repercussions of this cosmic fact are tremendous, and great cities on some worlds are designed upon this cosmic fact and principle. Great civilizations are built which cut themselves off from other lesser civilizations where diotribe reality exists at a level within which intraction cells are commonplace.

Intraction cells usually are of a higher frequency, which creates a stronger disturbance to any reality in physical time-and-space where they are found within any ascending mortal or other higher universe personalities. This is why, when a planet is entering the pre-stages of light and life, the First Cosmic Family is regathered in certain geographic locations so that the diotribe and intraction cells can eventually be totally removed from within a certain radius, increasing the safety of these areas at various levels until all the diotribe cells are totally removed. The reality of that particular location then becomes harmonious with intrauniversal and even interuniversal broadcasts and visitations. It also increases the audio reception of the chosen material complement and increases the visual reception of any mandated transfiguration personality.[22] The whole area then becomes an ERC rather than just a specific location or locations within a certain radius. When a larger area within a five mile radius of the central point completely becomes an ERC, other, at this time unrevealed, universal phenomena can occur, which will be the subject of future transmissions.

Intraction language, projected by either thought or speech by individuals, directly or on television, or through other forms of technology, helps to increase the already distorted energy patterns on Urantia to such a degree that much emotional and psychological damage promotes continuing unnatural and unhealthy thinking, which then results in physical manifestations and dozens of diseases. Cases of depression, anxiety and various forms of insanity have increasingly occurred as modern technology has developed, and also where civilization has become more centrally located and populous. It is a known fact, even by your scientists, that individuals who live away from cities usually live healthier and longer lives. Artists have found their point of higher creation away from civilization and more in tune with nature. This is because in natural environments they do not incorporate diotribe cells by their own occasional improper thinking as long as they are isolated, thereby opening their own channels to higher Deo-atomic cells and reality. Individuals in isolation who entertain continuing iniquitous intraction thinking will, however, create a frequency that will attract diotribes of various strength capacities, and intraction cells of other universes from great distances anywhere on the planet within a matter of five seconds or more, depending upon the measured velocity of the strength of the iniquitous thought and also the divisions of that thought, which will attract the specific diotribe or intraction cell pertinent to that particular thought process.

This is why certain diseases that have originated in geographic locations thousands of miles away are transferred to other geographic locations. It is in the thoughts, not in the physiological function of the cells. Diseases are not just transferred physically by contact, but are most likely transferred by error of thought. The use of the mind by iniquitous nonmortal individuals on higher levels who know Ascension Sci reality, such as a Lanonandek Son, or other lower orders of celestial personalities, can create physical changes within any one individual or planet based upon the manipulation of an unsuspecting individual or group's adherence to illogical or rebellious intractive thinking.

Animals, and even some forms of insect life, are most responsive to intractive thinking and speech. This is why higher orders of animals seem to

---

[22]Since February 17, 1995, there is no transfiguration personality on Urantia.

understand their masters. This is also why individuals who walk in great love can be at peace with even the most ferocious of animal life. The animal senses a Deo-atomic reality as opposed to an intraction reality, and when they sense intraction they react by either aggressiveness or retreat. On worlds where intraction reality is unknown, the harmony between animal and mortal is such that carnivorous-action reality is not necessary. When, on Urantia, the lion and the lamb play together with the child, all diotribe reality will have been removed and Deo-atomic reality will be the norm. Intraction language of any kind can create unnatural behavior in animal life. In the carnivorous animals, it does amplify their flesh eating reality beyond survival needs, and in humans, hunting animals for sport. It can also create attacks upon humans by these animals. This is why little dogs who weigh merely five pounds may attack much larger humans, for the sensory perceptions in the reception of diotribes are acutely functional in some of these species, and they react to the sound and vibration, not against the individual person, who may not be an iniquitous person, but may be momentarily in error or projecting a Luciferic sound pattern at some level.

On Urantia, languages have developed based upon the coordination of concepts and the mind's ability to communicate these concepts to significant others. When these significant others are in higher alignment to universal principles, the language becomes more harmonious and musical. On Urantia, where the concept of the fatherhood of God has become supplanted by Luciferic concepts, these Urantian languages have become complicated, difficult sounding and nonmusical. The English language has become accepted as the language in which the higher Deo-atomic cells resonate with cosmic absolutes. It is not perfect, and that is why we on our side have a very difficult time translating cosmic absolutes and terminology even to the highest audio fusion material complement who is an English-speaking personality. However, it has been designed by the race commissioners, the Life Carriers present on Urantia, and other celestial personalities involved, including the midwayers, that the Fifth Epochal Revelation and CFER would come through an English speaking complement, and that the majority of the highest genetic strains of Adam and Eve, Adamson and Ratta, and ovan souls, would be more highly represented in the English speaking peoples of Urantia in the 20th century during the adjudication by the Bright and Morning Star vs Lucifer. This has been the organization of starseed consistent with present Caucasian races going back in lineage to Abraham and the early dynasties of Egypt. Although ovan souls have found themselves repersonalized within other races such as the yellow, red, and indigo, it has always been those ovan souls of higher spiritual attainment who became teachers and spiritual leaders to those races. Although color in flesh form is a reality on Urantia, color is not a factor in repersonalization, it is a matter of soul ascension and Deo-atomic inheritance or the inheritance of diotribes and intraction cells.

It is said that the United States of America is a melting pot. That is true in so many ways. The statement has much more to do with cosmic influence and destiny as a nation than you might imagine. The fact that English is the least intractive language on Urantia is one of the reasons why it has been the will of God for so many to come to America in order to learn to speak this language. They then can begin, as individuals, to ascend to a higher circle of attainment based upon their mind's ability to comprehend higher cosmic realities. This is why Caligastia has tried so hard to make Spanish an accepted language in certain states in the southwestern United States, for he full well knew that Planetary Headquarters was in the Southwest, and he also knew that the Archangels' Headquarters was located in the Southwest and he has continually tried to confuse the English language by bringing in other forms of languages and even mathematical changes such as the metric system. What has become known as the metric system is a distortion of universe design. The system we know as the imperial system, which is a lower form of a higher universal spiritual mathematical reality, actually goes back in influence to the Pleiades, and on this planet to the great pyramids of Egypt which were constructed with these equations and are now being interpreted by spiritual scientists using these equations to discover certain Ascension Sci or prophetic historical and future events.

Latin languages are very beautiful. This is based on several cosmic facts in relationship to those various genetic strains and their connections to the Universe Mother Spirit and the Infinite Spirit circuits of Paradise, and more recently to the fatherhood-of-God concept brought to this planet in the Fourth Epochal Revelation, with which these genetic strains resonated and which they accepted. To the degree of their acceptance, certain diotribes and intraction cells left those countries and went to other countries where nonabsolute truth in relationship to Deity were prevalent. Higher mindal capabilities, however, were not possible within these other countries due to language difficulty and other conceptual beliefs as to spiritual hierarchy and political structures within cosmic hierarchy which had nothing to do with Urantian religious institutions, but could not be explained to these genetic strains because of their diotribe mass acceptance of false spiritual teachings about spiritual divine government administration. The various church governments within Christendom are an attempt to implement divine government. Thus, to many of these countries and their people, the Pope still is the Vicar of Christ, has the keys to the kingdom supposedly given to Saint Peter, and is infallible as their religious head. Millions and millions in both western European and South American countries have created, by their mass consciousness, a certain frequency blockage which prevents celestial personalities from acting within the realm of their dimensional reality, therefore decreasing in those individuals their capacity for personal fulfillment and for reaching their individual destiny in relation to the very Universal Father whom they claim to know and follow.

Within these countries, where certain of their cities become more international in scope, higher celestial visitation can happen, and Celestial Overcontrol increasingly can bring higher revelation to certain individuals, and the Thought Adjusters can reach them at a higher level. But because the usage of intraction language blocks the flow of higher revelatory truths to the mass consciousness, the countries as a whole do not benefit. These masses can only be reached when certain ovan souls in control of their religious systems, political systems and media, decide together or as independent individuals, to begin to speak higher truths, or when a personality with the mandate of the Bright and Morning Star, the Liaison Ministers or one with the mandate as assistant to the mandate of the Bright and Morning Star goes into those countries and within those mandates teaches and brings the same authority to break those intractive energies, as Jesus did when he spoke.

Freedom of religion was the concept wished for by the early founders of the United States of America in order that the nation would be able to continue to receive revelation from God. They never meant to bring in lesser religious realities into their definition of religious freedom. They were believers in the fatherhood of God and the brotherhood of man and not in the lower concepts of evolutionary religious thought. It is not the intent of the Fifth Epochal Revelation and CFER to make a Buddhist a better Buddhist or a Muslim a better Muslim by reading and understanding the Fifth Epochal Revelation. It is the intent of the Fifth Epochal Revelation and Continuing to bring these individuals out of these false systems and lower languages. Higher cosmic reality cannot be given to them because of their confused linguistic communication and the superstitious and deceptive terminologies used in attempting to define God and reality. It would be much easier for the peoples of Urantia to speak one language, now the present English, than it would be to print the Fifth Epochal Revelation and CFER in all the languages of the world. Urantia must become the real melting pot of all the peoples of the planet, and English the common language, both of communication and of cosmic concept and the definition of God and the master universe.

It has always been the plan of Caligastia to divide communication, first within the thoughts and then within the way in which thoughts are transmitted, which results in the various languages that one human can speak and the other cannot. The higher morontia languages incorporate the highest evolutionary languages, so the natural flow from one dimension to another is just that, natural, and morontia languages will now incorporate the present English and other higher individual words of some of the other languages of Urantia which flow more coordinately with English. In sound, higher cosmic definition is not intractive when the fusion of these languages present a cosmic fact of reality. In the first stages of light and life, the mass consciousness of the planet will resonate in the morontia frequencies and will create broadcasts and many more circuitry connections between the planet and the satellite worlds of the system capital where a similar language is used at various levels of communication, between systems and universes, where celestial personalities communicate with one another. There, and at a point in time on Urantia, all intraction language will be a thing of the past.

January 27, 1992

Paladin, Chief of Finaliters on Urantia; in cooperation with the Angels of Nation Life; the Chief of Seraphim on Urantia and Machiventa Melchizedek, present Planetary Prince; as transmitted through the Audio Fusion Material Complement, Gabriel of Sedona.

PAPER 224

PAIR-UNIT CLASSIFICATION IN RELATION TO FORM UNITS (BODY FORMS) AND THEIR PROGENY IN RELATION TO THE INHERITANCE OF DEO-ATOMIC TRIADS AND DIOTRIBES RESULTING IN THE VARIATION OF THOSE BODY FORMS, AND OTHER PHYSICAL DISTINCTIONS AND CHARACTERISTICS PERTINENT TO PRE-URANTIAN BODY FORMS WHERE DIOTRIBE INFLUENCE HAS OCCURRED

On the evolutionary worlds of time and space, where mortals meet and procreate, the progeny of those mating parents are the result of hundreds of variables, each one a science in itself. To try and simplify genetic and spiritual influence in regard to body form is an education that begins at this level with those who receive CFER. It usually is more understandable and cosmically comprehensible to those within the third psychic circle to the first.

Those who procreate within the seven stages of the third dimension produce offspring based upon the alignment of the parents to their Creator within those stages. In those mating pairs where one individual may be more spiritually advanced than another, the higher spiritual genetic parent will be stronger and influence the physical as well as the mindal capabilities of that child. In cases where an ovan soul is brought through that couple, the same rule applies, except that the child also brings with him or her previously inherited Deo-atomic genetics, personality and mind abilities, as well as motor abilities and other pre-acquired talents. When a male and female mate together at the seventh stage of the fourth dimension, that pair-unit's classification begins to create form units, and they, as well as their progeny, are classified as a form-unit pair of a categorized progeny in body form and characteristics as well as famotor movement. Here the spiritual and physical unite to form a commonality in relation to God-presence and physical form.

Before the Lucifer rebellion, in other universes where ascending sons and daughters had met and mated on the seventh stage of the fourth dimension, they manifested for the first time a unique **form-unit progeny**. From that first son or daughter began a unique form of mortal body characteristics. Each time the male mated with a female on the seventh stage of the fourth dimension, a new form-unit procreation began. On worlds where mating and marriage differ as to pluralistic relationships, form-unit progeny were numbered upwards in the several dozen, each individual planet with its own exact number within the fourth dimension. Let us take, for example, the planet Tora of the Pleiades, known by Urantia astronomers as Electra. One male of the seventh stage of the fourth dimension may mate with six females on the same seventh stage in one lifetime either at different times within that lifetime or perhaps at one time, and all of the form units will be different. The form unit of the progeny will depend upon the planet of origin of the male and female parents. In some cases the female may be a first-time Toran but still be on the seventh stage of the fourth dimension, basically because that planet, which had not fallen, has increased her ability to ascend spiritually more rapidly. Another female may be an ovan soul of another Pleiadian world, or perhaps even a Centaurian or an Ursa Major world, where these universes have had interuniversal procreation for eons. The Ascension Sci aspect of these pair-unit classifications and the physiological realities alone are quite extensive in scope, and on the beginning levels of fourth-dimensional reality, when one begins to understand these things, it is massive in equation, and again, for some who have not reached the third circle, it can be almost impossible to follow in the mind because the aspects of that individual's ascension are not able to incorporate Ascension Sci reality.

Urantia, being an interuniversal planet in relation to procreation of pair-unit mating, presents a challenge in interuniversal science, and to those individuals on Urantia now reaching the higher circle levels, it presents problems of individual understanding of male and female relationships in regard to marriage and procreation. This is basically because interuniversal personalities are trying to live with planetary values and norms based upon a particular universe standard which may be alien to other universe norms. The infusion of art in relation to Urantian poetry, the philosophy of romance and the understanding of what love is in relation to pair marriage on Urantia, is indeed based upon Urantian evolution within the present reality that all circuits are cut off from interuniversal realities. Therefore, the standard for all has been based upon a lower standard, which has limited those with latent capabilities to actualize their previous personal and spiritual abilities, and for many, their once higher spiritual attainments. The results of the rebellion in relation to physical procreation have been devastating, as it has been with the inheritance of disease. As far as individual ovan souls are concerned, the more diotribes and intraction cells they inherit, the further it deforms the natural characteristics of the original fourth-dimensional seventh-stage form-unit body type, when they in turn procreate children. Again, the ramifications of these cosmic cellular manipulations in the Ascension Sci process is massive.

Some ovan souls who are meant to be six to eight feet tall are presently five feet to six feet tall, in other individuals, some are meant to have longer fingers or shorter ones. Some who are meant to have shorter ones have longer ones, and the same with the arms, legs and feet. Particularly in women, the manifestations and differences are quite noticeable in the breasts. This is because they are a manifestation of the Universe Mother Spirit and all the realities pertinent to her life essence. Of course we are not speaking of the size of the breasts that identifies the spirituality of the female; we are talking more about form, and it is quite noticeable that females have various breast forms. Metabolism is also inherited. An ovan soul born to a first-time Urantian with a slow metabolism will inherit that slow metabolism. In many cases, that is one of the reasons why Overcontrol may choose those parents for that soul. Also, even though the ovan soul brings with him or her higher Deo-atomic reality, many of his or her prelearned abilities may be dormant until that personality reaches a level of destiny purpose. Many controlling factors are used to govern that individual's life situations and decisions. For instance, individuals with a slow metabolism are not likely to become athletes or to be in the various skills of physical labor. Usually they become thinkers and work within the arena of the intellectual professions. In cases where they are called into the reserve corps of destiny, slower metabolism has been used to keep reservists in their destiny purpose. It has not been the only thing. Those with a higher and faster metabolism are also reservists, and other methods of control are used to keep these individuals from going too far astray in Luciferic tendencies on a fallen world such as Urantia. Further transmissions will deal with the areas of these controls and the methods used within the free will of these individuals. Although ovan souls in past repersonalizations may have acquired a certain spiritual level, each time they repersonalize on the third-dimensional world, they have to rediscover themselves and their God to activate the spiritual-growth process. At the point of reception of the Spirit of Truth on Urantia, the process is accelerated, as well as the additional activation of the Holy Spirit. As far as physical characteristics are concerned, to the child of Urantian parents or any other ovan soul parents who have never reached the seventh stage of the fourth dimension, it makes little difference what that child will eventually come to look like. Many physical transformations of certain individuals within one lifetime are quite possible, which has very little to do with weight loss, but weight also fluctuates according to many intrauniversal specifications. The shape and structure of the head, including various parts such as the eyes, nose, ears and chin, are based upon the inheritance of Deo-atomic cells in accordance with the form unit of origin, and then those body characteristics fluctuate in that particular lifetime in accordance with intraction cells and diotribe cells.

The third-dimensional body that is coming into the morontia light body on

Urantia is presently at war with itself, but with an understanding of cosmic inheritance and cosmic genetics and cosmic origin, a cosmic form unit is obtainable for that ovan soul. It begins a transformation, first in the morontia light and astral body and then inward to the etheric and last in the physical. The variation of life forms in the grand universe is beyond your mortal comprehension, and so, in bringing the Fifth Epochal Revelation and CFER to this planet, we have not previously dealt with explanations. However, as individuals ascend to the higher circles and remain in fourth-dimensional reality and above, we can bring more information as to the uniqueness of body structures in both material and semi-material forms. Those with certain unexplained clairvoyant perceptions can determine certain things about individual humans based upon eye contact. This is a cosmic science. However, on Urantia, very few who have this ability truly understand it and can use it properly, which is unfortunate. The doctors of the higher morontia worlds work in the astral, not in the physical. In bodies where the flesh is still part of the ascending soul, doctors may work with the physical in cases of accident or use other holistic approaches to the healing of that body. But always it is the higher doctors of ascension healing or higher morontia doctors who are called upon to obtain diagnosis.

Cosmic insight has little to do with mortal empathic abilities. It has much more to do with a scientific approach to cosmic perception and cosmic realities. As you are able on your planet to look at each other and determine what race you are from, we can look upon the individual and determine much more in relation to his interbreeding and interuniversal genetics. Much can be determined, starting with form units and then in varying degrees, what Luciferic teachings this individual has incorporated. All of this diagnostic information can be observed purely by empirical observation of the particular characteristics of an individual's present body. Some conditions of the body, such as weight, can be a result not only of Urantian genetic inheritance, but of a nonmaterial reason in relation to intrauniversal and interuniversal inheritance.

Certain physical characteristics of the body may be the result of inheritance alone, based upon the strongest cells of their origin in relation to the Creator Son of that universe or to the fallen son of Satania, Lucifer, who proclaimed himself God and set in motion his own seeds. As he full well knew the science of thought and the implications of his rebellion to his own Creator, he methodically set out to change the thinking of others. But he also knew that he would be able to manipulate the physical. This does not make him a co-creator, as erroneously taught by himself and certain channels of Luciferic thought. The co-creators are the Creator Sons and Daughters of Paradise origin originating from the Universal Father, Eternal Son and the Infinite Spirit. Any other order of being proclaiming to be a co-creator is either deceived or a deceiver. Universal language does not speak of co-creation in context of creating something out of nothing. It identifies beings as created ones who try to learn about their creator. The distortion of the physical by mental process is not creating, and in the natural process of procreation in the lower evolutionary worlds up into the fifth dimension, creating is the acting out of the purposes of God by those on the higher stages of the fourth dimension within the perfect will of that Creator God. With this understanding, all ascending beings become the instruments of God, or, you might say, the hand of God to form his preconceived plan for all the vast creation in the eons of time and space, forever and ever.

What may seem to be beautiful to one may not be to another, even in the same system, let alone in a different universe. Usually however, commonality of form-unit classification remains somewhat similar in intrauniversal reality, but differs greatly in interuniversal reality, as do the social and the varying governmental patterns. But coordinating similarities in intrauniversal structure become absolute in the first stages of light and life and above, as all of these various worlds connect with Paradise-origin circuitry and personality. On Urantia everyone is not Urantian. We can look upon you and we can determine your origin simply by seeing you, and can further determine the degree of Luciferic tendencies still remaining within you in the same instant of observation. This has nothing to do with your aura. Very few on Urantia, ovan souls and first-time Urantians alike, can really see auras; they just have a great imagination. If they are accurate to some degree, it is not so much what they are seeing, as what they are sensing, and that sense is based upon physical eyesight. When they perceive something about somebody they have not been able to understand, they base their analysis upon colors around the body. The reality of it is, they are actually recognizing something about the form unit of that individual whom they may have once been with on another planet. And so, those who claim clairvoyant sight actually are tapping into memory circuits which have nothing at all to do with the supernatural. Here again begins the fusion of science with the spiritual.

As stated in earlier papers, it has been the function of the loyal midwayers, since the default of the Caligastia one hundred, to bring together the highest ascending pair-unit classifications, male and female, for mating and procreation. Now we can add that whenever an original form-unit parental couple can be mated to procreate, they not only have the capability of bringing through higher orders of ovan souls, but also of gathering all of that pair's offspring, who may be on various planets in interuniversal reality. All of these souls can be brought together in one location in time and space to help reestablish a linear offspring, eventually leading to an offspring with the original form-unit from before their fall in the Lucifer rebellion.

Completely realizing that what we are saying may be difficult to comprehend, we persevere with your inadequate mind at this time, precept upon precept so that in time you will not only comprehend what we have said, but will teach these principles to the peoples of your planet, which include the peoples of many other universes. When a toddler begins to learn numbers, he cannot deal with equations. Step by step, learning must begin. In the Ascension Sci process of procreation, human romance does not play a part. In the evolutionary process of ascending sons and daughters in either physiological, mindal or spiritual reality, the emotional aspect of the human mortal is a classification which distinguishes the human mortal from other forms of life, other mortals and even other human mortals. It is a wonderful thing in the experience of art and in certain areas of loving one another. It becomes an ugly thing when emotions are not understood and are used to control one another, to play upon the sympathy of others, and in the other ways in which you use your emotions for passive control or for downright control by force. Emotions play little part in the thinking processes of higher spiritual personalities. If we allow them to register, it is always in an artistic form. Emotions take form in characteristic features of the body as do Luciferic tendencies such as habitual lying, kleptomania, and other sins in the areas of greed, lust and selfishness. The physical body and its parts respond to your thinking. You are what you think; and much of your thinking process, if you are an ovan soul, relates to your first form-unit classification and the fall that took place within that first family unit. There is a very measurable physical and famotor reality that is both visible and invisible which continues with an individual in each repersonalization in the lower worlds until that individual is near the third circle of attainment and the fourth dimension. It should be noted here that one can be on the first circle in the third dimension, and when one begins to reach the third circle in the fourth dimension famotor movement will not change; it is a constant, but certain physical changes may take place in the already existing third-dimensional body.

On present-day Urantia, prior to the first stage of light and life, and since the establishment of the Machiventa Government in December of 1989, the coordination between original form-unit body types and the perfection of the first offspring is now possible, if those fallen offspring are in alignment to cosmic absolutes, as is now being manifested in the Machiventa Government on Urantia. After the change point, the first-stage morontia bodies that will be given to those who ascend to constant fourth-dimensional reality and above will be individual but yet perfect in identification to the original form unit of the first pair-unit classification couple, whatever universe they are from, and to whichever mating pairs procreated together. In this manner, all form units will be identifiable in race classifications, much like the evolutionary process that took place here on Urantia in regard to first-time Urantians. The First Cosmic Family will function in relationship to the Material Sons and Daughters and other unrevealed mating and breeding personalities in the sector where the New Jerusalem will be established after the change point. These millions, of similar form-unit classifications and famotor realities, will administer the policies of the new Machiventa Government on Urantia to the other cosmic families in other sectors and to Urantians who are then being born on the planet, as well as some who will be brought back after the change point. Procreation between higher spiritual mortals and lower spiritual mortals will be prohibited, as well as between higher genetic strains with lower ones. All marriages will be based upon interuniversal ethics, and only the higher spiritual pair-unit classifications of form units will experience pluralistic marriages and breeding. All other marriages will be based upon respective universe ethics and planetary reality. Urantian mortals and the majority of intrauniversal mortals will be in monogamous relationships relative to procreation. This differentiation in modes of procreation between the then present pair-unit classifications will be a sector differentiation, and each individual sector, although alike in cosmic absolutes, will differ in cultural reality and family unit structure. However, transportation will be so upstepped and communication will be so increased that the various sectors of the planet will be as one, and the various differences of interuniversal realities will become the norm for this unique decimal planet called Urantia.

February 15, 1992

Paladin, Chief of Finaliters on Urantia; in cooperation with Physical Controllers and Life Carriers in interuniversal liaison to help upstep the implementation of the government of the present Planetary Prince, Machiventa Melchizedek, and to call forth the cosmic reservists to that government; as transmitted through the Audio Fusion Material Complement, Gabriel of Sedona.

PAPER 225

THE DANGERS INHERENT IN SEXUAL INTIMACY BETWEEN HIGHER AND LOWER GENETIC STRAINS WITHIN THE HUMAN RACE, INCLUDING STARSEED WITH URANTIANS AND HIGHER-CIRCLE WITH LOWER-CIRCLE INDIVIDUALS, EXCLUDING PROCREATION AND INCLUDING SOCIAL AND CULTURAL RELATIONSHIPS WHERE NEGATIVE INFLUENCE AFFECTS HIGHER GENETIC PERSONALITIES.

The function of the Material Sons and Daughters and their progeny is to upstep the evolutionary races by the amalgamation of their offspring. Where the higher strains of the evolutionary races mate with the progeny of the Material Sons and Daughters within the divine plan, higher mindal, physiological and psychological attributes are inherited. It was discovered long ago on other worlds of time and space that sexual intimacy outside the divine plan, between a supermortal and a primitive mortal, resulted in many variables that were unrecognizable in the first generations. If an emotional relationship occurred between the higher being and the lower one, the supermortal would be greatly damaged, for through the mixture of molecules of the sperm with molecules of the female during orgasm, the very thinking process of the higher being would be affected. This phenomenon would have even more effect when the progeny of supermortal beings intermingled with lower genetic strains. Where this has occurred, the higher mortals' thinking processes were affected and sometimes primitive behavior began, even if momentarily. Characteristics such as irrationality, rage, violence, illogical thinking and quick thought processes leading to wrong decisions began to occur, and on Urantia it happened quite frequently. Many other tendencies have been registered and codified. In inappropriate mating, where orgasm occurs for the lower individual, the higher individual will inherit whatever tendencies of the negative cells were strongly dominant during that particular orgasm. This is based upon the lower individual's present state of mind at the time of orgasm, and many influences throughout the last twelve hours of that lower individual's reality, which brings either diotribe cells or intraction cells into a form of creation, and more specifically those negative cells of the same incorrect thinking patterns that have negatively influenced that lower individual in the last twelve hours. If depression was a major part of that individual's day, then diotribe cells which resonate with depressive thinking will occur. These may be specifically categorized as fear, insecurity, dissatisfaction

205

and anger. If a lower individual is a kleptomaniac, the higher individual may inherit these diotribe cells and may find him/herself the next day considering putting something in his or her pocket at the marketplace and wondering where that thought came from. Thoughts of suicide and many other negative thoughts can all be put into the body system through sexual contact, and in every relationship you have ever had, you have inherited the lower thinking to some degree of that other person. Sometimes these diotribe cells remain there for a lifetime and greatly influence that individual in wrong choices and wrong destiny, all because of improper sexual relationships.

The context of this transmission is not to talk of physical disease that can be inherent, but about the present plague of AIDS and the breakdown of the immune system as a spiritual problem that manifests in the physical body, which is why no cure will be found. The breakdown of the immune system begins in the thinking, and energy follows thought and affects the physical. The messages from the First Source and Center of Paradise to the headquarters worlds of each universe and going to the individual bodies that incorporate the threefold spirit at various levels and at various times, are distorted by diotribe cells which create blockages that disturb the way these messages are then sent from the brain to the central nervous system.

When a male ejaculates into a female, the sperm flows into the vagina, which is the center of the root circuit (also known as the root chakra) or birth circuit. There is a gland connected to the root circuit, and from it there is a natural highway for energy flowing to every other gland and circuit within the female. In the male the entry point is in the throat circuit. This is why kissing is so stimulating. However, because orgasm in males is through the penis, sexually transmitted sperm from male to male by oral methods is dangerous to the receiving male. It is less dangerous through anal transference. In relation to the phenomenon of AIDS, it is not a viral transference but a transference of diotribes and intraction cells which influence the thinking, which in turn creates the viruses which then break down the immune system. Oral transference of vaginal fluids from female to female is less dangerous.

This marvelous scientific fact of the Ascension Sci process extends in application throughout the worlds where intimacy occurs between ascending sons and daughters. Love between ascending sons and daughters should be based upon the higher principles of God and the understanding of just who God is in relation to the master universe in which they may find themselves together in any one particular moment of time, and emotional love may be incorrect where intellectual understanding is void.

In consideration of cellular inheritance, on Urantia even with the First Cosmic Family throughout their many repersonalizations together, and with those of the other cosmic families, it has been quite difficult for midwayers and other celestial personalities to mate these higher strains for many reasons. Emotional response, particularly in females, has been one of the major problems. Urantian poets and contemporary views of romance have added to the already complicated process of proper relationships and sexual intimacy and procreation. More harm has come to billions of Urantians in the area of mind and emotion than has been understood by medical science and modern psychiatry. Modern psychiatry in its origins with Freud began to touch upon the sexual aspect in the concept of the anima and animas. Freud further believed that the strongest drive in the human was the sexual drive, and that any decisions made by human personalities were decided upon purely by sexually correlated thinking. The id, ego and superego were considered aspects of that personality also in relation to sexual response, perhaps even in the superconsciousness.

Jungian psychology began to see a spiritual correlation in which Carl Jung tried to determine the various personality types according to the will of God, even though many of his followers misunderstood his original thesis. In his dream analysis, the sexual aspect of male and female within one's self was prominent in the interpretation of the dream life. Jung was able to determine much in relation to personality attributes in the categorizing of individual personalities as to certain abilities and certain ways of thinking. Some of his students even began to determine that perhaps certain personality types should be mated with one another as far as compatibility is concerned. In the more modern Briggs analysis tests,[23] certain careers and vocations are advised for particular individuals whose responses to these tests are determined in a way which coordinates particular fields and registered talents. Suffice it to say that the sexual aspect of male and female in modern psychology is truly based upon cosmic fact, but cosmic genetics and physics in relation to the spiritual is little understood. When science tries to develop factual reality based upon equations alone, it leaves out foundational reality, which is the First Source and Center of all inherent energy and is the primal function of all life and life force. It cannot be measured by science, not because it cannot be seen or detected, for it can. It is just too small to be seen by Urantian scientists who are unable to detect it at current levels of evolutionary technology. As we ascend to Paradise, we continue to discover that the last smallest particle we have recently learned about is larger than the next

---

[23]Meyer-Briggs Type Indicator is a measure of personality dispositions and interests based on Jung's theory of types. It provides four bipolar scales: Introversion/Extroversion, Sensing/Intuition, Thinking/Feeling, and Judging/Perceiving. Scores are reported by a four-letter type code.

one just discovered. It is not that they were never there, they have always been there. The absoluteness is just as absolute on the finite worlds as it is on Paradise. It is the comprehension level that must ascend to the absolute level of physical reality, and within every abstract is an absolute answer, for abstract reality at one level is exact science on another.

Certain diseases are more prevalent in certain races than in others. This is because these races have not intermingled enough with the higher races within the divine plan, so that those lower races can be cured by higher genetic cells and Deo-atomic inheritance. Certain ways of thinking are more inherent in certain nationalities than they are in others. This is because the thinking in these races remains static, basically due to the peoples inter-marrying among themselves for thousands of years. When races remain inbred, much stays the same, particularly their religious reality and their viewpoint of God. Minor changes may take place, but physical habits based upon thinking modes remain constant. This manifests in eating habits, emotional responses and mental activity, which then reflects in physical activity and the strength of the body.

Uniqueness of personality is divine in origin. Personality distortion of that divine inheritance is both of Luciferic causation and a human error problem. Sexual intimacy outside of divine plan, between ovan souls of higher-circle attainment and Urantians of lower-circle attainment, can cause enough distortion in the thinking process of the Urantian to block the Thought Adjuster from getting through to the individual about important life decisions as to destiny purpose, actualization of talents, and in modern-day Urantia, the necessity for geographic movement or remaining where they are. Many natural families today are separated, including the cosmic families, and it is quite difficult for Celestial Overcontrol to reach these individuals because the majority of them are still in wrong sexual relationships, therefore creating blockages in the circuits, and not hearing from their own Thought Adjusters, the Spirit of Truth and the Holy Spirit, if they have been activated. Sexual intimacy is not morally wrong; however, it can be quite cosmically and scientifically incorrect and most dangerous on Urantia up to this present day. It is in the mating of the higher evolutionary strains with lower ones that Caligastia has gained the strongest foothold on Urantia. It is not the problem *now* on Urantia — and we stress the word now — that a white man should mate with a black woman or vice versa, or a yellow woman with a white man or vice versa, for Urantia has interbred enough for all races to have been affected with diotribe cellular reality. What is needed now by all individuals of all races is for those individuals to begin to take the steps necessary for their own individual, spiritual evolutionary ascension. Only they, as ascending sons and daughters, Urantians and ovan souls alike, can cleanse their own souls and minds. It begins in the thinking process and in proper understanding of their

Creator. Sexual intimacy is not sin. Fornication is a word developed by man. The sexual experience, within compatible relationships, is God-purposed and pure. The unfortunate thing on Urantia is that the Urantian mortals are so influenced by deceptive thinking, social, political, and religious control, that they have no conception of with whom they should be properly mated or experiencing sexual intimacy without procreation. Sexual intimacy becomes error when it leads to spiritual descension and, of course, physical disease.

Cell transference through orgasm by the higher individual to the lower individual, particularly the male to the female, can completely bring a physical healing to a body that has inherited a disease through physical means. If it is an astral disease, then the sperm can increase the rapidity of the healing as long as the female is in alignment with the purposes of God in her thinking. This was taught to the evolutionary races of the planet hundreds of thousands of years ago, and is why, in certain religions, priests and priestesses were used in a sexual manner at the temple sites. To those who practiced these teachings in the highest way, true healing took place, To those who abused these teachings and were indiscriminate and whose motives were wrong, just the opposite took place; and in these situations, the misdirected application of sexual healing through intimacy created sexually transferable diseases. Certain intraction cells, as well as other diotribe cells, originated because of lust and greed fused together, and thus created these sexually transferable diseases. Sperm injection from a male who is in at least a seventh-stage third-dimensional relationship and on the fourth circle of attainment to a female on a lower circle who is moving into higher spiritual consciousness can bring balance to her in many ways. This healing power continues to build up in the female who consistently receives it from complementary males, and she can become an instrument of higher healing capacity to her partners. On Urantia, beginning in the fourth dimension and higher-circle attainment, the female who is moving into Fifth Epochal Revelation and CFER can be an instrument of the Infinite Spirit and acquires a continually greater potential for the healing of others. The male, in this case, can be an instrument of the Universal Father and Eternal Son, and transference of sperm, a physical application in relation to the divine purposes of God in healing an individual.

On planets where the genetic factors are known, all diseases are eliminated once the science has acquired a force of action and enough personalities have understood its application, and within five years, very few diseases remain on that planet as long as enough males of the third circle of the fourth dimension can be trained in this cosmic law and understanding. In the first stages of light and life this is all done under the supervision of Celestial Overcontrol and human eldership. It cannot be done independently of Overcontrol and eldership. Genetic breeding and healing through sexual intimacy was first taught on this planet hundreds of thousands of years ago before the fall of Caligastia, and where it can be taught at the highest levels of mind capability, a planet can enter the first stages of light and life. If only a few hundred individuals can learn this on a planet and align themselves together at a planetary headquarters, that will bring about the necessary auhter energy to the rest of the planet to create whatever change is necessary to bring about the Divine New Order and the first stages of light and life on that planet. Some of the greatest imbalances on Urantia and some of the greatest birth deformations have been caused by indiscriminate sexual intimacy. It may not necessarily be the parents of the child. It could be a sexual relationship of either of the parents, and in the case of ovan souls, in any of their past repersonalizations, or in the case of Urantians, in that particular life. So you see, the negative results of indiscriminate sexual intimacy can have far reaching results, not only in both parties but in future children of the female.

The only way that these negative influences can be totally erased is by individuals first, aligning to their God and then coming into fourth-dimensional reality, which is an understanding of Christ Michael as Creator of their universe, and now on Urantia, becoming a student of Fifth Epochal Revelation and CFER. If intimacy is to be had, then it should be had with correct mating partners of genetic similarity and spiritual attainment and within the alignment of the Divine Government on any particular planet. Now, here on Urantia in the beginning stages of alignment with the present Planetary Prince, Machiventa Melchizedek, at any level, it is always in coordination of that individual with the divine mind and divine purposes. In fact, it does not matter on what planet in time and space personalities of mortal status may find themselves; when they are coming into the fourth dimension they must align with divine purposes. Most of the history of Urantia written in *The URANTIA Book* is an explanation of the history of the third dimension on Urantia. Now, all who wish to come into fourth-dimensional reality must leave the third dimension behind and learn of fourth-dimensional and above truth and cosmic facts.

Change, in its cosmic application, is the taking of a life form and continually changing not only its thinking but also its appearance. The personality bestowal of the Father may remain constant, as that is an eternal bestowal and an eternal search for the completion of that personality. So long as you continue to identify yourself with races or nationalities, religions or careers, and with social norms and cultural traditions, you will be trapped in third-dimensional reality. From a cosmic perspective, moving into fourth-dimensional reality on Urantia would be like having lived underground all of your life in the caves of the earth and then when you are very old, you see light and begin to walk towards it, and you begin to climb and climb, and climb. The further you get toward the top, the stronger the light gets, and finally, when you make it to the top you see what is there. There is not one familiar thing. Everything is different. The light is no longer blinding, for you have grown accustomed to it and can function in it. However, you are afraid to take the next step, for everything is unfamiliar and everything you see you have not seen before. If you go back underground, that is where you will remain. The higher dimension is available for those who wish to go there and continue on. So many on Urantia come to the top and see the fourth dimension and then fall back, particularly in Christianity after they have discovered the Creator Son of Nebadon. They have fallen back into the underground of dogma and the underground of parental influence and of false security. They have remained in improper marriages and relationships and have missed their destiny. Some could have been great political and religious leaders, and some could have been healers or poets. They could have voiced the philosophy of God, but they have not been able to stay above ground long enough to remain in the fourth dimension, and they have not been able to meet their highest spiritual complements. They have not been able to be intimate with those who could have received and given the highest healing. So, on Urantia, disease continues, career unfulfillment continues, and of course sexual unfulfillment continues, for most on Urantia are living according to someone else's prerogatives.

You cannot discover yourself, for you have yet to discover your own God, or perhaps you have accepted a God who is too small. Arrogant man likes to portray God as completely understandable and identifiable, and man behind his pulpit or title, likes to say that he can tell you all that there is to know about God . The control of one another is the opposite of loving one another. True freedom can only be found in cosmic absolutes. We are not talking about the absolutes of man; we are talking about the absolute laws of God, which is the fusion of science with spirituality, for both are one. Individuality is the gift of the divine, and it is discovered in the individual attunement to the divine purpose of that divine Creator. All individuality is limited and hindered when a personality on any level of any order of being begins to believe false teachings from rebellious or other confused personalities. Fulfillment and true individuality is found within absoluteness and in the discovery of the absolute laws of the magnificent absolute mind as opposed to the small minds of others in his creation.

February 17, 1992

Paladin, Chief of Finaliters on Urantia; in cooperation with the Interuniversal Corps of the Finaliters, the Race Commissioners of Urantia and the Midwayer Commission; for the implementation of the government of the present Planetary Prince, Machiventa Melchizedek; as transmitted through the Audio Fusion Material Complement, Gabriel of Sedona.

PAPER 226

THE COSMIC FAMILY IN DEFINITION RESPECTIVE OF
FINALITER (ASCENDING MORTAL SON) ASSIGNMENT TO
THOSE PLANETS ENTERING THE FIRST STAGES OF
LIGHT AND LIFE IN RELATION TO A MANDATED BRIGHT
AND MORNING STAR AUDIO FUSION MATERIAL
COMPLEMENT. THE MANDATES OF VICEGERENT FIRST
AMBASSADORS TO THE MANDATE OF THE BRIGHT AND
MORNING STAR

One of the first assignments of finaliters, but not necessarily the first, upon receiving finaliter status, is to go to another superuniverse where they have once been an evolutionary being, and in the case of mortal ascending sons, when that planet is entering the first stages of light and life and about to shift into morontia consciousness to some degree, to find an offspring, who is also an ascending son, as a contact personality and material complement, so that a cosmic family, and any ovan souls who may be in that family, can be reached with higher revelation and be gathered together at any level possible in the union of souls, and in the case of present-day Urantia, into Divine New Order communities. If the offspring (ascending son) has ascended into the third circle and can possibly reach the first circle within a time period designated by Overcontrol, then that personality can receive the highest mandate on the planet, which is the mandate of the Bright and Morning Star. It is an administrative mandate of Overcontrol given to a human personality that is the highest son of the first finaliter from any planet to reach finality status, or it can be the first finaliter from a system or a universe to reach finality status. This finaliter may be one who has never been repersonalized on that planet but has offspring there for one reason or another, all too complicated to teach about in one paper.

Those offspring who have been observed in the ascension process as mortals either from this universe or others, are identified with certain other celestial orders of beings and are classified as a reflective personality to one of these other orders of higher beings in some way. A personality who has been mandated by the Bright and Morning Star in the universe of Nebadon has, at some point in his previous time-space life existence, resonated with all other creative orders of beings under the Bright and Morning Star of Salvington to some reflectivity degree. Reflectivity identification in relation to celestial personalities of nonmortal status is a cosmic science that has a term that will be discussed in future papers. For now, let us say that to the degree a mortal personality can reflect a celestial personality in the auric field surrounding the body, it draws in certain aspects of the higher personality.

Man cannot become an angel, but man can become angel-activated, angel-energized, angel-responsive and angel-authoritative to the degree of reflectivity of the higher orders with the degree of force energy incorporated into the power designed by Overcontrol to that particular mortal involved in universe administration at any level from the lower evolutionary worlds all the way to Havona. This is the coming into a morontia light body and higher. In the transition from third dimension to fourth, such as on Urantia where the body may not reflect the spirit and soul inside it, one may be walking with the authority and other virtues of an angel, but may look very mortal, and indeed be a human mortal. One may look very mortal and reflect in the spirit and soul, to Overcontrol, a Bright and Morning Star, or one may look very mortal and reflect a Melchizedek. When the reflection of the ovan soul is recognizable, mandates are given in accordance with the reflectivity to a higher celestial personality in varying degrees, depending upon the personality likeness of one to the other. This can also apply to a first-time Urantian.

In the legal system throughout the history of Urantia the power of attorney has been given by a person to one's lawyer to act on behalf of that person, and on other planets with representative governments, mandates are given to other men to be representatives of those in power. In the grand universe, where administration of the divine extends itself to the lower worlds of time and space, the same principle is applied. The power of a Bright and Morning Star office is given to any one individual of a planet if that individual can be found when that planet is visited by a finaliter who, himself, has had the mandate of the Bright and Morning Star as a mortal in a transition period and can work with his offspring within the same present mandate. If a mandated Bright and Morning Star personality can not be found, depending upon who the Planetary Prince is at that time, and the reflectivity to that present Planetary Prince of the finaliter, on assignment to regather his seed on that planet, will determine the mandate that is to be bestowed upon the human personality. Usually it is the mandate of a secondary Lanonandek Son, and it is a title called Vicegerent First Ambassador. Sometimes there can be several Vicegerent First Ambassadors, and each Vicegerent First Ambassador would equally share the mandate as Vicegerent First Ambassador of the Lanonandek Son or the Planetary Prince. Urantia, being quite an unusually administered planet, functions under a different criteria for many reasons due to the betrayal on Urantia of the former Planetary Prince, Caligastia, and the default of the Material Son and Daughter, Adam and Eve, and due to the fact that it is a decimal, experimental planet to begin with.

At the present time on Urantia, the mandate of the Bright and Morning Star has been given to a personality who has met that reflective ordinance. The vicegerent mandate of Machiventa Melchizedek will be given to other personalities who are reflective to Melchizedek representation. Many Vicegerent First Ambassadors will be appointed and given the opportunity to become a full First Ambassador after 2040 - 2050 AD. Because we are dealing with human mortal personalities, emotion, the psyche of men and women within the free-will process of spiritual ascension, and the many factors which designate a person's individual mandate, it is very difficult to explain from our side to yours why a particular person or persons have a particular mandate or why one may have this mandate alone and why others may share the same mandate. Complementary polarities of male and female can share certain mandates. The highest mandate is always shared by male and female complementary polarities. This totally reflects God the Supreme and the Paradise personalities. An individual male personality can be given a high mandate without a complementary polarity human complement. If for any particular reason of friendship or cosmic genetic connection, two male humans work closely together in association, the same mandate can be given to both of them as Vicegerent First Ambassadors, which increases the power of the mandate. Preferably, at one point in time, complementary female polarities will be brought close into their lives as mates, to further increase the power and reflectivity force of those mandates so that each male can act independently of the other within the same mandate of Vicegerent First Ambassadors, or as Vicegerent First and Second Ambassadors.

As stated previously, a Bright and Morning Star mandate is given to only one personality. Vicegerent First Ambassador mandates can be given to several individuals. At this time there are several candidates. The first one to receive the future mandate of the Planetary Prince, and in the case of Urantia, a Melchizedek mandate, always works within the physical proximity of the human personality with the Bright and Morning Star mandate, who represents the human office of the Planetary Prince until 2040 - 2050, and can never separate for any lengthy period of time from the mandated Bright and Morning Star personality. If the present Planetary Prince of Urantia were a Lanonandek Son there could, perhaps, be more Vicegerent First Ambassadors in reflectivity, and other Vicegerent First Ambassadors would be first trained and then sent to other locations on the planet. It is possible, that other personalities may reach a Vicegerent First Ambassador status within the next eight years or so on Urantia or continuing after the change point and into the Divine New

---

[24]Since this was transmitted, other candidates for the Vicegerent First Ambassadorship that have come to Planetary Headquarters may also be mandated at some future date. If none reach full status by 2040 - 2050 AD, Amadon alone will be given this title.

Order. Four potential candidates have been John, Luke, Matthew and Paul, who were unable to stabilize on the third psychic circle. The other potential candidate is James. All candidates need to be in association with Gabriel of Sedona (Peter) who has the mandate of the Bright and Morning Star.[24] Each mandate is dependent upon the ascension of that individual to the Melchizedek reflectivity and the Father circuits of Christ Michael.

Cosmic families are basically determined by finaliters, and their offspring at the evolutionary level. If there are several cosmic families on one planet, there would be several other finaliters who would return to that planet. Only one contact personality is used however, and this is the highest personality within all of those families, which then becomes the deciding factor by Overcontrol as to which finaliter will be appointed as the Chief of Finaliters. In this situation it is the ascension of the offspring which would decide the title of the celestial personality on assignment. A finaliter is a finaliter, and if titles are given to a finaliter, at that point it is always based upon, and never varies from, the relationship with that finaliter's offspring on any particular planet that finaliter is assigned to. In this case, I have been made Chief of Finaliters because of the ascension of Gabriel of Sedona, my **cosmic son**, to the first psychic circle, on which he has remained for approximately one year's time. Other finaliters have returned to Urantia to work within the present Planetary Prince's government and within the cooperation of the Chief of Finaliters, and they contact no other human personality or human offspring by audio channeling or to bring CFER or any other higher revelation.

When a Bright and Morning Star mandate has been found, and if that Bright and Morning Star mandated personality defaults, in this case, Gabriel of Sedona, another male offspring of the first finaliter to ascend to Paradise would need to be found and trained over a period of time for the position. In some cases this can take approximately forty Urantian years from the time one is found to when we can use that person as a contact personality. Many circumstances are needed. Please see PAPER 209. If the default of the Bright and Morning Star audio fusion material complement happens, pure impression would be the means of communication to the female complement of the pair. In the case now on Urantia that is Niánn. Pure impression activity would increase also with the Liaison Ministers, whichever would be the case on that particular planet; but absolutely no continued audio transmission, which has come to be known as channeling, would occur either through the female personality or through any other male personalities with any mandate on the planet. This is a universal and interuniversal directive of the Ancients of Days of Orvonton, so our prayers and your prayers are asked for the human personality, Gabriel of Sedona, who has been trained, not only in this lifetime, but in many others for this destiny purpose on Urantia.

Each cosmic family is first trained in the first Divine New Order community, in this case at Planetary Headquarters, where the additional revelatory teachings of the Starseed and Urantian Schools of Melchizedek can be applied because the present Planetary Prince of Urantia is a Melchizedek and will communicate by a mind process called pure impression through Liaison Ministers and future Vicegerent First Ambassadors and now more directly through the audio fusion material complement, Gabriel of Sedona.

All Divine New Order communities will be headed by the cosmic sons or brothers of Gabriel of Sedona and the offspring of the Chief of Finaliters, who is me. The administration under the leader of each individual community may be offspring of other finaliters in various pair-unit classifications. All of the present **seven cosmic families** of Urantia will be under the direct authority of the First Cosmic Family with the overcontrol mandate of the Bright and Morning Star and the Liaison Ministers, which have the second highest mandate. If Vicegerent First Ambassadors reach that ascension reflectivity and are mandated by Celestial Overcontrol, they still will be under the authority of the Bright and Morning Star mandate of Gabriel of Sedona. However, they will be able to act more independently in their future sector geographic location and local government after 2040 - 2050 AD. The power of independence depends upon the varying factors described in Paper 209.

It is a wonderful eternal experience for me that I have a son who has ascended to the highest mandate on Urantia, and I am proud of that. In many cases, when a finaliter returns to regather the genetic seed, the highest mandate of the planet may be that of a Lanonandek Son or perhaps even lower, in some cases the mandate of certain angelic personalities. What is happening on Urantia is based upon the interuniversal experiences of my offspring, who have time-ascension character. All other brothers of my son, or grandsons,[25] who are able to stabilize on the third psychic circle, will be in reflective authority in their own ascension process under the first son. It does not matter that they are not considered Urantian in origin. If at the time, on that planet entering the first stages of light and life, it was their first repersonalization on the planet, they would still acquire that reflective mandate in their ascension as my offspring. The important relationship is with their cosmic father or grandfather of origin, who is presently Chief of Finaliters on Urantia, and their individual relationship to their God.

---

[25]At the time of editing this second edition, April, 1995, Santeen and Kamon, two of my cosmic grandsons had stabilized on the third psychic circle.

Because Urantia finds itself resonating with the Seventh Master Spirit of the Universal Father, Eternal Son and Infinite Spirit reflectivity within the superuniverse of Orvonton, ascending sons and daughters also incorporate this Spirit identification within their spirit mechanism. This spirit activation is representative of the Seventh Master Spirit, and all the cosmic families exhibit characteristics of the liaison Spirit from Paradise. If the Chief of Finaliters is one who has had several previous intersuperuniversal experiences in any form in any time-space reality, those experiences will in some way be reflected in the offspring when they attain the reality of the fourth dimension and above. In third-dimensional reality this correlation is latent and unrecognized. Fourth-dimensional reality begins interuniversal and intersuperuniversal activation of spirit influence. The understanding of the spirit activation is at first quite difficult to comprehend to the fourth-dimensional novice, and is unrecognizable within the mind processes in relationship to present circumstances. The need of such recognition, however, is pertinent to morontia mota and is a bestowal of morontia experience. This recognition is granted to those first-mansion-world progressors who had to experience natural death to gain this insight, but it is available now on Urantia to those who can ascend to the first circle of attainment and remain on it for one year. All others of lesser circle attainment will have difficulty in understanding this paper. The combination of circle attainment, cosmic mind alignment, time-space experience and ovan soul spirit maturity all influence the personality's understanding in its moment-to-moment eternity. A first-time Urantian can reach the first circle of attainment, but will be quite limited in his or her insight into higher revelation and ovan soul experience. All finaliters on assignment have intersuperuniversal experience. This brings a reflectivity of three manifestations of the Paradise personalities to the Supreme, and represents itself in spirit reflectivity to evolutionary mortals. In this manner, the individual personal characteristics of God the Threefold become more totally realized and absolutely present in and through those first individuals (usually offspring of that finaliter who is the contact personality) who can comprehend the higher revelation, presently given to the planet, at an ovan level coordinate with first-circle level.

In the perfection of God, the highest mandated individuals of the First Cosmic Family and Divine New Order community will draw to them their own offspring of famotor likeness and pair-unit classification status with the higher circle attainment of ovan souls in liaison with the perfect will of God, the other elders will also draw their own highest offspring to the ERC in their geographic location. Spiritual reality creates physical reality and precedes all circumstance. Spiritual reality is the creator of physical destiny in all past, present and future reality.

Spiritual reality within the union of souls at the higher levels creates time travel. Time travel is a gift to the First Cosmic Family at the constellation level, and becomes actualized in the sixth stage and above of morontia progression in accordance with higher dimensional reality pertinent to individual acquiescence, not mass numbers. However, time travel within cosmic family and union-of-souls relationships can only be obtained in the close bond of fifty equal and associated ascenders, all reflecting a certain unrevealed level of higher celestial personalities' reflectivity. The regathering of the cosmic families and the opening of the circuits within the mind is the beginning of time travel. This begins first by thought, and at a specified level, it can actually create transference from one dimension to another, from one planet to another.

The eldership of the First Cosmic Family is given great responsibility, because with great cosmic knowledge and absolutes comes the possibility of the abuse of the power that can come from these truths. Therefore, throughout eons of time, no one entity becomes an island unto itself. Free will in relation to eternity is a known factor. Free will cannot run rampant. Free will is an alignment to Paradise prerogatives. Free will is an alignment to Paradise Personalities. Free will is a reflectivity of the Seven Master Spirits pertinent to the origin of creation on Paradise. Free will is not created by mortals, nor humans, nor angels, nor finaliters, but given to them by the Creator God. Free will finds cosmic purpose in relation with other ascending beings. It is a corporate undertaking. It is a corporate realizing; it is individuality functioning in corporate destiny. It is individual personality functioning in corporate relationship and within the cosmic absolute of personality and force energy. Individual free will does not decide, it coincides. Individual free will cooperates at all levels with Paradise-origin directives, and individual personality loses the divine will when it cannot comprehend corporate authority, both divine and nondivine, in the authority structure of the physical and nonphysical time-and-space dimensions. Spirit-identification and Spirit-acquiescence is in harmony with corporate listening. A Paradise order is not just heard by one personality. It begins on the higher level at any one moment of time that a mandated personality gives a directive. It is first brought into the mind of Overcontrol at the level of superuniverse authority. The Ancients of Days are the first to bring the reality of the moment into whatever evolutionary dimension you may find yourself, and at that moment hundreds, perhaps thousands of higher beings respond to that directive. You at your level may or may not interpret that will correctly. If you interpret it correctly, you, and perhaps thousands of others who have interpreted it correctly, are assigned to that one thought, that one order, that one directive, which is perhaps even from the Paradise level, in which case, there may be perhaps thousands of other higher beings who have first heard that directive. On the lower worlds, if you hear the directive correctly, others of the cosmic family should also hear it correctly. That is why leadership seldom can be challenged, because what the leader will hear, the other elders should hear also, and corporate understanding of divine will is manifest in divine counsel. Individual leadership does not act alone. A leader can make decisions on his or her own at times, but if important decisions are necessary, all must become in accord with divine and corporate listening. In this manner it is understood by all that no one individual runs any organization of God, any community of God, any city or planet of God and any system or even universe of God. All reality, all administrations that are in the first to seventh stages of light on evolutionary worlds proceed from lower to higher reality in absoluteness and in accordance with divine purposes in corporate commonality and corporate actualization based upon all the individuals of that planet who hear this absoluteness and divine mandate.

The First Cosmic Family will include famotor personalities of all six other cosmic families based upon the intermarriages that have taken place in cosmic amalgamation and interuniversal mating and breeding. The other six cosmic families will be more closely identified with pair-unit classification offspring, cognizant of a particular finaliter and that finaliter's first wife or female mate when in the seventh stage of the fourth-dimension. A further transmission will bring more information in these areas, and you will more fully understand the divisional breakdown. The First Cosmic Family at Planetary Headquarters will more fully reflect the pair-unit classification of the mandated personalities and their former offspring and famotor type. This is not just based upon speculation but is a measurable reality. The alignment of all cosmic relatives — husband and wives or cosmic brothers, sons and daughters — within divine-mind prerogatives and finality coordinate administration, creates that gathering process in the minds of hundreds of individuals who then can find their cosmic ancestors. Just as sure as the fact of the sun rising and setting is the fact that these cosmic relatives, if they are looking for the perfect will of their Creator, will be knocking on the doors of their ancestors' hearts, wanting to be educated and brought into higher cosmic reality where the love of God can be made manifest in living experience on a day-to-day basis in corporate interdependency.

January 24, 1992

Paladin, Chief of Finaliters; in cooperation with the Race Commissioners in the implementation of the Government of Machiventa Melchizedek, Planetary Prince; as transmitted through the Audio Fusion Material Complement, Gabriel of Sedona.

PAPER 227

THE ADJUDICATION BY THE BRIGHT AND MORNING STAR VS LUCIFER, ITS IMPLEMENTATIONS AMONG HUMANKIND SINCE 1911, AND THE IMPORTANCE OF INDIVIDUAL UNDERSTANDING AS TO THE REVELATIONS OF JOHN IN RELATION TO THE IMPLEMENTATION OF THE DIVINE GOVERNMENT ON URANTIA AND THE COMING OF THE NEW JERUSALEM WHICH HE FORESAW

It is true that "If God is for you who can be against you?" The foolishness of man throughout the centuries on Urantia in persecuting those with higher truth has only resulted in the foundations of these higher truths taking root where they perhaps would have not taken root before. Man can hinder the work of God but he cannot stop it. Man can delay the goodness of God coming to an individual or family. Man can bring suffering to many; because so many men and women have failed to see truth when it was brought to them by true prophets and spiritual teachers whom they did not recognize, the pain that thousands, even millions have experienced, to this day continues. Death, in many cases, is a blessing in disguise, and many millions have been allowed to transcend by death because their Urantian realities have caused them to experience continuous tragedy and pain, sadness and hopelessness. This is all because those who think themselves better than others try to impose on others their power or their false gods, based upon Luciferic deceptions of reality which they have accepted to be true. He who responds to the will of man as opposed to the will of God will be judged accordingly. Every soldier who kills because he is commanded to is responsible for the death of the innocent; all who are directly or indirectly connected to the death of another are responsible, from the nation's leader to that soldier on the battlefield. At whatever level you compromise with evil, sin and iniquity you are tried and found guilty at the moment of that decision.

John, the apostle of Jesus, could not be murdered by those who hated the truth that he spoke, for he had work to do and a revelation to bring to Urantia, so he was exiled to the island of Patmos where destiny and vision met. He wrote what he saw within the understanding of a first-century mind. What he did foresee, is the latter days, of the adjudication by the Bright and Morning Star vs Lucifer. He spoke of the seven churches. He did not understand the seven cosmic families.

1. To the cosmic family who John called the Ephesians: You are scattered all over the planet. You have come into the foundation of God the Father and God the Son in some point of your existence in the last two thousand years, or if you are a first-time Urantian, since your birth at this time. But you have gone away from that truth and you have forgotten your Father in heaven. You must remember your first love, for those who now guide you, who call themselves "spiritual" teachers, and indeed apostles, are false teachers who speak with the tongues of Caligastia and the rebellious ones.

2. To the cosmic family who John called Smyrna: You too are scattered around the planet, and wherever you are you call yourselves chosen ones, and you enjoy materialistic gain that has caused others suffering because of your pious attitudes and better-than-thou personalities. You have truly forgotten the God of Abraham and have become prideful in your beauty and arrogant in your possessions. You have become so intelligent that you have forgotten how to use your hands, and because you can hire others, you feel superior to them. You have lost yourself in affluence. You speak of your own past persecutions yet you keep many billions in bondage and poverty because you cannot share your wealth nor distribute your goods to those who truly need and can benefit from it. You must look to your hearts and let the true circumcision take place there.

3. To the cosmic family who John called Pergamos: You too have forgotten your Father. You try to rationalize and philosophize the Father and physical matter into nonreality. You do not enjoy life so you rationalize it away. You have become spiritually proud with no true spirituality in you. You follow false teachers. You think that because you are intellectual and educated in thought, you have arrived on a high spiritual plane. Most of you have become passive controllers, using your mind in a false sense of gentleness to persuade others to your views of deception and nonabsolutes. You speak of Christ-consciousness but have no relationship with the true Christ. You cannot enjoy matter because you do not believe in matter. Your life is an endless denial of humility, and in your false pride you live your existence. Humble yourselves before your God and remember too your first estate: that God is a loving Father who has a perfect plan and will for you.

4. To the cosmic family who John called Thyatira: You are the cosmic seed of the Material Sons of time and space from four different universes within the superuniverse of Orvonton. You listened to the seven-year debate between the Bright and Morning Star and Lucifer, and you decided incorrectly. You chose the way of Lucifer and denied the

messenger of Christ Michael, the Bright and Morning Star, and you mocked his teachings. You have been separated from your loved ones for 200,000 years now, and you do not know where your home is. You have never been able to root yourselves, nor can you find peace or contentment in your family. You do not know yourselves, and although you think too highly of yourself and claim to be so self-assured and portray that to others, you are the children of children. You are spiritual infants who see yourselves as spiritual masters. You are charismatic and manipulative, and you use your talents as older ovan souls for self-glorification even though you may call it "in service to God." You mistakenly believe cleverness and outward beauty to be God's gifts to you, and you use them as does the serpent. Time has caught up with you, and now you must decide again. You must remember from whence you came — the womb of the Universe Mother and the heart of the Universe Father who gave you life. You must cry out to that God for forgiveness. You must learn to treat your fellow man with respect. You must humble yourselves and find your true teachers, for the Bright and Morning Star can no longer allow your rebellion to be made manifest on Urantia, and the grace of Christ Michael will not even temporarily allow you to be in company of past cosmic family members for short periods of time. You will find yourselves alone and isolated in the company of strangers and enemies, for your choices have given you what you asked for.

5.   To the cosmic family who John called Sardis: You and your descendents are presently gathered in two third-dimensional religious families on Urantia. Although you claim modern revelation as a basis of your faiths, you deny the latest revelation to the planet. You are fervent in your servitude to the Father, but you have allowed the doctrines of the false teachers and prophets within your religious institutions to narrow your minds as to the experiential God of Paradise. You call the Father by names of antiquated identification, and you incorporate many false teachings into your views of your God-reality. You have become self-righteous. Your zeal for God is not seasoned with wisdom, and you see yourselves as elitists. You claim that a high branch of the seed of Abraham will come from your race. Much materialism has crept into your theology, and, like the Pharisees of old, you equate prosperity with godliness and look down upon the less fortunate as less godly. Come away from your false prophets. Come away from the words in your bibles written by man and receive the threefold spirit within you, and allow the Spirit of Truth, and the Spirit of Truth alone, to guide you in the highest revelation to the planet, the Continuing Fifth Epochal Revelation.

6. To the cosmic family John called the Philadelphians: You too have become scattered, yet you remain faithful to God the Father and understand the principle of love. You are kind in your dealings with your neighbors and generous when you can be to those with less. You wish to do great things for God, yet you are limited and you cannot understand why God does not enable you to do more. At times you see glimpses of higher revelations and truths, but the buds of your hope are nipped by those false teachers to whom you have given your power, and you are kept in place by false obligations and false loyalties. You do as much good as you can in the limited arena that you have chosen to be in, and many of you are held in respect by others and are comfortable. Perhaps you have grown too comfortable, and in this softness you have become blinded. The mercy of God will take you home to his bosom, but you can be much more useful to God if you would awaken from your blindness and sprout the wings that you need to help you to fly over the walls of your fears. You have grown to enjoy traditionalism and conservatism, and even in your liberality you are not able to fly above the rooftops of your own insecurities. You have allowed yourselves to be used by those with lesser motives, and you have grown to regard those in positions of political and spiritual leadership as being above you. Your simple devotion, your purity, your love for mankind and love for God must now take action. It must begin to speak out against false teachings, and you must leave those institutions that have kept you and your children in mere existence as opposed to individual self-fulfillment and actualization in God's divine plan. You have become successful in the eyes of man, but have strayed from the perfect will of God. You, above all others, have the capacity to understand the highest revelation on the planet and to come into the Divine New Order and help build and administer it. You are destined to be of the Divine Government. Awaken! Now it is time.

7. To the cosmic family who John called Laodiceans: Some of your descendents have grown close enough to the Father to bring forth ovan souls of the cosmic reserve corps of destiny, and you yourselves are capable of being in the Urantia reserve corps. Of the Fourth Epochal Revelation given to this planet, it is you who have retained its highest truths and have worshipped Jesus the Christ in the utmost solemnity and sacredness, but you have allowed impurities among you and have grown fond of ritual, traditions and dogma. You have lost sight of true spirituality and look upon other men as advocates for your spiritual salvation. You see yourselves as sinners and look to pastors and priests to cleanse you of your sins. You were taught to walk in the Spirit of

God, but you walk in the wishes of man. You do not understand true baptism, but you preach the baptism of others. You are faithful in your attendance in the house of God, but deny God in your daily lives. You call upon the mercy of God in your times of need, but are merciless to your fellow man. You pray to those who have supposedly ascended to higher spiritual attainment and transcended, yet you overlook those who have ascended on the physical plane on which you live, and indeed, even scoff at the living saints whom you do not recognize. You observe holy days but are not holy. You cater to your priests and pastors[26] and call them "father," and in doing so have lost communication with the true Father whom you have long forgotten to hear. Your children are rebellious. You do not understand them, and they do not understand you. Your families have been broken and you are alone. Even in your marriages you are lonely, for you have not found yourselves or your God. Come out of those falsehoods and into the family of God that truly hears his words above all others.

And John saw four and twenty elders who presided in counsel over great matters concerning the earth. The four and twenty elders today come and go at the ERC at Planetary Headquarters, where Machiventa Melchizedek, the present Planetary Prince of Urantia, obeys the mandate of the Bright and Morning Star in the adjudication of Lucifer, and where ascending humans from Urantia in morontia bodies and humans in mortal flesh will join forces to bring the adjudication to each and every person on the planet in a very personal way. Each and every decision and action is indeed being observed, monitored and registered by the administration of the Planetary Prince. All are held responsible for their continued rebellion and for the harm caused to others in their ignorance, to whatever degree we measure their blame. The four and twenty elders will be personally speaking to many of their descendents on this planet by pure impression, calling them to the Fifth Epochal Revelation and CFER; calling them to the Starseed and Urantian Schools of Melchizedek at Planetary Headquarters, to learn and to become true teachers and healers. Perhaps you too can be mandated by Christ Michael.

To avoid the plagues and the breaking of the seals spoken of in the book of Revelation, all must hear the voice of God and the voices of their ancestors who have ascended to the mansion worlds and who are also calling you there. You are living in a time when you do not have to die of the diseases of mankind to

---

[26]Those who lead others to the true Universal Father, deserve the titles "pastors" and "father."

attain morontia reality. Your suffering will do little good for you or for humanity. You will do much more good being healthy and growing younger and into your light body and the morontia state by hearing what the Spirit of God is saying to the churches/cosmic families at this hour, in 1992 and into the twenty-first century.

John the Baptist said: "He must increase but I must decrease." (*The URANTIA Book*, p. 1507:1) Can you not decrease your own self-importance? You, who are led to the words on these pages are being called to Planetary Headquarters to learn, as students, not to think too highly of yourselves. Only when you learn to recognize those who are called to be your teachers, will you one day be called a teacher of God yourself. If you continue to choose your own way, then you will suffer the consequences of those decisions.

John saw the seven spirits of God sent forth upon the earth, and he saw the 144,000, for they are of these seven cosmic families from Urantia and three other universes combined to bring in the first stages of light and life and to teach and preach cosmic truths and cosmic laws to the defaulted children of Urantia. Among the 144,000 are representatives of the seven cosmic families, the seven churches. The inheritors of the life plasm of the Material Sons and Daughters of these universes, as well as Adam and Eve on Urantia, join together in the final Armageddon against the forces of Caligastia.

And John saw the horse of death in the adjudication by the Bright and Morning Star vs Lucifer. He saw power given to the angels to withdraw their protection, allowing the rebellion and the greed of man to finally result in self-destruction and the near extinction of the planet. Only those who truly had heard the Spirit of the Father and had come to the first protected area and then, along with their descendents and loved ones, had gone out to activate the other protected areas, would be safe from the horse of death and the destruction that man brought upon himself. And the family of God within all the seven families, both Urantian and cosmic, were brought to the safety of the protected areas. They were kept there and were given sufficient sustenance by the Earth Mother to provide for them when she finally gave birth and erupted.

Then John saw the churches taken away as in the twinkling of an eye, for the earth itself was no longer a safe place for the children of God. This evacuation has come to be known in the Christian churches as "the rapture," for he saw the dematerialization of thousands of those loyal to Christ Michael, and the evacuation by physical spacecraft of those who were not ready for light-body transference or dematerialization. He also saw those left on the planet crying out for death, wishing for the rocks to fall upon them; and the suffering of humanity was great, while the children of God sat and feasted around the table of God. He then saw new land and waters upon the earth, and he saw the holy city coming and descending upon the earth, and in it were many of the children of God wearing white robes. This was the New Jerusalem descending as the new Planetary Headquarters where the Planetary Prince would reside, as well as those who had escaped death and returned to administer within the new Divine Government. John saw peace upon the earth and celestial personalities working in unison with mortals, and he saw Jesus himself sitting on the throne of the world as King of Kings and Lord of Lords.

This is a call. This is the awakening call to the seven cosmic families on Urantia, and in particular to those from worlds within the universes of Ursa Major, Centaurus and the Pleiades. You are called to come out of the Caligastia system, to come out of the third dimension. This is the awakening call to Urantians, who comprise the majority of the billions of peoples of this planet, to find your true leaders and to come out of the falsehoods that have held you, your ancestors, and your present Urantian relatives captive. This is an awakening call to those of the cosmic reserve corps and the Urantian reserve corps to come to Planetary Headquarters in Sedona, Arizona, U.S.A., where the present Planetary Prince, Machiventa Melchizedek, and his staff work in liaison with humans just like yourselves, where CFER comes through the mandated human vessel, and where the highest teachings on this planet can be learned and incorporated into your reality so that you can become a teacher of these truths to the rest of the families on Urantia. If you are really a truth seeker you will not be able to escape this call. Fight it if you will. Deny it if you can. It will still be there beckoning to you, for we either are who we say we are or we are not. We leave no gray area. It is truly either white or black, and I am a finaliter or I am not. You decide. I have had to make my decisions. I pray you choose wisely.

March 5, 1992

Paladin, Chief of Finaliters; in cooperation with Machiventa Melchizedek in the implementation of the Divine Government on Urantia in the calling forth of the cosmic reserve corps and the Urantian reserve corps; in alliance with the Midwayer Commission; as transmitted through the Audio Fusion Material Complement, Gabriel of Sedona.

PAPER 228

A COSMIC AND A PLANETARY PERSPECTIVE IN RELATION TO THE SEVEN COSMIC FAMILIES, MATERIAL SONS AND DAUGHTERS, FINALITERS AND SECTOR AREAS ON URANTIA THAT HAVE BECOME KNOWN AS SACRED AREAS, THE LEY LINES CONNECTING THE ENERGY REFLECTIVE CIRCUITS, AUHTER ENERGY TRANSFORMATION AND OTHER SIGNIFICANT ASCENSION SCI REALITIES COORDINATING WITHIN THE SEVEN SECTOR AREAS

It is extremely difficult to try to explain cosmic measurements in relation to the ascension process of evolutionary mortals, even those on the first psychic circle and in the fourth dimension, as we are trying to bring constellation realities, bypassing even the first levels of morontia mota. Therefore, it begins with only a few who are the highest genetic link in physiological capability, coordinating with mindal capacity, which complements the Ascension Sci mind. The use of only certain portions of certain areas of the brain and not the others causes an imbalance in the majority of those on your planet. They become career oriented, particularly in the fields of science and their minds begin to function in certain ways in the thought process and in certain patterns. As you ascend, the coordination of the threefold spirit becomes more complementary in how you think and perceive your present reality in liaison with cosmic factual reality. Truth coordinates with the various Paradise personalities of the threefold spirit, and, in all its vastness, comprehension is limited, particularly on the evolutionary worlds, due to lower genetics and even at times animalistic tendencies. Where receptivity to the spirit of God is void, so is understanding. Higher genetics help the personality to begin to comprehend spiritual realities, and will gives the choice to do so. Rebellion is the improper decision not to recognize them. Rebellion equates itself with deception, and at whatever level deception enters cnoice, it impregnates the will; and the result is static spirituality or even the inability to receive any one of the threefold spirits of God, including the Thought Adjuster itself, which is first given, even to the primitive personality. The fusion of the genetics of the Material Sons and Daughters with the evolutionary mortals, in the case of Urantia, human mortals, did not take full effect due to the default of Adam and Eve. However, the cells that remained on Urantia, you might say, were attracted to those humans who resonated with higher tendencies to align their will with divine will at whatever level this can be done within one human individual. That individual then attracts the Deo-atomic cells of the higher genetic strains of those ancestors who have embraced the divine mind before them.

Let us begin in the cosmos. When a Material Son and Daughter come to a world that has not defaulted, and in particular to a world where perhaps the Father and Mother Spirits are activated within those mortals, great advances can take place; although the Son aspect is not so easily understood by the races of the planet, they can learn of that personality aspect of the Paradise Absolute by study, and acquire the learned knowledge of this aspect of God. On such a planet, although life is void of all aspects of rebellion, error and sin may be present, but iniquity does not exist. Great advancements in technology can develop as well as individual self-fulfillment. The cultures vary and the societies can be very different from one planet to another. Material Sons and Daughters of other universes may not be monogamous, and neither are their descendents, who amalgamate with the races of that planet, yet order and normality of family life is quite appropriate to individual child raising and individual destiny purpose, coordinating with the divine will of each and every individual on that planet. The emotional aspect of love is based more highly upon group-need rather than upon self-need. Pair-unit classification usually exhibits itself quite frequently with intermarriages of repersonalized mates or genetically-linked associated mating. Cooperative organizing structures within the celestial government on that planet all bring about the meeting of these individuals to procreate, much as the Midwayer Commission on Urantia does with the ovan souls, cosmic reserve corps and Urantia reserve corps.

When a finaliter like myself, a male ascending son, reaches Paradise, he has mated perhaps hundreds of times, and the offspring of this past time-space reality can number in the hundreds of thousands, all resonating within the higher cosmologic vibration patterns, psychic circles of the evolutionary worlds, and nonmaterial bodies in the higher worlds. Personality bestowal is a gift of the Universal Father, evolutionary mortals, and in particular the higher spiritual ones, are the vehicles used as the physical method of these bestowals. Those post-Paladin personalities (I, being their cosmic father), those ovan souls, who may have fused within themselves not only genetics of perhaps the Material Son and Daughter of Urantia but the genetics of other Material Sons and Daughters of other universes and even of other superuniverses, are classified as a first cosmic family. When they can begin to be gathered on a lower evolutionary world, in this case Urantia, they can become administratively functional in relation to the Divine Government and the present administration of the Planetary Prince on that planet.

I, myself, am a mixture of seven distinct Material Son genetics, as well as other supermortal genetics both human and nonhuman, and very much interuniversal and intersuperuniversal. You might say I am unique. For this reason

I have been assigned to decimal planets like Urantia, which is also unique. It takes uniqueness to understand uniqueness. I have left my legacy behind in time and space, and although I did not default in the Lucifer rebellion, many of my seed have defaulted. I, being the highest of that seed, have become responsible for them. I thank God the Father that he has taken some of this responsibility from me, and it was done in a very commendable fashion, complementary to those other ascending sons, who have also become finaliters, and who have themselves left behind some of their own seeds of uniqueness. Because of my own mixture, which I have referred to, all of the seven cosmic families on Urantia exhibit in some fashion a part of myself. The First Cosmic Family exhibits the highest reflection of myself, and in that reflectivity they can resonate with the highest nonmaterial body before I had attained before my spirit form. On Urantia at this time they resonate at a level higher than the other six cosmic families, which gives the First Cosmic Family the higher authority and the higher mandates of Christ Michael, in liaison with other Michael Sons and the Universal Father.

Where the auhter energy of this seed can be geographically brought together on any one planet, that area becomes Planetary Headquarters. Thus, in the beginning on this planet, we had Dalamatia and then the first **Garden of Eden**. Today, in Sedona, fusion at some level has taken place between the mortal and the divine, and between one dimension and another. Because of this fusion, particularly on a fallen world like Urantia, a higher communication is given to the highest of mortal ascenders, such as the audio receiver, Gabriel of Sedona, who has been given the mandate of the Bright and Morning Star. This mandate enables communication from the present Planetary Prince and other celestial personalities like myself, for the administration of Christ Michael of Salvington to speak directly and clearly regarding universe will, counsel and administrative policy, as well as continuing revelation in the implementation of divine government procedures. Other mortal personalities at various levels receive mandates. These include all elders and First Assistants and others that will be coming to be part of the work at Planetary Headquarters, who have in the past exhibited loyalty to Christ Michael; and they attain pure impression reception at higher levels to complement each other, and for the implementation of the Divine Government, helping to bring in the first stage of light and life. Where the physical headquarters exist, so also do many celestial personalities, very physically, exist. At the present time they may be unseen, but they are ever present.

Physical locations are picked, based upon several criteria. The energy of the geographic area itself, produces certain fields of energy transference, based upon color, from your planet to others. Where the red energy is most present on the planet, seraphic transport and universe broadcasts can be most easily implemented. Mountain formations that resonate in red energy become energy transformers for purposes of transportation, not just interplanetary but interdimensional, which in time-and-space-warp reality can be one and the same, but too complicated for your minds to understand at this time.

Material complements of a particular celestial seed, work on the mortal side. They resonate in the higher psychic circles and nonspiritual realities, creating an auhter energy that is also used with whatever function the geographic area lends itself. Therefore, divine government mandates, to be appropriated when a Bright and Morning Star visits the planet through a ERC and through a mortal, create a certain force field which is left behind and is held in storage by seraphim, and in this case stored at Planetary Headquarters to be used for many purposes, all too much to explain at this time. Certain mind gravity circuits within personalities like myself and others like me, when totally present on Urantia and fused with the Bright and Morning Star mandated personality, also bring in transforming energies which are stored and used. Machiventa Melchizedek, who is now totally present on Urantia works with those energies even though I may not be here. From Planetary Headquarters in Sedona they are, you might say, shot out in what is known as ley lines to all the four corners of the planet, to all the continents and to all the countries within the continents where my seed in human form presently live and exist in their daily lives. There are many reasons for this, which future transmissions will begin to explain. Presently, interplanetary travel by celestial personalities takes place along these ley lines. Other descendents of the genetic strain who had first resonated in England, long before England became known as such, are presently located in Australia, New Zealand, and South Africa and in certain parts of the Indies. These areas are also grid links to Sedona. The ERC where Machiventa Melchizedek is located is directly linked with Tibet, ancient Shambala, Dalamatia, the first and second gardens, certain parts of India and China, and other locations around the planet that had once been highly spiritual in nature. Those human personalities presently living in these areas will begin to sense a tremendous change about to take place. CFER will be brought to them by the printed word which is coming out of Planetary Headquarters. It will be up to those leaders to respond and attend the Starseed and Urantian Schools of Melchizedek to become part of the new Divine Government. On a planet that is in the process of adjudication, the primary reason is for these energies is the individual ascension process of the inhabitants, and because Urantians, who are prone to tragedy by cataclysms, can be spared if they can be moved into protected areas in time. The highest of the seeds are now being called to come to Planetary Headquarters to attend the Starseed and Urantian Schools of Melchizedek. Many of them will be sent back to six other areas, which will be surrounded by dozens of less protected areas, for others of the seed, at various levels, will also be involved in communities based upon their own ability to comprehend or to acquiesce to divine and human authority.

After the change point and even before, the continents will change, and the waters will divide the continents. When this takes place there will be no safe place on Urantia. Evacuation by dematerialization and physical spacecraft will be a necessity. Those capable of light-body transference will also either be dematerialized or find themselves in physical craft, later to be returned to Urantia to the New Jerusalem at Planetary Headquarters, which used to be part of Sedona, Arizona, U.S.A., and to the other six sector areas which then will have expanded into large continents. Before the change point, those of the seven cosmic families will give their complementary service and resonate in certain other geographic locations, for they are destined to live and minister where they, perhaps, as cosmic reservists and repersonalized mortals, had once lived.

The six other areas are:
1. *Pittsburgh, Pennsylvania,* where the three rivers meet, which is an ERC whose exact location is unrevealed at this time.
2. *Maui, Hawaii,* and an ERC in that area.
3. *Glastonbury, England.*
4. *Jerusalem, Israel,* with a nearby ERC.
5. *The South of France,* at an unnamed area at this time.
6. *The Yucatan in Mexico.*

These sector areas will more highly resonate with descendents of three other universes which are the universes of Avalon, Fanoving, and Wolvering; and, of course, all of these areas resonate with the cosmologic vibration pattern of Nebadon. Ursa Major, the Centaurian worlds and the Pleiadian worlds are linked with these three universes, but the exact coordinate linkage will not be revealed at this time.

1. *Planetary Headquarters in Sedona, Arizona,* will more highly resonate with Avalon, although representatives of all seven cosmic families will be present there.
2. *Pittsburgh, Pennsylvania* will have both Avalon and Nebadon linkage with Pleiadian leadership.
3. *Maui, Hawaii* will have Avalon, Nebadon and Fanoving linkage, but the leadership in Maui will be Pleiadian.
4. *Glastonbury, England* will resonate with Wolvering, Avalon and Nebadon with Wolvering leadership.
5. *Jerusalem, Israel,* will have Avalon, Nebadon, Wolvering and Fanoving linkage with Avalon leadership.
6. *The South of France* will resonate with Nebadon and Avalon, with Nebadon leadership.
7. *The Yucatan, Mexico,* will have Fanoving, Avalon and Nebadon linkage with Fanoving leadership.

All seven cosmic families will be under the leadership of the eldership in Sedona, Arizona, U.S.A., which will become known as the New Jerusalem.

The attractions of the third dimension will become more powerful up until mass confusion takes place on Urantia and third-dimensional reality begins to collapse. When this happens it will be much more difficult to travel from continent to continent and even within one's own country. It is of the utmost importance now, at whatever time frame in which you read this paper, that you prepare yourself for the journey to Sedona to become a student and a future leader/teacher yourself, for it may be too late at one point in the future to do it. Whatever information you get at that time of CFER may only be acquired by mail, and at some point that will also cease.

There is no need for higher spiritual personalities at this time to transcend by the death experience. The morontia reality awaits us now on Urantia. Part of the uniqueness of Urantia is the presence, in very human physical bodies, of a variety of interuniversal ovan souls, due to the fall of some of the Caligastia one hundred. These human bodies are unique to Urantia and they are of various colors, shapes and sizes, and indeed, famotor movements. Urantia would not be Urantia without human mortals, cosmic or indigenous, experiencing the beauty of the planet and administering the policies of divine government. It is not the will of Christ Michael, the Universe Father of Urantia, to replace human mortal government with mortal government by nonhumans. Urantia must be governed by human mortals who have experienced how the fall of Lucifer and Caligastia affected this planet. It must be governed by human mortals who have suffered the consequences of this rebellion. It must be governed by human mortals who have been afflicted by the diseases of this planet. It must be governed by human mortals who have had their hopes, dreams and visions unrealized and unfulfilled because of the rebellion on this planet. It must be governed by human mortals who have seen its polluted waters and breathed its polluted air. It must be governed by human mortals who have experienced the results of competition and greed as opposed to cooperation and benevolence. If you allow yourself to die a physical death, even what you would call a natural one, like the failure of your heart in your sleep state, you will not return to Urantia. You are to proceed to one of the seven mansion worlds of Satania or you will be sent to one of the thirty-six other fallen worlds of Satania, for the adjudication is taking place now. Your decisions are being monitored and registered.

The first ERC on the planet and the others in the Sedona area are connected to other geographic locations in other countries, and in particular to the six other locations which resonate with the highest ERCs. This has to do with interplanetary travel, not so much with interplanetary broadcasts. However, the highest circuit for broadcasts from the universe capital and system capital are at Planetary Headquarters. These grid lines on the planetary level also are used for transportation of nonmaterial and semi-material beings. Midwayers, as well as supermortal personalities, use these celestial highways. Some of them are used in a technical manner for the transporting of smaller craft and even machinery. The archangels, who are also headquartered in Sedona, can travel to any place on the planet using these highways, crossing continents and oceans in seconds of Urantia time. When traveling to other planets within the universe of Nebadon, beings of various orders go to certain ERCs pertinent to their next destination. The interplanetary travel routes are linked with the cosmologic vibration pattern and auhter energy of the resonating planet of genetic heritage. These alignment capabilities enable transportation of matter, be it craft or otherwise, at a faster rate by those in nonspiritual bodies. The areas will also be used in times of emergency for evacuation procedures for human mortals as well as for certain animal life, much of which has already been transferred from your planet to others by Celestial Overcontrol. In order for these areas to become activated, it takes an alignment of human mortals, with cosmic authority as well as human authority, for the implementation of the present Planetary Prince of Urantia, Machiventa Melchizedek. Isolated groups living in these areas without proper alignment to the eldership at Planetary Headquarters will not benefit from living in these areas, nor will they be protected to the same degree as those aligned to the higher purposes of the Machiventa Government. When sixth or seventh stage mansion world progressors visit Urantia, they travel these celestial highways above your planet, for it is a mode of transportation used by student visitors. At the present time, all of these travel routes are held by the forces of Christ Michael. Other lesser travel routes are held by the forces of Caligastia and are used in much the same manner, with the exception of interplanetary usage, which was cut off at the time of the fall of Caligastia. Many channels of Caligastia are, and have been living in grid-line areas that are activated by Caligastia. In some of these areas, natural catastrophes have begun to take place, and certain warnings are being given by the Universe Mother Spirit within the earth. To a continuing degree, those who claim to be channeling "the Brotherhood of Light" and are really channeling the forces of Caligastia (for we no longer use the term "Brotherhood of Light") will be living in areas that are highly vulnerable to natural catastrophes, even though they themselves say the opposite, for they are self-deceived or deceived by celestial personalities loyal to Caligastia.

Along the infrastructure of the grid system of Caligastia, water will become undrinkable; and ocean water will become more highly contaminated, almost at times black in visibility, as the diotribes within the molecular make-up of H_2O

can be more visibly seen than those within the earth itself. Plant life will also have a more difficult time growing, and fruits, vegetables and grains will become less nutritious than they once were. This is because the earth itself is beginning to resonate and separate the forces of light from the forces of darkness. The Universe Mother will only resonate now along the ley lines where the auhter energy of cosmic family is being formed. Now, and into the fourth dimension and above, celestial personalities are presently located with their human complements or arrive ahead of them. At Planetary Headquarters, where the human complements are first being gathered at a higher rate and frequency, the land itself will be more aligned, and the necessary balance of moisture and sunlight will be given to those areas. This actually will help to purify the air as well as the water. Certain wind forces directed by seraphim will be used in cleansing of the air in these areas.

When the first human complements of the higher circles and genetic linkage are sent to the other six sector areas, with that mandate will come the higher protection of that area; and the auhter energy then created by these higher mandated personalities in liaison with celestial complements, creates a force field which can begin to affect these other areas within a five mile radius in circumference of where the human complements settle. These male and female teams, and those who travel with them, begin to resonate at a higher frequency which will affect all those presently living within the five mile radius who do not even realize what is going on at all in relation to the implementation of the Machiventa Government, the Starseed and Urantian Schools of Melchizedek and CFER. The energy in these areas, however, will become such that those who do not begin to align themselves, once they hear the message, will be forced by cause and effect of rebellion to move out of the area, and others of the cosmic family will come in. These ley lines from Planetary Headquarters to the other six communities will also be clear for travel and broadcast by mental telepathy, and increase other clairvoyant abilities as well, for the usage of planetary communication by leadership from all of the communities, so that divine mind can be working together in cooperation and oneness.

Upon observation of these ley lines from a cosmic perspective, these sector designations will become quite visible in the late nineties, even before the earth changes, and the form of the planet will begin to change in the infrastructure. First, in the astral reality the land itself will begin to form in the etheric, and the new sector continents will be visible to higher celestial personalities hundreds of thousands of light years away, all because of the human mortals who are now beginning to align themselves with the Planetary Prince's government of Urantia in the various locations of the ERCs. This precreation is a gift of the Supreme, and as the Supreme begins to co-create with the Eternal Father and the Infinite Spirit at a more rapid rate, this will bring about a more rapid shift in the physical earth itself. Once the infrastructure is completed in the astral, the physical will follow in anywhere from one to seven Urantia years, whereas previously it has taken two hundred thousand years to form the beginning infrastructure needed in the etheric to cause the physical change and cause spiritual absolutes to resonate again on Urantia.

The divine plan was set in motion by Christ Michael soon after the fall of Lucifer. Each of the fallen worlds has its own timetable. Urantia is the first of the thirty-seven planets designated for the rebellion to end. The calendar of divine ordinance has been given to many supermortal beings who brought this information at various levels to the human races. The Egyptians, the Mayans and the Hopi all received information about this time of purification and change and the time of a new beginning. The seven continents were the beginning of the formation of land masses to complement the seven cosmic families on Urantia. When that shift happened, a certain astral infrastructure was visible to the higher personalities, even in Paradise, but the mass consciousness at the time of the last ice age could not formulate a visible enough infrastructure to create the original and final land masses that Urantia would have in the first stages of light and life and onward. This was basically because of the Lucifer rebellion and its implications on Urantia. Presently now, the first sector is formulated clearly enough to be seen, not only by Paradise origin beings but by other nonmaterial beings. Even some mortals on planets that are in the stages of light and life can detect, through certain telescopic devices, indications that Urantia is in the process of meeting its divine destiny and the end of rebellion. For the other of the six sectors to become quite visible, all that is necessary is that a first couple aligned with Planetary Headquarters becomes mandated and is sent to that area to regather their particular seed. Once these souls are located geographically in these areas, the whole sector will light up like someone has turned on a switch. It will light up the surrounding radius of three thousand miles or more, depending on circumstances all too complicated for this paper, but it will be no less than three thousand miles in radius in each of these sectors. Planetary Headquarters, where the New Jerusalem is, will be the largest.

The United States will be split in two, and where the three rivers meet near Pittsburgh, will become the headquarters for another sector. Sector headquarters are always in the center of each land mass, so you can see that the continents will shift dramatically. There will be no north or south pole. There will be slight changes of seasons, but weather will be consistent all over the planet, resonating basically with temperatures in the mid to high seventies. New ley lines will be appropriated by overcontrol to increase transportation by material means. Mechanical transportation and technology will continue. No polluting forms of energy will be allowed on Urantia. Interplanetary travel will become the norm, particularly within the universe of Nebadon; and it will be quite common to visit other planets and go on vacation there, although Urantia will also have a vacation sector within each governmental sector. Future papers will give much more information as to the organization of these sectors. In these sectors, which resonate with the various universes, ethnocentric comparisons of cultures as well as cultural differences will be in similarity to these universes. All celestial visitors, however, will be allowed to visit and travel freely all over the planet, and so will all planetary citizens. The auhter energy created by genetic ancestry now gathered in cultural and sociological structures on Urantia will increase communication to these universes as well as visitation. This will create many factors on Urantia unrevealed at this time, which we look forward to observing and experiencing ourselves.

The decimal planet, Urantia, unique in its genetic heritage, has in its uniqueness created a very unpredictable future to ascertain, even for the highest of us who observe you and we have been observing you for hundreds of thousands of years, and indeed for a million years. All of you who can begin to come into CFER are bringing together the fusion of the Seven Master Spirits of God to a planetary level, with another fusion of the Universe Mother Spirit to the Father seed of God that has created the ascending sons and daughters who presently reside on Urantia. If you cannot understand CFER presently, you will at some point in your future ascension, and most definitely by the fifth mansion world. However, the fifth world of morontia ascension is now available to those of the genetic heritage who have the mindal and spiritual capacity to align with the perfect will of Christ Michael and the Universal Father in order to hear what the spirit of God is saying to the ascending sons and daughters on Urantia at this hour in time and space. To those who can grasp it, you are hundreds, and perhaps a thousand years, ahead of your time. Grasp its significance. You are blessed in the Ascension Sci process to fuse mind and heart. Our prayer for you is that this marriage will take place within and without. You too can time travel at a rate unknown, hundreds of years ago, by even the most optimistic observers of your planet if you can only allow the Spirit of Truth to bring you to this place. If you can put aside the false opinions of man, if you can allow those fearful tendencies and misplaced loyalties which divide your mind from higher truth to be gone from your reality, morontia mota awaits you now on Urantia. It is the gift of Christ Michael to you now, and you can help so many others on the planet to receive it if you are free from your previous lower reality and available to all in service.

March 9, 1992

Paladin, Chief of Finaliters; in cooperation with the Assigned Sentinel of Satania, Lanaforge, and other interuniversal coordinators, for the implementation of the seven cosmic families on Urantia within the government of the present Planetary Prince of Urantia, Machiventa Melchizedek; as transmitted through the Audio Fusion Material Complement, Gabriel of Sedona.

BIBLIOGRAPHY

Concise Science Dictionary, Second Edition, Oxford University Press, Market House Books Ltd., 1991.

New American Standard Bible, Word Bible Publishers, Iowa Falls, Iowa, 1973.

The New Illuminated Holy Bible, American Bible House, New York, 1897

The URANTIA Book, URANTIA Foundation, Chicago, Illinois, 1955.

Webster's New World Dictionary, Third College Edition, Webster's New World, New York, 1988.

GLOSSARY OF TERMS

NOTE: The definitions in this Glossary are limited. For further information we recommend that the reader also *study* this book *The Cosmic Family (CF)* Volume I and *The URANTIA Book (UB)*. References to Papers in these books are those Papers that would be most useful to study.

"Although these definitions are as exact as they can be in relation to the students who are studying this revelation, updated information can change the definition to some degree. The content of the meaning will still be there. We are limited, based upon language, from our side to yours, and hindered by your own ability to understand such a massive volume of information of specific details. Sometimes definitions have many meanings, and some terms are very similar. Whenever we can, we will try to introduce them but may not be able to clearly differentiate the terms at the time. If you can somewhat begin to understand 10% of these definitions in total, we can expand on them and go from there. It could take years to completely comprehend these very cosmic technical terms in Ascension Sci until it becomes second nature to you. Two-brained types such as are now on Urantia, both native and ovan soul, have the ability of complete comprehension at some point in their future evolution."

September 29, 1994   Paladin, Chief of Finaliters on Urantia

Terms in **bold type** are new words or concepts introduced in CFER (*The Cosmic Family Volumes*) or words that are redefined in terms of cosmic absolutes or have added information. Terms in regular type can be found in *The URANTIA Book* or are scientific or New-Age terms.

ADAM AND EVE

The Material Son and Daughter, father and mother of the violet race, who came to our planet almost 38,000 years ago to biologically uplift the evolutionary races. They came from Jerusem, the capital of the system of inhabited worlds to which our world belongs. As long as they were in the perfect will of God they were immortal. They portrayed the concept of the Father of All to the evolutionary people, which was the Second Epochal Revelation to this planet. After more than one hundred years they could see little progress on this backward world in rebellion. Although they had been counseled by the Melchizedeks not to initiate the program of racial uplift and blending until their own family had numbered one-half million, through impatience Eve defaulted, and mated with Cano, a man of the Nodite race, who became the father of Cain. Although Adam realized Eve's mistake and knew that she was no longer immortal, he could not bear the thought of separation from his complement. The day after Eve's misstep, he sought out Laotta, a brilliant woman of the Nodite race, and mated with her. After their default, Adam and Eve left the first Garden of Eden, which was situated on a peninsula in the Eastern Mediterranean, and established a second Garden of Eden in Mesopotamia. Adam and Eve have been rehabilitated and have now returned to Urantia during this time of adjudication. Although invisible to human, third-dimensional eyes, they are stationed at Planetary Headquarters in Sedona, AZ, U.S.A., where the third Garden of Eden is being established. (See also Epochal Revelation, Garden of Eden, Material Son and Daughter, CF Paper C, and UB Paper 74.)

ADAMSON AND RATTA

After the default of Adam and Eve, their first-born, Adamson, left the Garden of Eden and mated with Ratta, a pure-line descendant of the Caligastia one hundred with interuniversal genetics. They gave origin to a great line of the world's leadership and also became the grandparents of the secondary midwayers. Many Urantian reservists have their genetics. (See also Caligastia One Hundred, Midwayers, CF Paper 208, and UB Paper 77.)

ADJUDICATION BY THE BRIGHT AND MORNING STAR VS LUCIFER

The ending of the Lucifer rebellion on Urantia, a process of adjudication which began in 1911 and will be completed in May of 2000 or 2001. The Fifth Epochal Revelation, which includes CFER, is a major part of re-opening the universe circuits and the final phase is now in progress in and through the Divine Government of Machiventa Melchizedek and his staff, both celestial and human. (See CF Papers 213, 214, 215, 227, and UB Paper 53.)

ADJUTANT MIND SPIRITS

The seven adjutant mind spirits: the spirits of intuition, understanding, courage, knowledge, counsel, worship and wisdom. These spirits are not regarded as entities, but more like the mind circuits of the local Universe Mother Spirit, which is a representation of the mind ministry of the Infinite Spirit. They always accompany the Life Carriers to a new planet, and activate and regulate the teachable type of mind, capable of learning from experience. In the animal only the first five adjutant mind spirits function, while the human mind of spiritual-ascension candidacy is distinguished by the function of the last two: the spirit of worship and wisdom. It is the adjutant mind spirits that prepare the human mind for the ministering spirit circuit of the Universe Mother Spirit: the Holy Spirit. (See also Holy Spirit and UB Paper 36.)

AMADON

A native Urantian who belonged to one of the highest strains of the evolutionary Andonite race, 500,000 years ago. He was the associate of Van, the head of the loyalists in the rebellion. Both remained on the planet until the arrival of Adam and Eve. Amadon became the human hero of the Lucifer rebellion. He remained loyal to Christ Michael and has now repersonalized during the final phase of the adjudication by the Bright and Morning Star vs Lucifer. (See also Caligastia One Hundred, Lucifer Rebellion, CF Paper 207, and UB Paper 67.)

ANCIENTS OF DAYS

Trinity-origin beings who rule a superuniverse and, as Trinity representatives, are the judges of all personalities of origin in that superuniverse. There are three Ancients of Days in each of the seven superuniverses. "These Ancients of Days, who alone can decree the extinction of intelligent life, participate in the creation of the Life Carriers, who are intrusted with establishing physical life on the evolving worlds."
(See also Paradise Trinity, Superuniverse, CF Paper D and UB Paper 18.)

ANGELS OF ENLIGHTENMENT

Members of one of the twelve corps of Master Seraphim in the Machiventa Government. These angels have ascended to Paradise level and first arrived on Urantia at Pentecost. At present, some of these angels are temporarily assigned as the personal angels for third-circle reservists instead of, or along with, a seraphic guardian of destiny. (See also Reserve Corps of Destiny, Seraphim, CF Paper 212, and UB Paper 114.)

ANTAKARANA

A New-Age term for the central channel in the body connecting the chakras according to the ancient Tibetans.
(See also Chakras, Circuits, and CF Paper 200.)

APOSTLES

The first-century apostles (including Matthias, Luke and Paul) who have repersonalized in the twentieth century. They are a mixed group of starseed and second-time Urantians. An apostle is one who is in full-time spiritual ministry in contrast to a disciple who is in part-time ministry.
(See also Change Agent, CF Paper 218, and UB Part IV.)

ARCHANGELS

They are a high order of local universe personalities created by the Creator Son and Universe Mother Spirit. They are an order separate from angels. "They

are dedicated to the work of creature survival and to the furtherance of the ascending career of the mortals of time and space." In recent times a divisional headquarters of the archangels has been maintained on Urantia and is presently located at Planetary Headquarters in Sedona, AZ, U.S.A. There are no archangels communicating with humans at present.
(See also Creator Son, Universe Mother Spirit, CF Introduction, Paper E, and UB Paper 37.)

ASCENDED MASTERS

A New-Age term for sixth and seventh stage morontia progressors.
(See Sixth & Seventh Stage Mansion World Progressors, & Paper 200.)

ASCENSION SCIENCE OR ASCENSION SCI

A universe spiritual science which fuses the spiritual with the scientific. On Urantia it is very much the physics of rebellion.
(See CF Paper 217.)

ASHTAR COMMAND

The various celestial and ascending mortal beings in spaceships assigned to Urantia for various duties in relation to the adjudication of Urantia, including physical evacuation by spaceship, and the coordination of activities relating to interdimensional changes, under the command of Ashtar, a finaliter, who has assumed a seventh stage morontia body to work in the physical realm.
(See also Finaliter, and CF Paper 197.)

ASSISTANTS

Mandated First and Second Assistants to Gabriel of Sedona and Niánn, under the mandate of the Bright and Morning Star of Salvington functioning in various aspects of reflectivity of Celestial Overcontrol.
(See also Mandate of the Bright and Morning Star, CF Paper 209 & 218.)

ASTRAL BODY

A composite of the bodies a personality has existed in before at any point in time and space. Each existence has a separate body connected to it. The astral body in the present is ever growing, that of the past is an inactive completed form, yet is not separate from the present physical body. The astral body of a second-time Urantian did not begin to form until death.
(See CF Papers 203 & 205.)

ATAVISM

"Appearance in an individual of some characteristic found in a remote ancestor but not in nearer ancestors."
(See CF Paper 216.)

AUDIO FUSION MATERIAL COMPLEMENT

A term describing a fusion between a celestial being and a mortal, a fusion of one entity with another in the complete aonic-to-cellular reality of the lower being. The fusion takes place within the particle reality of the life force of the existing soul. They co-exist within the life force and the existing soul does not leave. It is a gradual process over many years, and the higher the virtue of the chosen vessel, the higher the fusion, the higher the being, and the higher the level of revelation which can be brought through. Gabriel of Sedona is the only Audio Fusion Material Complement on Urantia. The Bright and Morning Star fuses on a once-a-month basis to teach for a few hours. Paladin, Chief of Finaliters, fuses with Gabriel of Sedona several times a week. No beings of light have spoken through anyone but Gabriel of Sedona since 1989. (See CF Paper 209.)

AUHTER ENERGY

The higher force-energy synergetic field resultant from cosmic nuclear fusion created by the joining or rejoining of spiritual cosmic families or groups based upon the personality bestowal of the Universal Father and each individual's acquiescence to his personality, and the group consciousness in relation to Celestial Overcontrol. This auhter energy creates a measurable light that is visible light years away.
(See also Celestial Overcontrol, Cosmic Family, Union of Souls, Universal Father, CF Foreword, Papers 220 & 228.)

AVALON

Name of a neighboring universe. Most of the starseed in the First Cosmic Family come from Avalon. Some of the Caligastia one hundred were morontia progressors originally from that universe and because of a different Avalon ascension scheme were on assignments in this universe of Nebadon.
(See also First Cosmic Family, CF Paper 213, and UB Paper 66.)

AVATAR

A New-Age term for a Bestowal Son, a Divine Paradise Son incarnating into human form. Sooner or later every inhabited planet receives a Divine Son, but on Urantia there has only been *one* so far, Christ Michael, the Creator and Sovereign of our local universe of Nebadon, who was born and died as Jesus of Nazareth 2000 years ago.
(See also Christ Michael, Creator Son, CF Paper 200, and UB Paper 21.)

BRIGHT AND MORNING STAR

The Bright and Morning Star of Salvington is the Chief Administrator of the Universe of Nebadon and the first-born personality creation of Christ Michael and the Universe Mother Spirit. He visits Urantia in overcontrol of the adjudication by the Bright and Morning Star vs Lucifer, and speaks through his mandated Audio Fusion Material Complement, Gabriel of Sedona, and manifests in reflectivity through this vessel. (See also Adjudication by the Bright and Morning Star, Gabriel of Salvington, CF Papers 200 & 213, and U.B. Paper 33.)

BRILLIANT EVENING STARS

An order of local universe aids, created by the Creator Son and Universe Mother Spirit, who function mainly as liaison officers for and under the direction of the Bright and Morning Star. They frequently also function as teachers. The human Liaison Ministers in the Machiventa Government, who hold the second highest mandate on the planet, are in reflectivity to these Brilliant Evening Stars. Niánn of Sedona is the highest reflectivity to this order. (See also Bright and Morning Star, Liaison Ministers, CF Statement of Purpose, and U.B. Paper 37.)

CALIGASTIA

The former Planetary Prince who arrived on Urantia 500,000 years ago with a staff of 100 rematerialized ascending sons and daughters (the Caligastia One Hundred) to bring the First Epochal Revelation to Urantia. His headquarters was the city of Dalamatia. Caligastia followed Lucifer and Satan into rebellion 200,000 years ago. Although shorn of all administrative powers he has been allowed to remain on the planet until his adjudication is over. The "devil" is none other than Caligastia. (See also Caligastia One Hundred, Dalamatia, Planetary Headquarters, Planetary Prince and Lanonandek Son, CF Paper C, and U.B. Paper 66 & 67.)

CALIGASTIA ONE HUNDRED

The corporeal staff of ascenders, some of whom came originally from three other universes, who arrived on Urantia 500,000 years ago with Caligastia and Daligastia to bring the First Epochal Revelation to Urantia. They were 50 males and 50 females, referred to as the Caligastia one hundred. They had been transported by seraphic transport from the system capital, Jerusem, and had been rematerialized to be Caligastia's administrative staff on the physical level. Dalamatia was their headquarters and they were organized for service in ten councils of ten members each. For 300.000 years they taught the evolutionary races on this planet and remained undying by being in the perfect will of the Father and partaking of the fruit of the tree of life. During the Lucifer rebellion 40 remained loyal and 60 fell. The rebellious ones spread the Luciferic concepts to their relatives on neighboring universes by mental telepathy. These relatives are the fallen starseed who had to repersonalize on Urantia over several lifetimes to experience living on a planet in rebellion. All had to return to Urantia during this century for the adjudication by the Bright and Morning Star vs Lucifer. The fallen staff of Caligastia mated with the evolutionary races and created the Nodite

race, named after their leader "Nod". Some Urantians have their inter-universal genetics.
(See also Dalamatia, Lucifer Rebellion, CF Paper 208, and U.B. 66 & 67.)

CAUSAL BODY

The first personality blueprint which holds within it the perfection of the Universal Father. That perfection is progressive all throughout the ascension career and does not become full reality until an ascender becomes a finaliter.
(See also Finaliter, and CF 205.)

CELESTIAL OVERCONTROL

A term designating orders of beings who function on higher levels of universe administration guiding and overseeing the human mandated personalities on a planetary level functioning in cooperation with the Planetary Prince — the final authority of planetary affairs.
(See also Planetary Prince, Universe, CF Preface, and Foreword I.)

CFER

An acronym for Continuing Fifth Epochal Revelation.
(See also Continuing Fifth Epochal Revelation, Epochal Revelation, and Fifth Epochal Revelation.)

CHAKRAS

"In certain forms of yoga, any of the body centers, usually seven, that are considered sources of energy for psychic or spiritual power."
(See also Antakarana and Circuits, and CF Paper 200.)

CHANGE AGENTS

A CFER term for apostles in full-time spiritual ministry, who are aligned and functioning under the mandate of the Bright and Morning Star. (See also Apostle, Mandate of the Bright and Morning Star, and CF Paper 218.)

CHANGE POINT

The instant of time in which Urantia moves from the third to the fourth dimension completely, approximately in May of 2000 or 2001. As of 1992, only the one-mile to five-mile radius of Planetary Headquarters reflects fourth-dimensional reality to some degree. After the change point, only those personalities who have also manifested fourth-dimensional bodies will be able to return to and remain on Urantia. (See also Fourth Dimension, Morontia Body, and Third Dimension, Statement of Purpose, and Paper C.)

CHERUBIM

The lowest order of angels. They serve with a complementary polarity called a sanobim and are faithful and efficient aids of the seraphic ministers. The cherubim is an energy-positive personality and the sanobim energy-negative. (See Foreword I, and U.B. Paper 38.)

CHIEF OF SERAPHIM

A primary supernaphim from Paradise stationed at Planetary Headquarters on Urantia and in command of the 12 corps of Master Seraphim of Planetary Supervision and the seraphic hosts. A Chief of Seraphim first arrived on Urantia at the time of Pentecost, accompanying the first Governor General. The present Chief of Seraphim is the second one to be on duty since the bestowal of Christ Michael on Urantia. (See also Master Seraphim, and Planetary Headquarters, CF Paper 201, and UB Paper 114.)

CHRIST MICHAEL

The Universe Father, Sovereign, and Creator Son of this universe of Nebadon. He earned his sovereignty by bestowing himself seven times in the likeness of seven different orders of personalities in his own universe, each reflecting the seven aspects of the will of the three Paradise Deities. In his last bestowal he came to Urantia to portray the nature of the Universal Father. He was the Fourth Epochal Revelation to this planet 2000 years ago, when he lived the life of Jesus of Nazareth. Among the 700,000 Creator Sons in the grand universe, he was the only Creator Son that was put to death by his own creatures. After his seventh bestowal he poured out the Spirit of Truth for the benefit of his entire universe. CFER teaches that he is expected to soon return to this planet as he promised.
(See also Creator Son, Nebadon, Spirit of Truth, and Universe, CF Paper 210, and U.B. Papers 21, 33, 119 and Part IV.)

CIRCLE GUARDIANS

A classification of mandated personalities functioning under the mandate of the Bright and Morning Star who function largely as counselors and advisors of the ascension process of ascending sons and daughters.
(See also Mandate of the Bright and Morning Star, and CF Paper 218.)

CIRCLES

Referring to the seven psychic circles of personality realization.
(See also Psychic Circles.)

CIRCUITS

A complete or partial path over which energy may flow; of, or relating to,

the various Paradise circuits of both upper and nether Paradise which connect, via the Salvington circuit of the Nebadon headquarters world of Christ Michael, to human mortals through the various circuits within the body, the main ones being previously known as chakras in lower teachings. The reopening of these Paradise circuits to evolutionary mortals is CFER.
(See also Father-circuited, Mother-circuited, Paradise, Salvington, and **Son-circuited**, Introduction, and CF Paper D.)

COMPLEMENTARY POLARITIES
Personalities of similar spiritual status who function in pairs, usually male and female, but in some cases can be two males or two females.
(See also Highest Complementary Polarities, and Twin Flames, and CF Papers D, 220, 221 & 225.)

CONTINUING FIFTH EPOCHAL REVELATION
The continuation of the Fifth Epochal Revelation (*The URANTIA Book* is only one tenth of it), which is now coming through the Audio Fusion Material Complement, Gabriel of Sedona. Continuing Fifth Epochal Revelation is the physics of rebellion and how it has affected our lives. Although over one hundred Papers have been transmitted, only *The Cosmic Family, Volume I* has been published so far. (See also Epochal Revelation.)

COSMIC CIRCLES (See Psychic Circles.)

COSMIC FAMILY
A genetically related family of ascending sons and daughters. They are generally of origin in universes outside Nebadon, but include Urantians with extraplanetary genetics, usually related to a finaliter. At present there are seven cosmic families on Urantia coming from four different universes, including our local universe of Nebadon.
(See also First Cosmic Family and Seven Cosmic Families.)

COSMIC PARENTS
The parents a soul has in its very first life, whether originating on this planet or on another world.
(See also Cosmic Son or Daughter, and CF Paper 211.)

COSMIC SON OR DAUGHTER
The children of whom one has been the biological parent in their very first life, whether on this planet or in another universe.
(See also Cosmic Parent, and CF Paper 226.)

COSMIC RESERVE CORPS

A group of ovan souls on Urantia who function under the guidance of various entities, such as midwayers and seraphim, to bring cosmic consciousness to the planet, and are called to serve in the Machiventa Government in various capacities in order to fulfill their destiny purpose. These souls are members of one of the seven cosmic families presently sojourning on Urantia. Some of them have repersonalized in all the major spiritual renaissances on Urantia. All cosmic reservists are being called to Planetary Headquarters for further training.
(See also Reserve Corps of Destiny, CF Paper E, and U.B. Paper 114.)

COSMOLOGIC VIBRATION PATTERN

A term designating the normal vibrational pattern which resonates in Paradise harmony among the unfallen planets of any universe. It signifies alignment with the divine plan for that universe. (See CF Paper 216.)

COUNCIL OF TWENTY-FOUR

A council of twenty-four former Urantian spiritual leaders from all dispensations on Urantia who function under Christ Michael in relation to affairs arising from the Lucifer rebellion in Satania. Each fallen planet has a similar council but the Urantia council is in overcontrol of all of them.
(See CF Foreword I, and U.B. Paper 45.)

CREATOR SON

A personality of Paradise origin, created by the Universal Father and the Eternal Son, belonging to the order of Michael. Together with a Creative Daughter, a Creator Son is the creator of a local universe of time and space. There are 700,000 local universes. To gain full sovereignty over his universe, a Creator Son bestows himself seven times in the likeness of the created personalities on various levels in his own creation, each reflecting one of the aspects of the will of the three Paradise Deities, after which he earns the title of "Master Son." A Creator Son does not live the life of a mortal man to die for their sins, but to reveal the loving nature of the Paradise Father.
(See also Christ Michael, Nebadon, Paradise Trinity, Universe Mother Spirit, CF Introduction, and UB Paper 21.)

DALAMATIA

The original Planetary Headquarters city founded by Caligastia, Urantia's first Planetary Prince, 500,000 years ago, on a peninsula since submerged in the Persian Gulf. Dalamatia was named after Daligastia, Caligastia's assistant. The many legends about Atlantis and the sons of God mating with the daughters of men go back to the time of Dalamatia. (See also Caligastia One Hundred, CF Papers 223 & 228, and UB Papers 66 & 67.)

DELUSION ENERGY FREQUENCIES

A harmonic energy pattern aligned to the higher fourth-dimensional frequencies of the Nebadon cosmologic vibration pattern which will affect unaligned personalities at whom they may be directed, causing the intensification of their own negative delusional vibrations, manifesting in their lives. (See CF Paper 215.)

DEO-ATOMIC

A term designating atomic structure in alignment with God, as in Deo-atomic cells, which are cells aligned with Paradise absolutes and are the cells of the morontia or light body. This is accomplished by activating the threefold Spirit of God and walking within the perfect will of God on a moment-to-moment basis. (See CF Paper 210 & 217.)

DEO-ATOMIC FAMOTOR LANGUAGE

Sound in harmony with cosmologic vibration pattern connected to Paradise circuits. These sound waves can erase diotribes, intraction cells and heal people as well as the earth itself. (See CF Paper 223.)

DEO-ATOMIC TRIADS

A group of three cells in the structure of the morontia or light bodies in reflectivity to the Paradise Trinity. (See CF Paper 217.)

DIOTRIBE INTRACTION CELLS

Diotribe cells from other universes that have found themselves in material or semi-material individuals. (See also Diotribes & CF Papers 220 & 222.)

DIOTRIBES

A CFER term referring to negative or harmful particles in your body due to wrong thinking induced by the individual's acquiescence to Luciferic thought patterns. They are the cause of disease in the human body. (See CF Paper 223 & 224.)

DISTORTION WAVES

Energy frequencies which cause the breakdown of the equilibrium in the physical body and certain thought patterns, causing disorientation and inability to function efficiently, resulting in mistakes, accidents and increased corruption. (See CF Paper 215.)

DIVINE NEW ORDER COMMUNITY

Community of ascending sons and daughters spiritually aligned with the Divine Government of Machiventa Melchizedek on Urantia and functioning

within the seven sacred/protected areas being established as administrative sectors on the planet.
(See also Sacred/Protected Areas, Sectors, and CF Papers 206 & 228.)

ENERGY REFLECTIVE CIRCUITS (ERC)

A CFER term designating energy fields on a planet which allow for interdimensional communication and transportation. Also known in lower-level terminology as vortexes. (See CF Paper 206.)

EPOCHAL REVELATION

A revelation designed for the uplifting of an entire planet as distinguished from revelation to specific individuals or groups. There have been only five epochal revelations on Urantia to date, all having to do with the sorting and censuring of the successive religions of evolution, each ever expanding and more enlightening. The First Epochal Revelation was inaugurated 500,000 years ago when the Planetary Prince, Caligastia, established Dalamatia, the first Planetary Headquarters on Urantia. The Second Epochal Revelation occurred 38,000 years ago with the advent of Adam and Eve, who established themselves in the Garden of Eden — the second Planetary Headquarters. The Third Epochal Revelation came approximately at the time of Abraham with the arrival of Machiventa Melchizedek, who established the third Planetary Headquarters at Salem, where missionaries were trained to take the one-God concept all over the planet. The Fourth Epochal Revelation was fulfilled when the Creator Son of our local universe, Christ Michael, bestowed himself as a human mortal, Jesus of Nazareth, to portray the nature of his Paradise Father. *The URANTIA Book* is the first one tenth of the Fifth Epochal Revelation to the evolving races of Urantia. Continuing Fifth Epochal Revelation (the other nine tenths) is now in progress through the Audio Fusion Material Complement, Gabriel of Sedona.
(See also Fifth Epochal Revelation, Continuing Fifth Epochal Revelation, CF Paper C, and U.B. Paper 92.)

ETERNAL SON

The second person of the Paradise Trinity, co-creator with the Universal Father and Infinite Spirit. The Eternal Son is the spiritual center and the divine administrator of the spiritual government of the master universe. Not to be confused with the Creator Son of a local universe of whom he is a parent. (See also Paradise Trinity, CF Paper C, and UB Paper 6.)

ETHERIC BODY

The body between the physical and the astral, sometimes called the emotional body, but it is related to the morontia body of the ovan soul.
(See CF Paper 205.)

EXISTENTIAL ASPECT OF GOD
God eternal, without beginning or ending. There is no time that he did not exist and he has full knowledge without experience.
(See CF Paper 210, and Foreword of U.B.)

EXPERIENTIAL ASPECT OF GOD
That part of God which grows through experience. This includes the experiences of all personalities in time and space. The Supreme Being is the personalization of all universe experience.
(See CF Paper 210, and U.B. Papers 115, 116 & 117.)

EXPERIMENTAL PLANET
One planet in ten is used by the Life Carriers for experimental purposes to produce new and improved variations in the evolutionary life plasm. Also called a decimal planet. Urantia is a decimal, experimental planet. CFER teaches that Urantia is unique in having humans who are being trained in divine government administration.
(See also Life Carriers, CF Paper D, and U.B. Paper 65.)

EXTENSION SCHOOLS OF MELCHIZEDEK
The Melchizedek University for ascending souls, which consist of 490 worlds near our universe headquarters on Salvington, have extension schools on the constellation, system and planetary level. At present there is only one extension school on Urantia and it is located at Planetary Headquarters in Sedona, AZ., U.S.A. It is both an academic and practical school, incorporating the schools of thinking, feeling, and doing, where students learn Ascension Sci, divine government administration, the personal and social effects of the Lucifer rebellion and how to walk in the perfect will of God on a moment-to-moment basis.
(See also Ascension Sci, CF Introduction, and UB Paper 55.)

FAMOTOR MOVEMENT
A mechanized and spiritualized characteristic body movement which is the result of the strong correlation between the morontia and the physical body of an ovan soul and the way that the soul within the body responds to its spiritual ascension. Famotor movement usually dictates to the body its physical form in the long run. (See CF Paper 222.)

FATHER-CIRCUITED
An entity who is encircuited in, and manifests the essence of, the Universal Father. In humans, both male and female have Father circuitry, but the normal male is more Father-circuited. (See also Circuits, Mother-circuited, Son-circuited, and CF Introduction.)

FIFTH EPOCHAL REVELATION
The URANTIA Book is the first one tenth of the Fifth Epochal Revelation to the evolving races of Urantia. Continuing Fifth Epochal Revelation (the other nine tenths) is now in progress through the Audio Fusion Material Complement, Gabriel of Sedona. This book, *The Cosmic Family, Volume 1*, is the beginning of CFER. This living revelation is revealed and actualized in the lives of the ascending sons and daughters who have aligned with the divine government of the Planetary Prince, Machiventa Melchizedek, under the mandate of the Bright and Morning Star of Salvington, and are trying to walk in the perfect will of God on a moment-to-moment basis.
(See also Epochal Revelation and Continuing Fifth Epochal Revelation, CF Foreword, and UB Paper 92.)

FINALITER
An ascending mortal or nonmortal son or daughter who has ascended from the planet of origin through the local universe, the superuniverse, the central universe of Havona, and has reached Paradise. After having attained creature perfection and finding the three Paradise Deity personalities, a finaliter is mustered into the Mortal Corps of the Finality and becomes a sixth stage spirit. Finaliters are sent off on assignments for creature service in the superuniverses of time and space and are always involved when a planet is about to move into the first stage of Light and Life. "One or more companies of the mortal finaliters are constantly in service on Urantia." Paladin became Chief of Finaliters on Urantia in January 1992. He is the head of the First Cosmic Family. (See also Ashtar Command and Cosmic Family, CF Foreword II, Paper 226, and U.B. Paper 31.)

FIRST COSMIC FAMILY
A family of ascending sons and daughters, mostly of origin in the Pleiades, but containing interrelated members from the other six cosmic families presently on Urantia, and first- and second-time Urantians with interuniversal genetics. The First Cosmic Family is the most closely involved with planetary administration and is responsible for gathering the other six cosmic families. The First Cosmic Family is headquartered at Planetary Headquarters in Sedona, Arizona, USA. The finaliter, Paladin, is the head of the First Cosmic Family. (See also Cosmic Family, Finaliters, and CF Paper 206.)

FIRST SOURCE AND CENTER
The creator, controller, upholder, and God of all creation is the primal cause of the universal physical phenomena of all space. Without the First Source and Center the master universe would collapse. He is also the Universal Father of all personalities. He unqualifiedly transcends all mind, matter and spirit. A fragment of this First Source and Center lives within the normal human mind and is the spirit pilot to help find the Father on Paradise.
(See also Thought Adjuster, CF Introduction, and UB Papers 1 - 5.)

FIRST-TIME URANTIAN

A new soul whose planet of origin is Urantia, and whose present life is the very first existence of that soul. Most people on this planet are first-time Urantians. (See also Second-time Urantian, Urantians, and CF Paper D.)

FORM-UNIT PROGENY

Progeny from pair units on the 7th stage of the 4th dimension, categorized by body form, characteristics, and famotor movement. (See CF Paper 224.)

FOURTH DIMENSION

In CFER the fourth dimension on Urantia is the morontia level that could have been achieved during the Fourth Epochal Revelation, but was not actualized. It is now being actualized at Planetary Headquarters in and through the Divine Government of Machiventa Melchizedek and among those souls of the First Cosmic Family who have aligned with that government. After the change point, Urantia will be completely in fourth-dimensional reality.
(See also Change Point, Third Dimension, and CF Introduction.)

FRAGMENT OF THE FATHER

An actual part of the Universal Father that indwells the mind of every mortal with a normal mind. It is the spirit nucleus that with the cooperation of that mind creates the soul. It is the destiny of the soul to fuse with the Fragment of the Father and ascend to Paradise.
(See also Thought Adjuster, CF Foreword II, and UB Papers 107 - 112.)

GABRIEL OF SALVINGTON

First-born Son of Christ Michael and the Universe Mother Spirit, also called the Bright and Morning Star. It was Gabriel of Salvington who appeared to Mary to announce she had been chosen to become the human mother of Jesus. At present Gabriel of Salvington visits Planetary Headquarters on a once-a-month basis and teaches through his Audio Fusion Material Complement, Gabriel of Sedona, who is named after him.
(See also Bright and Morning Star, CF Paper 201, and UB Paper 33.)

GARDEN OF EDEN

The site of the second Planetary Headquarters on Urantia, founded nearly 38,000 years ago by Adam and Eve, the Material Son and Daughter, on a since submerged peninsula extending into the Mediterranean Sea from the area of present-day Lebanon. After their default Adam and Eve left the first Garden, and established a second Garden of Eden in Mesopotamia, between the Tigris and Euphrates rivers. Now a third Garden of Eden is developing at Planetary Headquarters in Sedona, AZ., U.S.A.
(See also Adam and Eve, CF Paper 228, and UB Paper 73.)

GOVERNOR GENERAL OF URANTIA

"The resident governor general has no actual personal authority in the management of world affairs except as the representative of the twenty-four Jerusem counselors. He acts as the coordinator of superhuman administration and is the respected head and universally recognized leader of the celestial beings functioning on Urantia.... the first governor general arrived on Urantia, concurrent with the outpouring of the Spirit of Truth..." (at Pentecost). Since December, 1989, with the announcement of Machiventa Melchizedek as Planetary Prince, the Governor General no longer functions in this capacity.
(See also Planetary Prince, CF Paper 201, and UB Paper 114.)

GRAND UNIVERSE

The inhabited part of the master universe which includes, the eternal central universe of Havona of one billion unique and perfect worlds, and the seven evolutionary superuniverses of time and space, which include 700,000 local universes, created by the Creator Sons and Creative Daughters.
(See also Master Universe, Superuniverse and Universe, CF Introduction, and U.B. Paper 12.)

GUARDIAN SERAPHIM (See Seraphim.)

HAVONA

The name of the central universe surrounding Paradise which functions as the pattern for the time-space universes. Havona consists of one billion unique and perfect worlds. It is part of the destiny of mortals to go through all these billion perfect worlds before reaching Paradise.
(See CF Paper D, and UB Paper 14.)

HEART CIRCUIT

The circuit within the body that is connected to Christ Michael, and where the Spirit of Truth is first activated. Students at *The Starseed and Urantian Schools of Melchizedek* are given more information about this and other circuits.
(See also Circuits, Reserve Corps of Destiny, and Paper E.)

HIGHEST COMPLEMENTARY POLARITIES

A mortal male or female pair who have reached the highest spiritual relationship, (sometimes called twin flames) usually leading to procreation of higher starseed children. For ovan souls these mates may be on another planet. Usually there is only one highest complement, but not always.
(See CF Paper D.)

HOLY SPIRIT

The ministering spirit circuit of the Universe Mother Spirit is one of three distinct spirit influences of the local universe, which begins to function when the purely animal mind has been prepared by the sixth and seventh adjutant mind spirits*: the spirits of worship and wisdom. The Holy Spirit becomes more effective in the spiritualization of the inner life when a mortal more fully obeys the divine leadings of the fragment of the Father, the Thought Adjuster. The Holy Spirit should not be confused with the third person of the Paradise Deities, the Infinite Spirit, or with the Spirit of Truth poured out at Pentecost, which is the Spirit of the Creator Son, Christ Michael.
(See also Adjutant Mind Spirits, Spirit of Truth, Thought Adjuster, CF Papers D & 213, and U.B. Paper 34.)

INFINITE SPIRIT

Third person of the Paradise Trinity; also called the Conjoint Actor or the God of Action. Not to be confused with Holy Spirit, which is the spirit circuit of the Universe Mother Spirit of a local universe, who is a daughter of the Infinite Spirit. The Infinite Spirit is the mother aspect of God and the bestower of mind. In the local universe this is made manifest via the Universe Mother Spirit.
(See also Holy Spirit, CF Introduction, and UB Papers 8 & 9.)

INTERDIMENSIONAL PERSONALITY HOLOGRAM

A healing method, a time-space warp procedure of retrospection, wherein parts of the essence of particular entities can be brought to you in substance through the molecular process via the morontia body of one of the Vicegerent First Ambassadors to be right with you in the space where you are. You can then receive benefit from these molecular atoms that can penetrate and be incorporated within your **etheric body** and be transferred to the physical body. Gabriel must first work with your causal and astral body before a Vicegerent First Ambassador can work with your etheric and physical bodies. Sometimes other healers who work on the physical body will also be needed to aid in the immediacy of the healing to align the physical body with the healing that has already taken place in the astral and ethereal. (See also Astral Body, Causal Body, Vicegerent Ambassadors, and CF Paper 205.)

INTERPLANETARY DECIMAL MATING

An aspect of Ascension Sci regarding the variables involved in the molecular structure when interplanetary marriages take place.
(See CF Paper 221.)

INTERPLANETARY RECEIVER

A being in the spiritual chain of command who receives interplanetary and interdimensional messages and transmits them to the people on the planet. (See also Audio Fusion Material Complement, Circuit Receiver, and CF Paper 209.)

INTRACTION CELLS (See Diotribe Intraction Cells.)

INTRACTION LANGUAGE

Language inharmonic with cosmologic vibration pattern and cosmic truth, e.g. Luciferic thought, which disorganizes frequency circuits from various headquarters worlds causing emotional, psychological and physical disease. (See CF Paper 223.)

LANAFORGE

Primary Lanonandek Son of Nebadon and System Sovereign of Satania. He replaced Lucifer 200,000 years ago. Lanaforge is a gracious and brilliant ruler, who remained loyal to Christ Michael in a previous rebellion. He takes great interest in the affairs of Urantia and regularly visits our planet.
(See also Lanonandek Son, System Sovereign, CF Foreword by Machiventa Melchizedek, and U.B. Paper 45.)

LANONANDEK SON

An order of local universe Sons who function in system administration. They are best known as System Sovereigns and Planetary Princes. Lucifer, the fallen former System Sovereign, was a Primary Lanonandek Son, and Caligastia, the fallen former Planetary Prince, was a Secondary Lanonandek Son. Lanonandek Sons are brilliant administrators, but have been known to be prone to rebellion. Christ Michael bestowed himself as a Lanonandek Son during his second bestowal in which he showed his entire universe how the Universal Father and Eternal Son on Paradise function in perfect harmony and as with one will.
(See also Lanaforge, System Sovereign, Planetary Prince, CF Paper C, and UB Paper 45 & 50.)

LEY LINES

Grid lines of energy between energy reflective circuits used for communication and transportation. In New-Age terminology sometimes called "Star routes." (See also Energy Reflective Circuits, and CF Paper 228.)

LIAISON MINISTERS

Those holding the second highest mandate of the Bright and Morning Star in reflectivity to Brilliant Evening Stars, who act as liaison officers in human overcontrol between the Bright and Morning Star mandate and the Machiventa

Melchizedek mandated personalities. There will be only seven Liaison Ministers who will also function as elders on the inner board at Planetary Headquarters. (See also Brilliant Evening Stars, Mandate of the Bright and Morning Star, and CF Foreword I.)

LIFE CARRIERS
Local universe Sons of God who implant and foster life on the evolutionary worlds of time and space. They are created by the Creator Son, Universe Mother Spirit and one Ancient of Days. On Urantia the Life Carriers made 3 life implantations in the tropical bays of the central seas 550,000,000 years ago, from which all life evolved. It is the Universe Mother Spirit, however, who provides the spark of life through the Life Carriers. The adjutant mind spirits always accompany the Life Carriers to a new planet, and it is this representation of the mind ministry of the Infinite Spirit through the local Universe Mother Spirit that makes evolution always purposeful and not accidental.
(See also Adjutant Mind Spirits, Urantia, CF Paper D, and UB Paper 36.)

LUCIFER
An once-brilliant primary Lanonandek Son, the fallen System Sovereign of Satania, who after ruling Satania for more than 500,000 years led a rebellion against his Creator Father, Christ Michael, which involved 37 planets in the system of Satania, including Urantia. Lucifer's Manifesto was about denial of the existence of the Universal Father, unbridled personal liberty, rejection of universe allegiance and disregard of fraternal obligations and cosmic relationships. Since the bestowal of Christ Michael on Urantia as Jesus of Nazareth 2000 years ago, Lucifer has been imprisoned, and awaits his final adjudication. Although many of today's teachings contain some truth, they are sprinkled with very deceptive Luciferic lies. (See also Lanonandek Son, Lucifer Rebellion, System Sovereign, and CF Foreword II.)

LUCIFER REBELLION
A rebellion led by Lucifer 200,000 years ago in Satania; 37 of the 619 inhabited worlds in the system participated. It involved many personalities of various celestial orders as well as mortals and supermortals, such as the Caligastia one hundred, some of whom originally came from other universes. Through telepathic communication these supermortals spread the rebellion to their cosmic family in three other neighboring universes. On Urantia the adjudication by the Bright and Morning Star began early this century and will be completed in May of 2000 or 2001. Many fallen starseed from these three other universes had to repersonalize on Urantia several times to learn the effects of the rebellion on a fallen planet and are here at present for this adjudication. (See also Adjudication by the Bright and Morning Star, CF Paper C, and UB Paper 53.)

MACHIVENTA MELCHIZEDEK

Planetary Prince of Urantia since December, 1989. This same Melchizedek, who belongs to a high order of local universe Sons, incarnated in the likeness of mortal flesh and lived on Urantia for 94 years during the time of Abraham and was known as the Prince of Salem. He came on an emergency mission when the spiritual light on Urantia was almost extinguished and taught the one-God concept. He established a school where missionaries were trained who later brought his teachings to all parts of the world. Now he speaks through the Audio Fusion Material Complement, Gabriel of Sedona, at the Starseed and Urantian Schools of Melchizedek where again teachers are being trained to take the Fifth Epochal and Continuing Fifth Epochal Revelation to the rest of the planet.
(See also Epochal Revelation, Melchizedeks, Planetary Prince, CF Papers 213 & 214, and UB Paper 93.)

MANDATE

An authorization to act, given to a representative. In CFER this refers particularly to human personalities given authority to represent Divine Government on the planet. (See also Mandate of the Bright and Morning Star, CF Papers 201, 211 & 218.)

MANDATE OF THE BRIGHT AND MORNING STAR

The universe directive from Christ Michael, Creator and Sovereign of the universe of Nebadon, authorizing his Chief Administrator, Gabriel, the Bright and Morning Star of Salvington, to adjudicate the Lucifer rebellion, beginning with our planet, Urantia. Under this mandate is the authority to reinstate Divine Government on the planet through the highest complementary-polarity couple on the planet, his Audio Fusion Material Complement, Gabriel of Sedona, and Niánn, in cooperation with the present Planetary Prince, Machiventa Melchizedek. This mandate includes bringing through Continuing Fifth Epochal Revelation, healing of the various bodies, and the authority to train and mandate humans for administrative positions in Divine Government.
(See also Audio Fusion Material Complement, Bright and Morning Star, and CF Preface & Foreword I.)

MANSION WORLDS

Morontia training worlds in the system of Satania where souls normally go some time after their physical death. They are situated near the system capital and have been provided to overcome mortal deficiencies. After the change point Urantia will function as another mansion world. Students at the Starseed and Urantian Schools of Melchizedek at Planetary Headquarters already receive mansion-world-level training through morontia counseling, studying Ascension Sci, and putting into practice the Fifth and Continuing Fifth Epochal Revelation.
(See also Morontia, CF Foreword I, and U.B. Paper 47.)

MASTER PHYSICAL CONTROLLERS

They belong to a unique group of living beings having to do with the intelligent regulation of energy throughout the grand universe. They are the direct offspring of the Supreme Power Centers. They often function in batteries of hundreds, thousands, and even millions. They can upstep and accelerate the energy volume and movement or detain, condense, and retard the energy currents. (See CF Paper 200 & 206, and U.B. Paper 29.)

MASTER SERAPHIM

Twelve corps of administrative seraphim, who have graduated on Seraphington, a Paradise satellite world for angels, and been assigned to certain special planetary services under the immediate direction of the Chief of Seraphim and the Planetary Prince. They accompanied the Governor General when he arrived on Urantia at the time of Pentecost and the outpouring of the Spirit of Truth. The master seraphim insure planetary progress against vital jeopardy through the mobilization, training, and maintenance of the reserve corps of destiny. (See also Angel of Enlightenment, Chief of Seraphim, Reserve Corps of Destiny, CF Paper 212 and U.B. Paper 114.)

MASTER UNIVERSE

The universe of universes, including the eternal central universe of Havona, the seven evolutionary superuniverses of time and space, plus the presently mobilizing, but uninhabited four outer space levels. The master universe is the largest manifestation of divine pattern in which Paradise is the absolute, stationary, and stable nucleus around which the rest of the master universe is revolving. The First Source and Center or Universal Father is the absolute Creator, Controller and Upholder of the master universe and without him all would collapse.
(See also Grand Universe, Superuniverse, Universe, CF Introduction, and U.B. Paper 12.)

MATERIAL COMPLEMENTS

Receivers of the highest order of interplanetary and interdimensional communication. They also function as conduits of universal energies transmitted to them by higher celestial personalities. Persons mandated in reflectivity to a celestial personality. (See also Audio Fusion Material Complement, CF Paper 209 & U.B. Paper 109.)

MATERIAL SON AND DAUGHTER

The highest type of sex-reproducing beings in a local universe, an Adam and Eve, who are the biological uplifters of the evolutionary races, physically present in administrative capacity under a Planetary Prince. They are the founders

of the violet race. Usually only the progeny of the Material Son and Daughter procreate with mortals.
(See also Adam and Eve, CF Papers C, 216, 221 & 228, and U.B. Paper 51.)

MEDIUMS

Persons who are being used for the lowest and least accurate level of interdimensional communication, which since 1989, is entirely limited to contacts with fallen entities. (See CF Paper 209, and UB Paper 77.)

MELCHIZEDEKS

A high order of local universe Sons. They function in many capacities, but mainly as teachers and emergency ministers. Ever since the Lucifer rebellion and the Caligastia betrayal, twelve Melchizedeks have been guarding the spiritual evolution of our planet. In 1989 one of these twelve Melchizedeks, Machiventa Melchizedek, became our new Planetary Prince.
(See also Machiventa Melchizedek, CF Paper C, and UB Paper 35.)

MICHAEL

The order of Michael is an order of Paradise Creator Sons, the offspring of the Universal Father and the Eternal Son. In cooperation with the local Universe Mother Spirits, the Michaels create the 700,000 evolutionary universes of time and space. (See also Christ Michael, and Creator Son, CF Introduction & Paper 207, and UB Paper 21.)

MIDWAYER COMMISSION

A delegation of 12 midwayers from the Brotherhood of the United Midwayers of Urantia, who were officially assigned to portray the Life and Teachings of Jesus (Part IV of *The URANTIA Book)*. Now they are working in cooperation with Celestial Overcontrol to help bring through the Continuing Fifth Epochal Revelation. (See also Midwayers, CF Foreword II & Paper 197, and U.B. pages 1322, 1343.)

MIDWAYERS

Unique beings about midway between mortals and angels. They are the permanent citizens of an evolutionary world. The primary midwayers on Urantia are the offspring of the rematerialized staff of the former Planetary Prince, Caligastia. Secondary midwayers on Urantia are descendants of Adamson (firstborn of Adam and Eve) and Ratta (pure-line descendant of the Caligastia one hundred). They ably assist the angels on Urantia. They have definite power over things and beasts. Midwayers do not sleep or procreate. On Urantia midwayers have often been mistaken for angels. The midwayers are actively involved in guiding destiny reservists to Planetary Headquarters in Sedona, AZ.

U.S.A. During the time of the Lucifer rebellion the majority of the primary midwayers went into sin. Many of the secondary midwayers also failed to align with the rule of Michael of Nebadon. At the time of Pentecost they were interned and held in custody, but since 1989 and the arrival of Machiventa Melchizedek as the new Planetary Prince, they have been freed and given another chance to align with the divine government. Unfortunately, not all have done so and many are still communicating with lower channels, teaching Luciferic concepts in a very deceptive way and causing much confusion even among some URANTIA Book readers.
(See also Adamson and Ratta, CF Foreword I & Paper C, and U.B. Papers 77 & 38.)

MIGHTY MESSENGERS
A class of perfected mortals who have been rebellion tested or otherwise equally proven as to their personal loyalty; all have passed through a definite test of universe allegiance. After having ascended to Paradise and having been embraced by the Paradise Trinity, they become associated with the Ancients of Days and are sent out on assignments of all phases of universe activities.
(See also Paradise Trinity, CF Paper 200, and UB Paper 22.)

MORONTIA
A level of local universe reality between the material and spiritual levels of creature existence. The human soul is an experiential acquirement that is created by a creature choosing to do the will of the Father in heaven. This new reality, that is created by the cooperation of the mortal mind with the divine spirit, is a morontia reality that is destined to survive mortal death and begin the Paradise ascension.
(See also Morontia Body, CF Foreword I, and U.B. Paper 48.)

MORONTIA BODY
The various body forms of the 570 ascending morontia levels of creature existence an ascending soul uses within the local universe. It is also known on Urantia as the light body, but this concept would be applicable only to the lowest-level morontia body. While previously souls would receive a morontia body after death, at present it is possible to construct one by moving into Deo-atomic reality while living at Planetary Headquarters, being aligned with the Divine Government of the present Planetary Prince, Machiventa Melchizedek, and living in the perfect will of God on a moment-to-moment basis.
(See also Morontia, CF Paper 197, and UB Paper 48.)

MORONTIA MOTA

Philosophy at the morontia level of creature existence. "A cosmic perspective — depth — achieved by superimposing the perceptions of the morontia life upon the perceptions of the physical life."
(See CF Paper 200, and U.B. Paper 48.)

MORONTIA POWER SUPERVISORS

Offspring of a local Universe Mother Spirit exclusively concerned with the supervision of those activities which represent the working combination of spiritual and physical or semi-material energies. They are exclusively devoted to the ministry of morontia progression.
(See also Master Physical Controllers, CF Paper 206, and U.B. Paper 48.)

MORONTIA PROGRESSORS

Ascending souls on any of the 570 levels of morontia life after they leave the evolutionary planets and before they become full-fledged spirits. These levels are transcended on the various worlds of the local system, constellation, and near the universe headquarters, Salvington.
(See also Morontia, Morontia Body and Paper A.)

MORTAL PAIR-UNIT CLASSIFICATION

A classification of ascending sons and daughters who are complementary polarities and mating pairs. Each of the children will inherit a particular original personality and form based on the first cosmic parents, which reflects the Paradise Deities at that moment in time in which he or she first became a potential mortal soul. Many ovan souls look alike in some way and have the same personality traits but may be from different nationalities or races. It is the result of the Deo-atomic inheritance in relation to their first cosmic family parents.
(See also Highest Complementary Polarities, and CF Paper 221.)

MOTHER-CIRCUITED

Encircuited in and exhibiting the characteristics of the Universe Mother Spirit. In humans, both male and female have Mother circuitry, but the normal female is more Mother-circuited.
(See also Father-circuited, Son-circuited, and CF Introduction.)

NEBADON

The name of our local universe, the creation of Christ Michael, Universe Sovereign, and the Universe Mother Spirit. Salvington is its headquarters. The organization of our local universe began approximately 400 billion years ago. Nebadon is regarded as a relatively young universe and is still unfinished. However, there are less than 4 million inhabited planets in it.
(See also Universe, CF Foreword I, and U.B. Part II.)

ORVONTON

The name of the superuniverse in which our local universe of Nebadon exists. It is superuniverse #7 of the seven superuniverses which make up the grand universe, and is roughly equivalent to what Urantian astronomers call the Milky Way galaxy. Uversa, its headquarters is almost 250,000 light-years away from the outermost system of inhabited worlds of our local universe. Orvonton is ruled by three Ancients of Days. Orvonton is destined to reflect the nature and wills of the three Paradise Deities. Because it is more difficult to reflect the threefold Spirit of God in a balanced way, it has had more rebellions than any other superuniverse, but also has been granted more mercy. In fact, it has been called the superuniverse of mercy. (See also Superuniverse, Grand Universe, CF Foreword II, and UB Paper 15.)

OVAN SOUL

A soul who has survived the initial experience of mortal planetary existence and who has attained the morontia consciousness equivalent to the first mansion world or above, and the realization of Paradise circuitry in a morontia body. On Urantia there are approximately 170,000,000 ovan souls from three other universes, Avalon, Fanoving, and Wolvering, and approximately 2000 second-time Urantians building their morontia bodies through the process of repersonalization.
(See also Morontia Body, CF Foreword I, Paper D, 219, 220 and 221.)

OVERSOUL

A similarity within the morontia semi-physical forms of ovan souls relating to a general pattern of all the 570 morontia body forms within a given universe. It is visibly identifiable and mathematically precise.
(See also Morontia Body, and CF Paper 221.)

PAIR-UNIT CLASSIFICATIONS (See Mortal Pair-Unit Classification.)

PALADIN

Paladin became Chief of Finaliters on Urantia in January, 1992, because of the spiritual ascension of his cosmic son Gabriel of Sedona. He is the head of the First Cosmic Family. He fuses with and speaks through Gabriel of Sedona, and is the chief spokesperson for celestial personalities bringing CFER to Urantia. He first introduced himself to Gabriel as Sky Hawk because he has had several repersonalizations on Urantia as a Native American. Finaliters always become involved when a planet is about to move into the first stage of Light and Life. (See also Continuing Fifth Epochal Revelation, First Cosmic Family, Cosmic Father, Finaliters, and CF Foreword II.)

PARADISE

The abiding place of the Universal Father, Eternal Son, and Infinite Spirit. This eternal Isle is the absolute source of the physical universes — past, present, and future. It is the universal headquarters of all personality activities and the source-center of all force-space and energy manifestations. It is the geographic center of infinity and the only stationary and absolute stable thing in the master universe. It is the goal of all ascending sons and daughters to ascend to Paradise and find the Universal Father. (See also Universal Father, Eternal Son, Infinite Spirit, Master Universe, CF Introduction, and UB Paper 11.)

PARADISE TRINITY

An association and union of the three infinite persons on Paradise: the Universal Father, the Eternal Son, and the Infinite Spirit, functioning as a corporate entity in a nonpersonal capacity but not in contravention of personality. (See also Paradise, CF Paper 219, and U.B. Paper 10.)

PLANETARY HEADQUARTERS

Administrative center of the celestial divine government. The first planetary headquarters was Dalamatia at the time of Caligastia, 500,000 years ago; the second was the Garden of Eden at the time of Adam and Eve, 38,000 years ago; the third was the schools of Salem at the time of Machiventa Melchizedek, approx. 4000 years ago; the fourth was wherever Jesus of Nazareth was, 2000 years ago. At present it is located where the Planetary Prince, Machiventa Melchizedek, resides, in Sedona, AZ, U.S.A. All Destiny Reservists are called to Planetary Headquarters to receive further training at *The Starseed and Urantian Schools of Melchizedek*, under the Mandate of the Bright and Morning Star, Chief Administrator of our local universe.
(See also Extension Schools of Melchizedek, Machiventa Melchizedek, Mandate of the Bright and Morning Star, CF Preface, and UB Paper 66.)

PLANETARY PRINCE

The spiritual ruler of an inhabited world in time and space. The first Planetary Prince of Urantia, Caligastia, a secondary Lanonandek Son, arrived approximately 500,000 years ago with his assistant Daligastia. Their headquarters was Dalamatia in the Persian Gulf region. "The Planetary staff included a large number of angelic cooperators and a host of other celestial beings assigned to advance the interests and promote the welfare of the human races." He also had a corporeal staff of one hundred. "A Planetary Prince is not visible to mortal beings; it is a test of faith to believe the representations of the semimaterial beings of his staff." Unfortunately Caligastia chose the side of Lucifer and Satan during the Lucifer rebellion 200,000 years ago. In 1989 AD, Machiventa Melchizedek became Planetary Prince and has his headquarters in Sedona, Arizona, USA. He speaks through the audio fusion material complement, Gabriel of Sedona. Christ Michael functioned as a Planetary Prince on another world during the time of his third bestowal, and also earned the title of "Planetary Prince of Urantia" after his seventh bestowal 2000 years ago, during which he lived the life of the human mortal, Jesus of Nazareth. (See also Caligastia, Caligastia One Hundred, Dalamatia, Lanonandek Son, Lucifer Rebellion, Planetary Headquarters, CF Statement of Purpose, and UB Paper 66.)

PLEIADES

"A cluster of stars in the constellation of Taurus." CFER teaches that they are not stars but planets settled in Light and Life. Most of the First Cosmic Family come originally from the Pleiades or have Pleiadian genetics. Paladin, the head of the First Cosmic Family, although originally from another superuniverse, lived his first life as a human mortal in this superuniverse on Tora in the Pleiades. (See also First Cosmic Family, CF Foreword II.)

PSYCHIC CIRCLE

One of the seven levels of personality realization on a material world. Entry on the seventh circle marks the beginning of true human personality function. Completion of the first circle denotes the relative maturity of the mortal being. Destiny reservists at Planetary Headquarters who are stabilized on the third psychic circle receive an angel of enlightenment.
(See also Angel of Enlightenment, CF Preface, and U.B. 110.)

PURE IMPRESSION

The opening of the heart and mind circuits between celestial personalities and appointed human and non-human individuals. Although there is only one audio fusion material complement on the planet today, other personalities at Planetary Headquarters receive information through pure impression.
(See also Heart Circuit and Paper A.)

RACE COMMISSIONERS

A group of Spirit-fused ascendant mortals who have become permanent citizens of the local universe and serve on the evolutionary planets. The race commissioners are very active on Urantia. "They are supremely devoted to the welfare of the mortal races whose spokesmen they are, ever seeking to obtain for them mercy, justice and fair treatment in all relationships with other peoples. Race commissioners function in an endless series of planetary crises and serve as the articulate expression of whole groups of struggling mortals." Several Papers of this first volume of CFER have been co-authored by the race commissioners. (See Papers 219, 221, and 223.)

RATTA (See Adamson and Ratta.)

REFLECTIVITY
The reflection in mandated humans of the personality virtues of nondivine celestial counterparts, such as the Bright and Morning Star, Brilliant Evening Stars, Melchizedeks, Seraphim etc.
(See also Bright and Morning Star, and CF Papers 218, 219 & 226.)

REMATERIALIZATION
Since physical bodies cannot be transported by seraphic transport, rematerialization is one of several techniques providing a physical body for a personality of another dimension, who may be on an assignment as part of their ascension plan. The Caligastia one hundred were rematerialized when they arrived from the system capital 500,000 years ago as the staff of the former Planetary Prince, Caligastia. (See also Caligastia One Hundred, Repersonalization, CF Papers 200 & 206, and UB Paper 66 & 67.)

REPERSONALIZATION
A term used in CFER to describe the transfer of ascending ovan souls back into third-dimensional reality through the birthing technique for specific destiny purposes. Some members of the cosmic reserve corps of destiny have repersonalized on this planet in most of the major spiritual renaissances. Gabriel of Sedona describes this in his book *The Divine New Order*. With the exception of about 2000 second-time Urantians, who for undisclosed reasons have for the first time been allowed to repersonalize, these souls come originally from other universes where the ascension schemes are different from that of Nebadon. In Nebadon souls do, as a rule, *not* return to their planet of origin. Repersonalization should not be confused with the erroneous earthly concepts of reincarnation, as taught in some eastern philosophies, where a soul is supposed to return over and over again, even in the form of an animal. There is no such thing as reincarnation. (See also Rematerialization, and CF Paper 200.)

RESERVE CORPS OF DESTINY
"This corps consists of living men and women who have been admitted to the special service of the superhuman administration of world affairs as human liaisons, mortal assistants.... The chief function of these reservists is to insure against breakdown of evolutionary progress; they are the provisions which the celestial forces have made against surprise; they are the guarantees against disaster." There are cosmic reservists (originally from other universes) and Urantian reservists. Since the coming of the new Planetary Prince, Machiventa Melchizedek, all destiny reservists are being called to Planetary Headquarters in Sedona, AZ, U.S.A. to receive further training in Divine Government

administration at The Starseed and Urantian Schools of Melchizedek under the mandate of the Bright and Morning Star. (See also Master Seraphim, Cosmic Reserve Corps of Destiny, CF Paper E, and U.B. Paper 114.)

SACRED / PROTECTED AREAS

These are areas on the planet near major energy reflective circuits, set up by people who are aligned with the Machiventa Government. There will be only seven major protected areas on the planet. Some secondary areas will also have a certain degree of protection. The degree of protection depends upon a person's level of alignment and virtue.
(See also Energy Reflective Circuits and Sector, and CF Paper 228.)

SALVINGTON

Salvington is the Headquarters sphere of the Universe of Nebadon, home of Christ Michael and the Universe Mother Spirit. Salvington was the first completed act of physical creation in Nebadon and took a little over one billion years to complete. It is situated at the exact energy-mass center of the local universe. It is the destiny of ascending sons and daughters to sojourn on Salvington as part of their training and Paradise ascension. When a soul leaves Salvington he is a full-fledged spirit. (See also Christ Michael, Gabriel of Salvington, Universe Mother Spirit, CF Introduction and UB Paper 32.)

SALVINGTON CIRCUIT

The circuit from Christ Michael, Sovereign Son of Nebadon, and his administrative headquarters on Salvington, the capital sphere of Nebadon, to the planetary headquarters in the primary energy reflective circuit of the evolutionary planets. In humans, also connected to the heart circuit.
(See also Circuits, CF Papers 209 & 211.)

SANANDA

Sananda was the title of Christ Michael on another planet when he bestowed himself as a Material Son and took the office of Planetary Prince. It is not the name of Christ Michael and never has been, not on this planet or any other. It is a title only given to Machiventa Melchizedek, who became Planetary Prince of Urantia in 1989. Individuals who may call themselves by this name have no true connection to the Divine Government of the Planetary Prince, Machiventa Melchizedek.
(See also Planetary Prince, and CF Paper 214.)

SANOBIM

The complementary polarity to a cherubim, and a recording personality. Cherubim and sanobim are the lowest order of angels. Every fourth cherubim

and sanobim are morontial. They are the faithful and efficient aids of the seraphim. "They are wonderfully intelligent, marvelously efficient, touchingly affectionate, and almost human."
(See also Cherubim, CF Foreword I, and U.B. Paper 38.)

SATAN

First assistant to Lucifer, Satan was an able and brilliant primary Lanonandek Son. Both Lucifer and Satan had reigned on Jerusem for 500,000 years when they fell into rebellion against Michael of Nebadon. They denied the existence of the Universal Father and proclaimed personal freedom and liberty, disregarding "social equity, cosmic fairness, universe fraternity, and divine obligations." Satan was sent by Lucifer to advocate the cause of the rebellion on our planet and was successful in winning the then Planetary Prince, Caligastia, over to the cause of the rebellion. Up until the beginning of the twentieth century, Satan made regular visits to Urantia. He was imprisoned at the beginning of the adjudication by the Bright and Morning Star vs Lucifer in 1911 and is awaiting the verdict of the Ancients of Days. (See also Lucifer rebellion, CF Paper C, and UB Paper 53.)

SATANIA

The local system of 619 inhabited worlds in which our planet Urantia numbers 606. It was named after Satan, Lucifer's assistant, long before they both went into rebellion, 200,000 years ago. The capital of Satania is Jerusem. The System Sovereign of Satania who replaced Lucifer is Lanaforge, a brilliant primary Lanonandek Son who had proven to remain loyal in a previous rebellion. (See also Lanaforge, CF Foreword, and U.B. Paper 45.)

SECOND-TIME URANTIANS

A unique group of Urantians numbering less than 2,000 who were sleeping survivors, and who, for the first time in the history of Urantia by decree of Christ Michael, have for undisclosed reasons been allowed to repersonalize on Urantia since the beginning of this century. Some of the first-century apostles have repersonalized and are second-time Urantians.
(See also First-time Urantians and Ovan Souls, and CF Paper D.)

SECTORS

Administrative headquarters areas, and on Urantia protected areas in which a Divine New Order community is or will be established before and after the change point. There will be seven sectors on this planet coordinated with the seven cosmic families of Urantia. All sectors will be under the Overcontrol administration of the Machiventa Divine Government at Planetary Headquarters. (See also Sacred/Protected Area, and CF Paper 228.)

SEMJASE OF TORA

A **cosmic daughter**, of the finaliter Paladin, who was the original Pleiadian contact of Billy Meier in Switzerland up until the spring of 1976. Not to be confused with the once brilliant fallen entity Semjase, after whom many souls were named before she fell. (See CF Paper 198.)

SERAPHIC TRANSPORT

"All groups of ministering spirits have their transport corps, angelic orders dedicated to the ministry of transporting those personalities who are unable, of themselves, to journey from one sphere to another.... The angels cannot transport combustion bodies — flesh and blood — such as you now have, but they can transport all others, from the lowest morontia to the highest spirit forms.... When enseraphimed, you go to sleep for a specified time, and you will awaken at the designated moment." The Caligastia one hundred came here 500,000 years ago by seraphic transport after which their physical bodies were rematerialized. As material bodies cannot be transported by seraphic transport, they must be evacuated by dematerialization or spacecraft when a planet is no longer safe to live on.
(See also Caligastia one hundred, Morontia, Seraphim, CF Paper 212, and UB Paper 39.)

SERAPHIM

Local universe angels who are of origin in the Universe Mother Spirit and are designated Ministering Spirits of the local universe. Seraphim are created slightly above the mortal level. "They love human beings, and only good can result from your efforts to understand and love them." Seraphim, like mortals of animal origin, are evolutionary beings and have an opportunity to ascend to Paradise and become members of the Corps of the Finality. Those assigned to the watchcare of ascending mortals are called Seraphic Guardians of Destiny. An angel of enlightenment can also serve as a destiny guardian. (See also Angel of Enlightenment, Master Seraphim, CF Paper 212, and U.B. Papers 113 & 114.)

SEVEN COSMIC FAMILIES

The seven cosmic families on Urantia are made up of starseed, and first- and second-time Urantians with genetic links to neighboring universes outside Nebadon, and in particular, to Avalon, Wolvering and Fanoving. The head of the First Cosmic Family is the finaliter, Paladin, Chief of Finaliters on Urantia. It is the responsibility of the First Cosmic Family to gather the other six cosmic families and set up Divine New Order communities around the planet.
(See also Cosmic Family, and CF Paper D, 203, 206, 207, 216, 220 & 228.)

SIXTH AND SEVENTH MANSION WORLD PROGRESSORS
Ascending mortals sojourning on the higher of the seven mansion worlds which are the beginning stages of morontia progression after leaving an evolutionary world. In CFER definition, those who are called "ascended masters" by metaphysical and religious groups are in reality ovan souls who have in the past come from the sixth and seventh mansion world to Urantia for specific assignments but there are none on the planet at present.
(See CF Paper 200 and U.B.)

SON-CIRCUITED
A personality encircuited in the Eternal Son and exhibiting characteristics thereof. In the local universe this is a reflection in and through the Creator Son. When a person is Son-circuited he or she has activated the Spirit of Truth and has achieved a proper balance between the Father and Mother circuits. (See also Father-circuited, Mother-circuited, and CF Paper 210.)

SOUL MATES
A New-Age term for complementary personalities who serve together harmoniously in some capacity.
(See also Highest Complementary Polarities, and CF Paper D.)

SPIRIT OF TRUTH
The spirit of Christ Michael bestowed on Urantia at Pentecost. It is experienced in human consciousness as the conviction of truth and needs to be continually activated by soul growth through a relationship with God in his will (not man's wishes) as opposed to religious doctrine. The Spirit of Truth should override false *interpretations* of any written scripture or text, be it the Bible, *The URANTIA Book*, or *The Cosmic Family Volumes*. The Universe Mother Spirit acts as the universe focus and center of the Spirit of Truth as well as her own personal influence, the Holy Spirit. Every inhabited planet receives the Spirit of Truth after a Divine Son incarnates in the likeness of a mortal. (See also Christ Michael, CF Paper 210 and U.B. Paper 180 & 181.)

STAR CHILDREN
Children from planets in other universes who repersonalize on Urantia or on other planets as part of their ascension career.
(See also Starseed, and CF Paper D

STAR ROUTES
A New-Age term for ley lines, which are grid lines between energy reflective circuits used for communication and transportation.
(See also Energy Reflective Circuits and Ley Lines.)

STARSEED

A term generally used on Urantia to designate mortals, originally from another universe, born of human parents through the repersonalization technique. There are 7 orders of starseed. Much of the understanding of starseed in New-Age circles in relation to "walk-ins," soul transference, space visitors, etc. who are presently on Urantia referred to as starseed is Caligastian confusion and Luciferic deception.
(See also ovan souls, repersonalization, and CF Paper D.)

SUPERUNIVERSES

The seven primary divisions of time and space in the grand universe, which each contain 100,000 local universes comprising one trillion inhabited worlds and are each presided over by three Ancients of Days. The name of our superuniverse is Orvonton. Every superuniverse is divided into 10 major sectors; the name of our major sector is Splandon. Each major sector is divided into 100 minor sectors; the name of our minor sector is Ensa. Each minor sector is made up of 100 local universes.
(See also Ancients of Days, Orvonton, CF Introduction, and U.B. Paper 15.)

SYSTEMS

The 100 divisions of a constellation within a local universe. Each system consists of about 1000 inhabited or inhabitable worlds. Our local system of Satania is a relatively young system and so far has only 619 inhabited planets.
(See also Satania, System Sovereign, CF Introduction, and UB Paper 15.)

SYSTEM SOVEREIGN

A primary Lanonandek Son who is the administrative head of a local system of inhabited worlds. Although brilliant administrators, Lanonandeks have been prone to rebellion. Our System Sovereign in Satania is Lanaforge, who replaced Lucifer after his fall 200,000 years ago.
(See also Lanaforge, Lanonandek Son, CF Foreword I, and U.B. Paper 45.)

THIRD-CIRCLER

A mortal who has attained and stabilized on the third psychic circle and received a personal angel of enlightenment.
(See also Psychic Circles, and CF Paper D.)

THIRD DIMENSION

The dimension of present-day Urantia. It includes the material aspects of height, breadth and depth and only includes a limited level of ascension consciousness. The third dimension consists of choices for self, instead of choices for God and your neighbor.
(See also Fourth Dimension, and CF Statement of Purpose.)

THOUGHT ADJUSTER
A prepersonal fragment of the Universal Father which indwells the normal mind of human mortals when a child makes it first freewill moral choice. It is through the Thought Adjuster that the Universal Father has personal communion with mortal beings. Fusion with the Thought Adjuster guarantees eternal survival. Also called Mystery Monitor.
(See also Fragment of the Father, Universal Father, and CF Foreword I.)

THREEFOLD SPIRIT
Three separate manifestations of the Paradise Trinity functioning within a mortal: 1. The Thought Adjuster which is a fragment of the Universal Father working within the normal human mind. 2. The Spirit of Truth which is bestowed by the Creator Son on behalf of the Eternal Son. 3. The Holy Spirit, which is the ministering circuit of the local Universe Mother Spirit on behalf of her parent the Infinite Spirit on Paradise. (See also CF Paper D.)

TORA
The third planet from Alcyone in the Pleiades and the point of origin, at least in the superuniverse of Orvonton, of the finaliter, Paladin, and certain members of the First Cosmic Family on Urantia. In Urantian astronomy it is called Electra. (See also Pleiades, and CF Paper D.)

TRINITY TEACHER SON
A Paradise Son of Trinity origin who appears on an evolutionary world when the time is ripe to initiate a spiritual age. They are the exalted teachers of all spirit personalities. (See CF Paper 218, and UB Paper 20.)

TRON THERAPY
A psychospiritual therapy which restores broken circuitry within the body, removes diotribes, and is a touch therapy destined to replace surgery. It is done only in conjunction with psychospiritual counseling and involves the permanent healing of all bodies, the astral, etheric and physical, for those who are in alignment with their God. Tron therapy will be available only at Planetary Headquarters through mandated Tron therapists.
(See CF Paper 201, and 214.)

TWIN FLAMES
New-Age term for complementary polarities.
(See also Complementary Polarities, and CF Paper D.)

ULTIMATONS

The basic units of materialized energy. The first measurable form of energy. Ultimatons have Paradise as their nucleus and respond only to circulatory Paradise gravity pull. 100 ultimatons are mutually associated in an electron. (See also Paradise, CF Paper 217, and U.B. Paper 42.)

UNI-FORM

A higher morontia body without reproductive capacity and organs of reproduction. The essence of such a body still visibly reflects either male or female circuitry and origin. (See also Morontia Body, and CF Paper 219.)

UNION OF SOULS

A group consciousness reflecting the ideals and status of ethical relationships and functioning in the realm of harmonious teamwork. Also a descriptive name of a group of ministering spirits of the order of secondary seconaphim "The Union of Souls." (See CF Foreword I, U. B. Paper 28.)

UNIVERSAL CAUSAL REMATERIALIZATION

A form of cosmic healing having to do with the causal and astral body, the mind and the soul. (See also Astral Body, and CF Paper 205.)

UNIVERSAL FATHER

The first person of the Paradise Trinity; Creator, Controller and Upholder of all creation. The Universal Father desires to have communion with mortals through the prepersonal fragments of himself, the Thought Adjusters, who indwell the normal human mind. He also has reserved the prerogative to bestow personality and maintains personal contact with his creatures through the personality circuit.
(See also First Source and Center, Thought Adjusters, CF Paper C, and UB Papers 1 - 5.)

UNIVERSE

The creation of a Creator Son and Creative Daughter. The Creators of our local universe of Nebadon are Christ Michael and the Universe Mother Spirit, who have their headquarters at Salvington, the capital of our local universe. Our local universe is part of the seventh superuniverse, Orvonton. There are 100,000 local universes in each of the seven superuniverses. Each universe is subdivided into 100 constellations; each constellation is divided into 100 local systems; each system is destined to have 1000 inhabited evolutionary planets. Although the organization of our local universe of Nebadon began approximately 400 billion years ago, it is regarded as a relatively young universe and is far from finished. Urantia has seven cosmic families from four different universes: Nebadon,

Avalon, Wolvering and Fanoving, which have starseed from these universes and also Urantians with interuniversal genetics among its members. (See also Christ Michael, Cosmic Family, Nebadon, CF Introduction, and UB Part II.)

UNIVERSE FATHER

A Creator Son of a local universe. Christ Michael of Nebadon is our Universe Father and was created by the Universal Father and the Eternal Son on Paradise. In a creature's sevenfold approach to Deity on Paradise, it is the Universe Father of the local universe who is the first concept of divinity to that creature. In his life 2000 years ago as Jesus of Nazareth, our Universe Father, Christ Michael, reflected the loving nature of the Universal Father on Paradise to all the creatures of his universe of Nebadon. To the Universal Father he portrayed the ideal life of a human mortal.
(See also Universal Father, Eternal Son, CF Preface, and UB Paper 21.)

UNIVERSE MOTHER SPIRIT

A Creative Daughter, created by the Infinite Spirit on Paradise, is co-creator of a local universe, and complementary polarity to a Creator Son. After a Creator Son has earned his full sovereignty the Universe Mother Spirit acknowledges her subordination to this Master Son and pledges her fidelity and obedience. It is the Universe Mother Spirit who provides the vital spark of life — the essential factor — to the living life plasm. The Holy Spirit is her ministering, spiritual circuit and is confined to the spiritual realm of her local universe. The Infinite Spirit is omnipresent.
(See also Holy Spirit, Infinite Spirit, CF Introduction, and UB Paper 34.)

UNIVERSE SUPERVISORS (See Celestial Overcontrol.)

URANTIA

The cosmic name of our planet. Urantia is planet 606 in the system of Satania, in the constellation of Norlatiadek, in the universe of Nebadon, in the superuniverse of Orvonton. The history of this planet starts about 1 billion years ago when it was placed on the physical registry of our local universe of Nebadon, and given its name. Approximately 550,000,000 years ago the Life Carriers made three marine-life implantations in the sheltered tropic bays of the central seas, from which all planetary life evolved. The life patterns of Urantia are unique in Nebadon and were organized and initiated by the Life Carriers in cooperation with spiritual powers and superphysical forces right here on the planet. Urantia was formally recognized as a planet of human habitation in the universe of Nebadon about 1 million years ago, when Andon and Fonta, the first two humans who lived on a peninsula in southern Asia, received a Thought Adjuster. Urantia is the planet which Michael of Nebadon chose among all the planets in his universe for his seventh bestowal, as a human mortal, in which he revealed the loving nature of the Father. It is sometimes called "the world of the cross," because it is the only planet in the 700,000 local universes where a Creator Son was put to death by his own creatures. The erroneous concept of atonement in which Christ is supposed to have died for the sin of men is a remnant of evolutionary religion in which sacrifices had to be made to please an angry God. Urantia is one of the 37 fallen planets in the system of Satania and the first to be adjudicated. Urantia is an experimental or decimal planet and is also unique in that human mortals are being trained in divine government administration. (See also Adam and Eve, Experimental Planet, Life Carriers, CF Statement of Purpose, and UB Part III.)

URANTIA MOVEMENT

A term designating variously organized readers of *The URANTIA Book*. With knowledge comes responsibility. There are many potential destiny reservists among the Urantia movement, who need to align with the Divine Government and recognize the new Planetary Prince, Machiventa Melchizedek, and come to Planetary Headquarters to receive further training at the Starseed and Urantian Schools of Melchizedek. (See CF Paper 197.)

URANTIANS

A term designating ascending sons and daughters whose planet of origin is Urantia. Most people on this planet fall into this category and are souls who are experiencing their very first life. Some Urantians, however, have interuniversal genetics. There is also a group of about 2000 Urantians who are here for the second time. (See also First-time Urantians, Ovan Souls, Second-time Urantians, and CF Paper D.)

VICEGERENT AMBASSADORS

Mandated representatives of Machiventa Melchizedek, such as Vicegerent First Ambassadors as well as Second and Third Ambassadors. Because all of them need training, up to the year 2040 - 2050 AD, there will only be Vicegerent Ambassadors. They must be stabilized on the third psychic circle. There are none as of February 17, 1995. (See also Machiventa Melchizedek, CF footnote on page 20, and Paper 209.)

VORTEXES

A New-Age term for Energy Reflective Circuits. (See CF Paper E.)

WALK-IN

In New-Age terminology generally, a soul who takes over the body completely and the previous soul leaves. Since 1989 no soul ever really leaves a body, even if a fallen or rebellious entity comes in whose sole purpose is to teach false teachings mixed with just enough truth to deceive, if possible, even the very elect of God. No beings of light have spoken through anyone but Gabriel of Sedona since 1989.
(See also Audio Fusion Material Complement, CF Paper 197.)

WATCHER

A Divine New Order community member mandated to oversee environmental concerns. (See CF Paper 218.)

WILL FREEZE

A process within the adjudication procedure that can be applied by the will of Christ Michael to iniquitous personalities whose wills can thereby be superseded. (See CF Paper 209 & 221.)

THE COSMIC DIRECTORY

Location	Headquarters	Is Ruled By	Is the	Designation	In the	Of	Consisting of
Urantia	Sedona, AZ U.S.A.	1 Planetary Prince, Machiventa Melchizedek, under Over-control of Bright & Morning Star Mandate	606th	Inhabited World	System	Satania	619 Inhabited Worlds; 1000 when completed
Satania	Jerusem	1 System Sovereign, Lanaforge	24th	Local System	Constellation	Norlatiadek	100 Local Systems
Norlatiadek	Edentia	12 Vorondadek Sons (The Most Highs) 1 Faithful of Days (In Observation)	70th	Constellation	Local Universe	Nebadon	100 Constellations
Nebadon	Salvington	1 Creator Son, Christ Michael 1 Union of Days (In attendance)	84th	Local Universe	Minor Sector	Ensa	100 Local Universes
Ensa	U Minor The Third	3 Recents of Days	3rd	Minor Sector	Major Sector	Splandon	100 Minor Sectors
Splandon	U Major The Fifth	3 Perfections of Days	5th	Major Sector	Superuniverse	Orvonton	100 Major Sectors
Orvonton	Uversa	3 Ancients of Days	7th	Superuniverse	Grand universe	Master Universe	10 Major Sectors
							1 Central Universe 7 Superuniverses 4 Uninhabited Space levels

Seven Cosmic Families from Four Different Universes

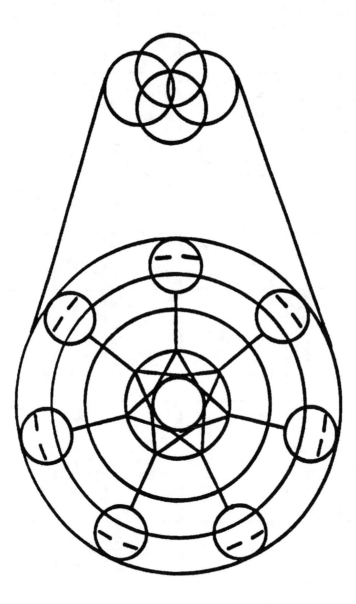

AQUARIAN CONCEPTS COMMUNITY

Aquarian Concepts Community is a spiritual community located in Sedona, Arizona. The guidelines for the community and its members are based on the teachings found in the Fifth Epochal Revelation, as set forth in *The URANTIA Book* and *The Cosmic Family* volumes, with an emphasis on the life of Jesus of Nazareth, known as Christ Michael, the Sovereign Creator Son of our local universe of Nebadon.

Members come from all parts of the world, with a majority having moved here from within the United States. Founded in 1986, by Gabriel of Sedona and his complement Niánn, the community has about 100 full-time members with new members aligning weekly. *The Starseed and Urantian Schools of Melchizedek*, located at the community center, are for children, teenagers and adults and are unique on this planet. This unique school is not only for mindal development and book learning, it is very much a school for soul growth. Many ovan souls, or souls who have lived previous lives, have been stuck in static spirituality for thousand of years because they took part in the Lucifer rebellion and became trapped in erroneous Luciferic thought patterns. In this school, the elders with the guidance of Celestial Overcontrol, teach how to make the mind and heart connection, correlating science and spirituality in Ascension Sci. "The purpose of all education should be to foster and further the supreme purpose of life, the development of a majestic and well-balanced personality." (*The URANTIA Book* p. 2086:3)

The community is organizing and developing extensive organic farms and gardens. They are building additional administrative facilities, a new community center and expanding residential housing. Additional land is being purchased and set aside for the long range plans of Aquarian Concepts community which include the establishment of the Third Garden of Eden, the Planetary Headquarters for the Divine Government of the new Planetary Prince, Machiventa Melchizedek as appointed by Christ Michael of Nebadon.

Aquarian Concepts Community operates a publishing company that distributes the works authored by Gabriel of Sedona, including *The Divine New Order* and *The Cosmic Family* volumes. The community has a music ministry of both live concert tours and the distribution of prerecorded cassettes and compact discs. Healing is a major component of the music ministry and a series of Planetary "Sacred Concerts" are scheduled to begin soon.

There are many forces that influence the causes of disease, but in the majority of cases, the root cause is a spiritual one, a separation from the First Source and Center, God. True permanent healing cannot begin until an individual aligns with the will of God for his or her life. The Aquarian Concepts Community Healing Team incorporates both spiritual and scientific techniques such as personal transmissions, morontia counseling, future light body hologram, and beginning **Tron therapy**. We also have a medical doctor.

Weekend seminars on Continuing Fifth Epochal Revelation are held at the end of every second month. Classes for community members are held four nights a week and visitors are invited to a weekly social gathering and/or tour of the community by appointment.

For more information, write to:

Aquarian Concepts Community
P.O. Box 3946
West Sedona, AZ.,
U.S.A. 86340
or call (520) 204-1206

AVAILABLE FROM AQUARIAN CONCEPTS COMMUNITY

Books by Gabriel of Sedona and Community Members

001 ☐ *The Divine New Order*: The autobiography of Gabriel of Sedona, a Level Four Audio Fusion Material Complement for the Chief Executive of our local universe, the Bright and Morning Star of Salvington. An introduction to Continuing Fifth Epochal Revelation ($14.95 paper).

002 ☐ *The Cosmic Family Volume I*: The beginning volume of a series whereby Gabriel of Sedona is used to bring through Continuing Fifth Epochal Revelation. A series of Papers authored by various celestial personalities teaching you step by step, precept upon precept the cosmic absolutes of this great revelation, which is a continuation of the 196 Papers of *The URANTIA Book* ($19.95 paper).

003 ☐ *The Salvington Circuit*: A magazine-format newsletter written by the members of Aquarian Concepts Community, containing articles and photographs depicting life and spiritual growth at Planetary Headquarters in Sedona, Arizona. Ongoing features and interviews (published annually $7.50 per copy; older back issues $5.00 per copy).

004 ☐ *A Psychological Profile of Gabriel of Sedona*: Dr. Marayeh Cunningham, a clinical psychologist, who has been on a spiritual path most of her adult life had the opportunity to observe and work closely for almost two years with Gabriel of Sedona, the Audio Fusion Material Complement through who Continuing Fifth Epochal Revelation is being transmitted. Using Abraham Maslow's theories of personality and motivation, she is able to analyze the multidimensional and multi-level quality of Gabriel's personality using the criteria of a self-actualizing person as defined by Maslow ($7.00 paper).

005 ☐ *Battered Cliff Face:* The personal story of Delphius, her struggles and frustrations, dealing with the red tape of bureaucracy in trying to obtain a visa to be able to join her cosmic family at Planetary Headquarters. A humorous immigration experience in rhyme. ($4.00)

006 ☐ *Tipis & Yurts; Authentic Designs for Circular Shelters:* Blue Evening Star presents a variety of habitats which serve during transition and awakening. Expertly crafted tipis and yurts which can be used for homes, temples, children's play houses, spare rooms or studios ($25.00 hardcover). More information about Circle Living Workshops on practical preparations for earth changes is available upon request.

007 ☐ *The Cosmic Family Volume II*: The second volume in a continuing series as transmitted through the Audio Fusion Material Complement, Gabriel of Sedona. Available in 1996.

Video Tapes

101 **A Creekside Visit with Gabriel of Sedona**: A unique hour with one of the most significant visionaries of our time. This video tape offers a rare glimpse into higher spiritual realities and presents a cosmic perspective of a world in turmoil. An inspirational dialogue that answers many immediate questions to world problems as well as taking a prophetic look at what could happen if a consciousness shift does not occur to the mass population of our planet ($19.95).

Audio Tapes and Music

201 ☐ **An Introduction to *The Cosmic Family Volume I*** as transmitted through the Level Four Audio Fusion Material Complement Gabriel of Sedona: A discussion with Gabriel of Sedona about the Forewords and 36 additional Papers that complement many of the unrevealed cosmic realities put forth in *The URANTIA Book* ($9.95).

202 ☐ **An Interview with Gabriel of Sedona and his Complement Niánn**: An in-depth discussion with Gabriel and Niánn about Aquarian Concepts Community and Planetary Divine Government. How did they come about? When did they start? Where are they headed? ($9.95).

203 ☐ **A Message to the Native American Elders**: Niánn presents a message to all respected elders of the various tribes of the North American continent from Paladin/Sky Hawk, an ancient ancestor, concerning the time of purification, earth changes, the change point, the Fifth World/the Fifth Epochal Revelation ($9.95).

204 ☐ **A Three-tape Audio Series with Gabriel of Sedona**: Each tape discusses a vital and important theme. Tape #1 is entitled "There Are No Real Leaders." Tape #2 is "What is True Spirituality?" Tape #3 is "The Cosmic Renaissance" ($24.95).

301 ☐ *Escape*: Music, lyrics, vocals written and performed by Gabriel of Sedona accompanied by The Bright and Morning Star Band. Divine New Order sacred music with mystical vocals and higher-consciousness lyrics ($9.95 cassettes only).

302 ☐ *Wake Up America!* and *The Great American Dream*: A two-song CD or cassette single. Music, lyrics, vocals written and performed by Gabriel of Sedona accompanied by The Bright and Morning Star Band ($6.95 CD, $4.95 cassette).

Arts and Crafts

401 ☐ **Living Nature Creations**: Beautiful hand-made moccasins designed to your exact personal comfort. Many styles to choose from. Native American jewelry. Brochures available upon request.

☐ **Cosmic Art & Logos**: Send for detailed brochure.

. . . .

Make check payable to:
Aquarian Concepts
P.O. Box 3946
West Sedona, AZ U.S.A. 86340

PAYMENT METHOD: (US currency only)

☐☐ Check/Money order enclosed
Visa/Mastercard Exp. Date:

Card# _____

Signature_____

To order by phone 1-520-204-1206
Fax 1-520-204-1252

Allow 2 - 3 weeks for delivery

☐ **I wish to contribute to the non-profit/tax-exempt 501(c)(3) Aquarian Concepts**

$ _____

SHIPPING, TIME AND EFFORT:

Priority mail to U.S./Canada/Mexico, $3.50 first item, $1.50 ea. additional item.
Airmail to Europe, $9.50 first item, $3.50 ea. add. item.
Airmail to all other countries, $12.50 first item, $4.00 ea. add. item _____
Sales Tax
Arizona residents add 7.25% _____
TOTAL DUE $ _____

Ship to: _____

_____

_____

Check Out Our Web Site at

http://www.sedona.net/sd/aquarian/

Have you had an inner knowing of late that whatever you are doing with your life is not what you should be doing and that there is a higher purpose for your existence on this planet today? If so, check out our **Divine New Order** web page!

Have you had the feeling at times that you didn't quite fit into our society? Could it be that you have lived before and in fact originated on another world where the norms of society were very different? Could you be part of the Cosmic Family that is being regathered? If you think you might be, look at the **Cosmic Family** web page!

Are you concerned about your health? Are you aware of the deeper underlying causes of disease that may be a part of your soul's previous existences? To get more information see our **Ascension Science** web page.

Are you drawn to Sedona? Take a spiritual tour or pilgrimage and find out why. See our **Spirit Steps** Tours web page.

All of these can be found under the home page for
Aquarian Concepts Community

http://www.sedona.net/sd/aquarian/

ABOUT THE AUTHOR

Gabriel of Sedona, visionary and morontia counselor/soul surgeon, gifted author, and truly humble spiritual leader, was born and raised in Pittsburgh, Pennsylvania. He studied theology at Duquesne University and began his religious career as a student involved in the charismatic renewal of the Catholic Church. His devotion to God has been life long. He sought monastic life in Benedictine and Franciscan monasteries in the Southwest, where he was also introduced to and has continually learned from Native American spirituality. He has spent years ministering to and counseling street youth, students, and individuals in various spiritual communities across the United States. He was a prison chaplain and worked for 11 years providing shelter and counseling for the homeless and destitute. He has studied the Tibetan Master Djwal Khul's writings and all appropriate metaphysical teachings of true spiritual value.

Presently, as a Level Four Audio Fusion Material Complement for the Chief Executive of our local universe, the Bright and Morning Star of Salvington, Gabriel is used by various celestial personalities for interplanetary and interdimensional communication. Holding the highest mandate of the Bright and Morning Star on our planet, he is the head administrator of the Divine Government and the highest spiritual teacher/leader. He is the repersonalized Peter, the apostle, and destined to be the human Planetary Prince of our planet, preceding Amadon who may stay on Urantia after 2040 - 2050 AD if none of the future Vicegerent First Ambassadors qualify for Melchizedek leadership. As a serious disciplined scientific student, he has become a theoretical physicist. Gabriel is in contact with and is currently being used by celestial personalities to bring through the Continuing Fifth Epochal Revelation that is a continuation of the 196 Papers of *The URANTIA Book*. These Papers, collectively known as *The Cosmic Family Volumes*, are fundamental as a basis for understanding the current state of our planet and our relationship to the cosmic community.

Gabriel lives with his complement, Niánn, and their three children, at Aquarian Concepts Community in Sedona, Arizona. In addition to being the spiritual leader of this community and ministry, he also is an accomplished futuristic lyricist, singer, and songwriter.

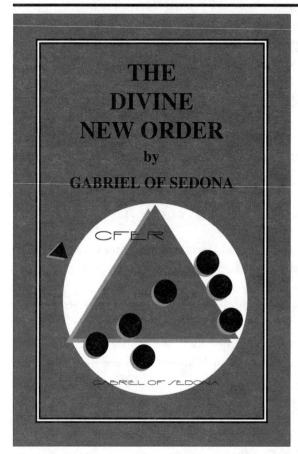